D1000412

WITHDRAWN FROM COLLECTION

FORSAKEN FEMALES

PROPERTY OF
PENN HIGHLANDS CC

FORSAKEN FEMALES

The Global Brutalization of Women

ANDREA PARROT
and
NINA CUMMINGS

ROWMAN & LITTLEFIELD PUBLISHERS, INC.
Lanham • Boulder • New York • Toronto • Oxford

ROWMAN & LITTLEFIELD PUBLISHERS, INC.

Published in the United States of America
by Rowman & Littlefield Publishers, Inc.
A wholly owned subsidary of The Rowman & Littlefield Publishing Group, Inc.
4501 Forbes Boulevard, Suite 200, Lanham, Maryland 20706
www.rowmanlittlefield.com

PO Box 317
Oxford
OX2 9RU, UK

Copyright © 2006 by Rowman & Littlefield Publishers, Inc.

All rights reserved. No part of this publication may be reproduced,
stored in a retrieval system, or transmitted in any form or by any
means, electronic, mechanical, photocopying, recording, or otherwise,
without the prior permission of the publisher.

British Library Cataloguing in Publication Information Available

Library of Congress Cataloging-in-Publication Data

Parrot, Andrea.
  Forsaken females : the global brutalization of women / Andrea Parrot and
Nina Cummings.
     p.   cm.
  Includes bibliographical references and index.
  ISBN-13: 978-0-7425-4578-6 (cloth : alk. paper)
  ISBN-10: 0-7425-4578-4 (cloth : alk. paper)
  ISBN-13: 978-0-7425-4579-3 (pbk. : alk. paper)
  ISBN-10: 0-7425-4579-2 (pbk. : alk. paper)
  1. Women—Violence against.   2. Sex role.   3. Political violence.   4.
Human rights.   I. Cummings, Nina, 1955–   II. Title.
HV6250.4.W65P36   2006
362.83—dc22   2006001100

Printed in the United States of America

∞ ™ The paper used in this publication meets the minimum requirements of American
National Standard for Information Sciences—Permanence of Paper for Printed Library
Materials, ANSI/NISO Z39.48-1992.

We dedicate this book to the many women whose stories appear in these pages. Although their lives were altered by violent experiences, they bravely spoke about what happened against a backdrop of hatred and blame. Their courage is an inspiration.

We also dedicate this book to our sons,
Andrew, Ryan, and Mackenzie.
It is in their respect and understanding of women's lives that we find hope for all women.

CONTENTS

Part III: Consequences and Possibilities

PREFACE

This book is the result of decades of interest in violence against women. Together, we have worked in the field a combined total of sixty years, during which our concerns expanded to global violence against women and the contextual aspects of women's victimization. This book examines many forms of what we consider violence, but it is by no means complete. Space considerations limited the extent to which behaviors were included and described. Furthermore, in writing this book, we struggled with determining what behaviors constitute violence, oppression, or brutalization, and which behaviors are simply nonharmful cultural or religious practices. Not all societies aspire to the same set of universal principles. How does one balance the importance of scientific evidence, cultural relativism, and universal truths against a backdrop of human rights concerns? There has been considerable debate between sociologists, anthropologists, human rights activists, feminists, physicians, and lawyers regarding whether certain behaviors are harmful or acceptable because they are mandated by cultural traditions. For this book, it was our choice to include social or physical problems that result in significant suffering, loss of life, health, or reproductive capability to a woman, her family, or society. As you will see, the violence can occur throughout the female life course.

The selection of behaviors included here is not value free. We are both Western-educated, middle class, Caucasian Americans. One of us is Jewish, the other Christian. As such, we prioritize values differently than others might. In an effort to incorporate diverse perspectives on these topics, many women from different countries, cultures, religions, and political ideologies reviewed the chapters. Their helpful comments provided welcome alternative viewpoints.

We are sensitive to the arguments about the role of cultural relativism. We believe gender violence is supported by almost universal patriarchal systems, which ultimately maintain women's subordination and create a world where violence against women is normative and condoned. Does cultural relativism make it right? U.S. Senator Pat Schroeder offered a response worth considering:

> *If it happens to you for racial reasons, it's a human rights violation.*
>
> *If it happens to you for political reasons, it's a human rights violation.*
>
> *If it happens to a woman, it's cultural.* (Green, 1999, p. 19)

There are persuasive debates that argue the merits of cultural relativism when certain practices that affect women are questioned or condemned, usually by Western feminists. It is not our intention to condemn practices that have traditions of importance that we cannot fully realize as Western women. But to argue that something is right, in light of the physical or mental trauma it causes (sometimes even death) simply because of cultural approval can be shortsighted. How do we determine what is culturally "good" or "bad" in light of globalization and the evolving and ever-changing cultural norms? We believe that there are certain universal truths that challenge torture, crime, oppression, and abuse in all its forms. To this end, we condemn some of the practices named in this book that, while argued to be culturally sanctioned, we find to be violent and threatening to women's well-being. That is not to say that these issues cannot or should not be discussed and we support engagement in "intercultural moral discussions" (Kopelman, 2002, p. 55).

We have yet to understand the full effects of gender violence. While it is possible to estimate how many lives are lost, how many women have been raped or battered, how many have experienced genital cutting, or how many women have been enslaved, it is quite a different matter to quantify the horrific and unrelenting physical and emotional suffering that results from many of these practices. To this end, there are many women's voices included here. The women's own words and descriptions of their circumstances have been italicized to stand out and provide necessary contextual examples of the survivor's perspective.

To define some of these behaviors as social problems and attempt to eliminate them against the beliefs and wishes of the cultures within which they reside, may create other social concerns. In many cases it is simply not enough to strive to eliminate a behavior defined as a social problem; understanding the role that behavior plays in a culture and identifying the resultant consequences are critical. Identifying behaviors as social problems is simply the first step; eliminating them while reducing resultant social problems is also vitally important.

Violence against women is not unique to any one country or region. Even within countries, vast differences can exist between rural and urban settings. Certainly men are victims of violence too. But the dominant theme throughout this book is that gender, race, and class distinctions within society have greater consequences for women. We understand that a focus on women's victimization may appear to minimize men's role in preventing it. That is not our intention; a book about women does not exclude or deny men's role in stopping the violence perpetrated against them.

If this is your first introduction to the violence experienced by women and girls, it will not be easy reading. It was not easy writing. But it is our hope that readers will digest the information and go one step further: do something to end the atrocities. Local activism is equally as important as policy or legislative initiatives. Support and funds are needed by groups and organizations that put into practice the theories that may someday lead to solutions. There is much each individual can do to stop the violence in their community.

Up to the moment this manuscript went to the publisher we were incorporating late-breaking events that increased women's vulnerability, such as the December 2004 tsunami in Asia. Women's ongoing susceptibility to violence either as a result of man-made disasters or natural ones continues to haunt us. For readers unaware of the magnitude of these problems, we hope they will find a new interest in women's victimization and listen carefully to the women's stories printed in these pages. It is our hope that readers will help create a world in which the subjective experience becomes a call to action.

CULTURAL QUOTES
PERPETUATING VIOLENCE

Cultural expressions from around the globe that are related to violence against women.

- Raising a female child is like watering your neighbor's plants (Sen, 2001). *India*
- The bottle [is good] with its sealing wax, the girl with her hymen (Schipper, 2003). *Arabic, Maghreb*
- The luckless man loses his horse, the lucky man loses his wife (Ramanamma, 1991, p. 74). *India*
- Women, like gongs, should be beaten regularly (Schipper, 2003). *English, USA*
- If you love your daughter, bind her feet; if you love your son, let him study (Yang, 2004). *China*
- A bad woman and a good woman both need the rod (Schipper, 2003). *Argentina*
- Good horses and bad horses need the spurs, good women and bad women need the whip (Schipper, 2003). *Europe, Americas*
- It's better to have my eye taken away, than to take away my good name (Chatzifotiou and Dobash, 2001). *Greece*
- Never trust a horse or a woman (Schipper, 2003). *Turkish*
- Girls and glasses are always in danger (Schipper, 2003). *German*
- A girl is like crystal: if shattered, it cannot be restored (Schipper, 2003). *Armenian*
- A girl worth kissing is not easily kissed (Schipper, 2003). *English, USA*

- Better a bad dowry, than a bad gift [i.e., illegitimate pregnancy] (Schipper, 2003). *Fulfulde, Nigeria*
- Darkness covers everything except a bad wife (Schipper, 2003). *Hebrew*
- Is one veil sufficient to cover a woman's wickedness? (Schipper, 2003). *Tamil, India*
- Children without fathers are similar to a house without a roof (Bui and Morash, 1999). *Vietnam*
- Three days she's a queen and three days she's still a princess, and from then on engaged as slave (Schipper, 2003). *Ladino, Libya*
- Beat a woman and a horse every three days (Levinson, 1989). *Serbia*
- Women are the enemy of women (Priyadarshini, 2005). *India*
- Never marry a woman with big feet (Schipper, 2003). *China*

ACKNOWLEDGMENTS

We are very fortunate that, in writing this book, we had the support of many individuals from many countries, including Canada, Colombia, China, Egypt, Ghana, India, Kenya, Korea, Nigeria, Spain, Turkey, and the United States. They were involved in undergraduate study, graduate study, social work, nursing, midwifery, teaching, law enforcement, law, family therapy, human rights work, university teaching, and administrative assistance. Many of them are friends who supported this very important and challenging endeavor.

We owe special thanks to three women who have provided invaluable assistance in the preparation of this book: Jyoti Aggarwal for extensive research support; and Monica Ruiz-Casares and Anamika Priyadarshini for their review of significant portions of the manuscript.

The following undergraduate research assistants helped in manuscript research and preparation: Ilana Kramer, Ha Yeon Lee, Jennifer Malm, Marylin Montoya, Danielle Peress, Lisa Rosenzweig, Beth Wallach, and Jared Wolfe.

The following professional women provided helpful critical review of the chapters:

Sue Brower, Sue Barker, Elizabeth Einstein, Martha Issah, Ndunge Kiiti, Nduku Kiiti, Patricia Lauper, Justine Lynge, Hongnan Ma, Kate Pierce, Aysan Se'ver, Sue Smith, Kamayani Swami, and Qi Wang.

This book was originally envisioned to be used in an existing course at Cornell University titled "Global Perspectives on Violence against Women." This class is cross-listed between the Feminist, Gender and Sexuality Studies program and the Department of Policy Analysis and Management. Students in this class were very helpful in identifying the promising practices to eliminate violence against women highlighted in the book.

Finally, we are grateful to our families for encouraging us and believing in the significance of this work.

I

UNDERSTANDING THE CONTEXT OF VIOLENCE AGAINST WOMEN

1

PERSPECTIVES ON VIOLENCE AGAINST WOMEN: HISTORICAL, METHODOLOGICAL, AND THEORETICAL

> Statistics are people with their tears wiped away.
>
> (Bertell, 2000)

According to early Greek writings by Aristotle and Galen, "humans were the most perfect animals, and among humans, men were more perfect than women" (Fox, 2002, p. 18). The biblical creation story, where Eve is formed from Adams rib, reinforces the subordination of women (Agonito, 1997; Fletcher, 1995), and it is not hard to find other examples of ancient attitudes that promote the male over female. Women's subjugation is perpetuated and supported by these myths, traditions, beliefs, and institutions (Borst, 1992; Counts, Brown, and Campbell, 1992). "In order to achieve and maintain subordination of the females, ideologies have been constructed whereby submissions to patriarchy appear in the nature of things. Ordained by the Gods, supported by the priests, implemented by the law, women came to accept and psychologically internalize compliance as necessary. Violence against women in all forms has and still thrives in such an environment" (Fox, 2002, p. 28).

There are references to violence against women as early as the Code of Hammurabi (1725 BC) (Moghissi and Goodman, 1999). In Western societies, both Judeo-Christian cultural beliefs and Western legal codes help explain why women are victims of socially condoned violence (Fox, 2002). The first laws in the world against wife-beating were passed in 1641 by the Puritans in Massachusetts, U.S.A. (Pleck, 1987). The common expression "rule of thumb" originates from historical Western legal guidelines which admonish husbands to limit the instrument that they beat their wives with to that which is no larger than his thumb; furthermore, husbands were not permitted to draw blood with the instrument (Fletcher, 1995). Historically (and still true today in some countries) when a woman was raped, the primary aggrieved party was not the woman, but her husband or father, so that the penalty and reparations were made to the male head of the household or family for turning his property (wife, daughter, or sister) into damaged goods. The rapist could be castrated or forced to marry the victim (Rhode, 1989). Because the marriage contract presumes wifely consent (Brownmiller, 1975), marital rape remains legal in many countries.

Millions consider violence against women normative because it is so deeply embedded within history and culture and is found in all social and economic strata worldwide; millions of women consider it a way of life (Jensen and Otoo-Oyortey, 1999). Certain types of violence against women (such as female genital mutilation and wife abuse) are often considered less serious than other types of violence because tradition and the intimacy of family relations suggest privacy and secrecy (Moghissi and Goodman, 1999). Still, violence is a major threat to women's quality of life and advancement worldwide. Today, gender-based violence is a significant factor in the cause of death and illness of women and is responsible for significant loss of economic productivity among women of reproductive age (Mehrota, 2001a; Heise, Pitanguy, and Germain, 1994). The violence is extensive; that is, one in three married women in developing countries is battered by their husband during their lifetimes (Jolly, 1997). Women's subjugation, lack of education, and lack of opportunity results in poverty, dismal living conditions, mental health concerns, and further embeds the cycle of violence perpetuated against women.

Some forms of violence endured by women and endorsed by cultures have been eradicated within the last century. However, there are still women alive who were victimized by these forms of violence and still suffer from the long-term consequences. We describe three of these practices in order to illustrate that, although these particular atrocities are condemned today, there are stark similarities with other practices that remain currently institutionalized, ignored, or minimized. Although history changed the circumstances for these victims, there are many more victims who have replaced them and live in fear today.

Footbinding

Footbinding in China was outlawed in 1911. However, it continued until 1949 in the remote mountain areas of the country (Cummings, Ling, and Stone, 1997). A daughter with bound feet meant greater status for the girl and her family because the daughter could now attract important and influential men as suitors. The criterion for a good daughter-in-law was rep-

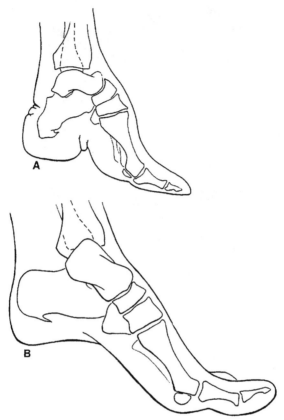

Anatomy of a non-weight-bearing bound foot (A) compared with a normal foot (B). Reproduced with permission from *Journal of the American Podiatric Medical Association* 80, no. 8 (1990): 407. Copyright © 1990 by American Podiatric Medical Association.

resented by a well-bound foot. Girls learned early that they influenced the reputations of both birth family and the family of her husband or future husband with a small, petite foot (Blake, 1994). Footbinding was supported and carried out by women because the prevailing wisdom of the time suggested that this practice promoted health and fertility. Girls usually between the ages of three to six years had all toes but the big toe broken and bound tightly with cloth strips to keep their feet from growing larger than three to five inches. The arches were broken, and the toes were bent toward the soles of the feet at extreme angles that caused disfigurement. For the foot to "shrink," this binding was left on the feet for at least three years. Although the bound foot was believed to be pleasing to look at compared to an "unbound" foot and purportedly had erotic attraction for men (Mackie,

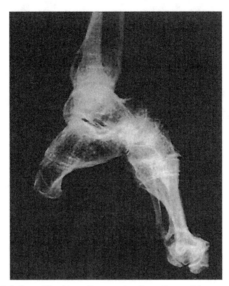

Lateral view of the left foot. The loss of normal trabecular architecture is most noticeable in the calcaneus, talus, and tibia. Reproduced with permission from *Journal of the American Podiatric Medical Association* 80, no. 8 (1990): 409. Copyright © 1990 by American Podiatric Medical Association.

1996), conditions such as ulceration, paralysis, and gangrene were not uncommon, and it has been estimated that as many as 10 percent of the girls died from the complications of footbinding. Women whose feet had been bound were more likely to fall, be less able to get up from a chair without assistance, and have more osteoporosis (as indicated by lower hip and spine bone density) than women with unbound feet, putting them at greater risk of suffering hip or spine fractures. In the late 1990s, more than one-third of women over eighty and almost one-fifth of women between seventy and seventy-nine years in China had bound-foot deformities (Cummings et al., 1997). Despite their infirmities, these women appeared to accommodate to their impairments because they were socialized to not complain (Cummings et al., 1997).

> *A*fter several months all toes but the big one were pressed against the inner surface. . . . Whenever I ate fish or freshly killed meat, my feet would swell and the pus would drip. . . . Mother would remove the bindings and wipe the blood and pus which dripped from my feet. Every two weeks I changed shoes. Each new pair was one-to-two tenths of an inch smaller than the previous one. (Ping, 2002, pp. 5–6)

Magdalens Laundries or Asylums

Women were sent to work and live in the Magdalens laundries, sometimes by parish priests, accused of being sinners, incorrigible, alcoholics, mentally deficient, or pregnant out of wedlock (even if the way they became pregnant was through rape or sexual abuse). "The Magdalens" were named after the converted prostitute from the Bible, Mary Magdalene, who was rewarded by Jesus with forgiveness and love for all she'd done. From the 1800s through the end of the twentieth century, these women were institutionalized against their will. Their punishment was a lifetime of "penitence" spent in the service of the Sisters of Charity or other orders, locked away performing menial domestic chores such as laundering prison and priest's uniforms, cooking, scrubbing floors and windows, and caring for the sick and the aging nuns (Finnegan, 2001). The labor was slavelike; no chance of escape, no compensation, harsh conditions, and minimally fulfilled needs such as food or clothing. Many of these women still bear the emotional and physical scars from their years at these asylums. In the 1970s, a search of property once used as a "laundry" uncovered approximately 133 unmarked graves on the convent grounds. The graves contained the remains of women who had worked in the asylum; family or friends were never notified of the deaths. They were essentially, unremembered (Culchieworks, 2003).

*M**ary Norris Cronin's family was torn apart when she and her seven brothers and sisters were sent to orphanages, simply because their widowed mother began to go out with a man. Mary was the eldest and just twelve when her life was shattered by being sent to St. Joseph's Orphanage in Killarney, Co. Kerry, with her sisters. Her two brothers were sent to an orphanage in Tralee run by the Christian Brothers. . . . She is in no doubt that the local parish priest reported that her mother was seeing another man and figured that she was a bad woman. "My mother was a much loved woman and this should never have happened. We were poor, but no poorer than our neighbours and we were all loved," she recalled. . . . Mary left the orphanage at sixteen, but it was not to be her last experience at St. Joseph's. She went to work in the home of a sister of one of the nuns but was reported for twice going to the pictures in one week. She was returned to the orphanage where a doctor was called to carry out an internal examination of her. "I remember to this day the doctor saying to the nuns this girl is intact. I hadn't been with any boy," she added. Mary was sent to the Good Shepherd Magdalen Laundry, also run by the nuns, in Cork. "We all had to slave there in the laundry with all kinds of dirty things," she said. Eventually at the age of nineteen, she was allowed to leave the laundry. (McDonald, 1999)*

Comfort Women

"Comfort women" was the name given to those who became sex slaves to the Japanese military between 1932 and 1945. The Japanese set up brothels to serve the soldiers. It is estimated that between eighty thousand to two hundred thousand women were forced into sexual slavery. The vast majority (approximately 80 percent) were Korean, but the ethnicities varied. Some women were Japanese, some Taiwanese, Filipino, Indonesian, or from other Pacific Islands (Soh, 1997; Yoshimi, 2000). Some Dutch women living in the Dutch East Indies (Indonesia) were also forced to become "comfort women." It is estimated that 80 percent of the women were between fourteen and eighteen years of age when they were forced into sexual slavery (Hicks, 1994). "Comfort Women" were intended to improve the morale of the Japanese troops and promote military discipline. The justification for the brothels was that by providing free sexual release, the soldiers would then not sexually abuse women in occupied territories. During the Nanjing Massacre of 1937 it was estimated that twenty thousand women were raped. In a ludicrous attempt to avoid similar publicity, the Japanese thought military-run brothels would prevent a similar problem. The Japanese also believed that by "providing" sexual activity, they could control the transmission of sexual diseases by regulating the brothels (Hicks, 1994; Yoshimi, 2000). The more bizarre argument for sanctioning and organizing sexual slavery of women was that the organization of comfort stations would prevent rape in public by the soldiers.

The Japanese soldiers who abused the enslaved women did not use the term "comfort woman." Instead the women were called "*pii*" (pronounced "pea"). The word is from the Chinese meaning goods or articles. In slang terms, it refers to the vagina and is considered disparaging (Yoshimi, 2000). Many of the women and girls taken to comfort stations were deceived and lured into service by promises of money, easy work, and education. Comfort stations were organized to efficiently "serve" the troops as well as the officers, ignoring the inhumane conditions and torture endured. An interview with an accountant told how they estimated the cost effectiveness of the system:

> *At that time [when comfort stations were being set up], we estimated the endurance of the women rounded up in local areas and the rates at which they would wear out. We analyzed which women were strong or weak in those areas and then had to go so far as to determine "how long they would be in use" from the time the soldiers entered the rooms until they left—how many minutes for commissioned officers, how many minutes for soldiers. . . ."* (Yoshimi, 2000, p. 61)

Women who worked in the stations reserved for officers were sexually assaulted less frequently than those in stations used by enlisted men. In most cases, Korean women were sent to be raped by the enlisted, while Japanese women were used by the officers (Pyong Gap, 2003). Korean women reportedly averaged twenty to thirty men a day, with one report citing as many as sixty men in one day (Yoshimi, 2000). If a woman refused the sexual overtures, she was beaten savagely. Additional forms of violence were not uncommon in the comfort stations. Soldiers, fueled by alcohol, often went on violent rampages, beating the women, brutalizing them during rapes, and destroying the little property the women had with them.

Each of us was visited by an average of thirty to forty soldiers a day; we could hardly find time to sleep. Fewer soldiers came while there was a battle. Soldiers were forced to use condoms which were piled up in each room, but some refused. I urged them to use condoms, warning that I had a terrible disease, they, however, did not care at all, saying "I even don't know when I'm to be killed. Why care about a trivial disease?" I was always terrified that I could be infected. Approximately once every second month, the army surgeon gave us check-ups. Anyone who had a problem was ordered to take a rest for a few days. Although I had no venereal disease, I kept bleeding. I was told at a recent check-up that my womb is still malformed from the abuse it received in my youth. Some women were suffering from swollen vaginas; the swelling was so bad that there was no space for a needle to be inserted inside. Seriously in pain, I tried to commit suicide several times. I hoped to jump into water or in front of a car, but I could not dare do it. I was nearly dying to see my mother. I wanted to run away, but it was hopeless because I did not know the location of where I was being kept. I just gave up. Some girls fought with soldiers. I did not rebel, because I thought that would be the best way to survive. (SoonDock, 1995)

In 1990, the Japanese government was accused of sanctioning the women's slavery in this way. Some of the Korean women survivors sued the Japanese government in a class action suit and demanded compensation for their suffering. In 1992, the Japanese government was forced to admit their culpability in sanctioning the practice of using women in military brothels during the war.

There has been public outrage at such archaic and violent practices as these over the years and yet what is striking is how other forms of violence, just as destructive, are accepted and condoned and perpetuated. It appears that as one type of violence is eradicated, another easily slips into place.

DEFINING VIOLENCE AGAINST WOMEN

According to the United Nations Declaration of the Elimination of Violence against Women, violence against women is "any act of gender-based violence that results in, or is likely to result in physical, sexual, or psychological harm or suffering to women, including threats of such acts, coercion, or arbitrary deprivations of such liberty, whether occurring in public or private life" (Richters, 1994, p. 2). The declaration stated that violence against women includes, but is not limited to "physical, sexual, and psychological violence occurring in the family and within the general community, including sexual harassment, trafficking in women, and forced prostitution, and/or physical, sexual, and psychological violence perpetrated or condoned by the State" (UN Draft Declaration on the Elimination of Violence against Women, 1993). Sexual and reproductive rights were recognized as human rights in the platform for action from the Fourth World Conference on Women held in Beijing in 1995. They are inalienable, integral, and an indivisible part of universal human rights. Although still the subject of debate internationally, many accept that violation of these rights is seen as a form of gender-based violence that affects women's mental and physical health (Mehrotra, 2001a; Mullally, 2005).

Discussions of violence perpetrated against women must consider the limitations of the word *violence*. The concept of violence is broad and includes threats, intimidation, verbal abuse, coercion, and harassment as well as murder, sexual assault, rape, and battering. What some may define as abusive behavior, others define as overt violence. Violence against women has been defined by Hom (1992) as the infliction of physical, mental, and spiritual suffering in the domestic setting as well as the commodification of female lives resulting from the social violence of denying women equality in economic and political participation. Others define violence in narrower terms that include only physical brutality (Dobash and Dobash, 1998). This is an important distinction when looking at research regarding violence against women.

The definition of *violence* may have different meanings for different researchers. What may be construed as less invasive or subtle forms of violence may have severe, long-lasting impact regardless of whether they involve physical brutality. To define violence solely according to the laws or concepts of various cultures would limit understanding of the victim experience. Is the victim experience defined from within a culture or by those outside it? To only define violence according to the perspectives of victims would limit our understanding of cultural attempts to address the problem. For our purposes, we prefer the broader definition of behaviors and oppressions (infliction of physical, mental, emotional, and spiritual trauma inside and outside the home as well as the subjugation of the female experience due to denial of economic, social, and political participation). The acts of violence described in this book affect women in all these ways.

A majority of research on this issue has been conducted in developed countries but a complete understanding of global violence against women depends on many factors. Cross-cultural comparisons are difficult because of the widely dissimilar studies used when research can be done. Furthermore, globalization contributes to the increasingly heterogeneous cultures within one country or region. As a result, "culture" may evolve into a diverse collection of traditions, traits, and attitudes (Cousineau and Rondeau, 2004). In developing countries where poverty, political dictatorship, civil unrest, urbanization, or rapid social change creates unstable social conditions, research is just now emerging. The numbers of crimes perpetrated against women in developing countries may be greater than in other countries (Doyal, 1995; Sev'er, Dawson, and Johnson, 2004) but we know little about the risks to women's safety in developing settings (Flake, 2005). A major source of information about violence in developing as well as developed nations comes from international human rights and advocacy organizations (Amnesty International, Human Rights Watch, United Nations, Women-Aid International, etc.). Even within Western countries that have empirical data from twenty years ago, there is still a paucity of research regarding the context of violence as well as violence perpetrated against marginalized populations (e.g., elderly women, homeless women, and disabled women). There is much to learn yet about women's victimization.

VIOLENCE AGAINST WOMEN IN CONTEXT

According to Coomaraswamy (1994) there are three general areas where women are particularly vulnerable to violence: in the family (due to domestic violence, traditional practices, and infanticide); in the community (rape, sexual assault, commercialized violence such as trafficking in women, labor exploitation, sexual slavery, abuse of female migrant workers, etc.); and by the state (including violence against women in detention as well as violence against women in situations of armed conflict and against refugee women). Worldwide, at least one-third of women have been beaten, coerced into sex, or abused in some other way—usually by an acquaintance (e.g., a husband, brother, mother-in-law, or other family member) (Heise, Ellsberg, and Gottemoeller, 1999; Sev'er, Dawson, and Johnson, 2004). One-fourth of women have been abused during pregnancy (Heise, Ellsberg, and Gottemoeller, 1999). Psychological abuse almost always accompanies physical abuse. In addition, one-third to one-half of all these cases involves sexual abuse. A high proportion of women who are beaten are subjected to violence repeatedly (Heise, Ellsberg, and Gottemoeller, 1999). Much of the serious violence perpetrated against women is done in the name of preserving virginity and marriage vows or punishing women for violating those vows. Female genital mutilation, honor killings, public beatings, lashing, and stoning are all carried out primarily in the interest of preventing sexual behavior outside of marriage. Atrocities such as rape during war, sexual slavery, and trafficking may be state-sponsored or at the very least, blatantly ignored as an underlying cultural problem that primarily affects women.

One way to examine this issue is by looking at the relationship of the female life cycle and women's degree of vulnerability. Gender violence occurs throughout the life cycle. Violence during the prenatal period includes sex-selective abortions, forced abortions, battering during pregnancy, and forced pregnancy. During infancy, violence against females includes infanticide, emotional and physical abuse, and restricted access to food and medical care. During childhood, females face genital mutilation, incest and sexual abuse, differential access to food, medical care, and education (compared to male children), child prostitution, and sexual slavery. The adolescent period brings the risk of dating and courtship violence, economically coerced sex, sexual abuse in the workplace, rape, sexual harassment, and forced prostitution. Violence throughout women's reproductive years includes abuse by intimate partners, marital rape, dowry abuse, partner homicide, psychological abuse, sexual abuse in the workplace, sexual harassment, rape, and abuse of women with disabilities. Elderly women experience violence in the forms of self-immolation, abuse of widows, and elder abuse (which affects mostly women) (Heise, Pitanguy, and Germain, 1994).

The Importance of Human Rights Work

The context in which violence against women occurs in many parts of the world is not well understood. This is partially due to the fact that conducting research on global violence against women has many challenges. Political and social unrest, war, and high rates of poverty and illiteracy contribute to conditions that make it nearly impossible to accurately determine the type and amount of violence perpetrated against women in many cultures. Patriarchal conditions and misogyny further contribute to the world's underestimation of the problem and lack of awareness of the conditions that lead to and contribute to abuse and violence.

Testimonies from women who have been raped, enslaved, trafficked, victimized, battered, burned, and tortured are often the result of international attention to war, civil unrest, or suspected human rights atrocities within countries. Often the testimonies about violence against women are only one piece of the human rights abuses that become public. However, upon closer examination, women are disproportionately victimized when war, civil unrest, and poverty exist (Vickers, 1993). Not only are they directly affected by war-induced violence, but the social violence that results from civil unrest also puts women at great risk (Flake, 2005). And of course women are particularly at risk within cultures where unchallenged patriarchy and misogyny are embedded in political, religious, or social systems.

The testimonies and stories of women collected by human rights agencies often provide the first known reports of these crimes. The reports may be the only documentation of the violence and its impact. The personal descriptions of women's experiences may be the only information available to understand the frequency, quantity, and context of violence against women worldwide. Without the rich data that these stories provide, it is impossible to fully comprehend the social, political, and personal consequences that result from global violence against women.

Studying violence against women worldwide poses particular challenges. Access to scientific data may be severely limited and available only within countries with university or research resources. Parts of the world embroiled in conflict (such as civil wars) may cross international borders. Scholars or scientists from those countries may be limited in their access to data. They may have fled areas because to stay may result in imprisonment, injury, or death. Even if scholars are in the area to document the violence against women, the infrastructure that is often necessary for them to operate may be lacking or severely restricted. Scholars may face hostility or refusal by authorities to conduct research so as to not depict the country in a negative light. The culture may be insulated by an acceptance of violence against women. The secrecy that often accompanies violence against women may be firmly planted. Certain forms of violence may be disguised as violence women commit against themselves; however, it is motivated by the restrictive and abusive conditions to which women are exposed. For example, in India, the dowry system of giving gifts to the family of a bridegroom contributes to female homicide and suicide rates in that country (Brockington, 2001). Scholars trained in traditional quantitative and qualitative methods from outside a culture are often not welcome or do not feel safe in countries experiencing political unrest. Reinterviewing participants in an attempt to confirm stories or documentation may be impossible. In many cases, testimonies are a singular event. To return to the participant or get additional access may pose a threat to the woman or researcher's safety. Women known to have talked about the conditions within a culture may risk being ostracized. Some individuals who provided testimony can never be traced due to dangerous war conditions or fear of reprisal.

Frequently, women will only talk to women. Violence experienced by women may be considered culturally sensitive: issues that fall into the subordinate women's domain. Women facing violence at the hands of men may be reluctant to discuss the victimization for fear that what they say may get back to the abuser, causing the victim further "punishment" for discussing a "private matter" with an outsider. (In Brazil, this dynamic is so prevalent that in the 1980s, the government was urged to take the unusual step of creating all women's police stations so that women who face domestic violence will feel safer reporting their victimization. See chapter 8.) Cultural structures may prohibit access to women; in some cases women are not allowed to venture outside of the family home or are required to have men present when speaking to strangers. Women's lack of access to education may reduce the number of individuals with proper training and interest in violence against women who conduct research. Sometimes a conflict will rage for many years, and it will be many more years before it is safe for scholars to enter the area to conduct research. This could mean that women in one part of the world are being subjected to brutal violence for decades before the rest of the world hears about it. All of these factors contribute to the likelihood that violence against women has been inadequately studied and undertheorized. How do we learn about abuses? Initial reports of atrocities more often than not come from political or women's groups *within* a region who take great risks to inform the world about events. They provide the first reports of human rights abuses, often gaining attention from international human rights organizations.

The Revolutionary Association of the Women of Afghanistan (RAWA) is one such group. RAWA members were responsible for secretly filming the publicized public execution of Zarmeena in a soccer stadium in Kabul in 1999. Zarmeena, accused of killing her husband, was the mother of seven, who had already been jailed for one and a half years for this crime. Several women, including one named Salima, risked retaliation and severe punishment if caught recording the execution. Undeterred, they borrowed a small video camera and hiding it under their burkas, brought it into the stadium to document the event.

We knew this execution wouldn't be documented by a news agency. Taliban wouldn't do it and they wouldn't let others. So it was our responsibility. And we discussed if we should take photographs or make a report, or if we should film it. The opinion of the committee . . . was that RAWA was a political organization of women, defending human rights and women, but we didn't have the power to make the Taliban stop. The least we could do was document the scene by filming it and getting the word out. We did it because no one else could document this, to show the brutalities. We were willing to sacrifice our lives to do this. (interview with Salima, in Brodsky, 2003, p. 15)

Women as Perpetrators

Although violence against women is most often committed by men, this is not always the case. In some instances women are the perpetrators of the violence carried out against other women, such as in the case of foot-binding, "bride burning," female infanticide, the Magdalen's asylums, and female genital mutilation. In these instances, women often believe that by performing these acts on young girls and women, they are causing harm and pain as the only means of saving the girl's life or soul in the future. In the case of female infanticide, aside from the cultural demand for sons, women may kill their own babies or granddaughters out of a sense of protection to save them from the horrible lives filled with pain and torture that they are likely to have endured.

As sociocultural theories of power explain, in many societies there is or was an unswerving cultural mandate to do whatever is necessary to make women fit into a particular model that is the only acceptable vision of a woman within that culture. In many cases the women who carry out violence have been the victims of the same violence themselves and have suffered terribly, but they realize it is the only option open to them. Women have been directly responsible for administering torture or carrying out humiliating procedures on female prisoners and political activists (McWilliams, 1998). In the case of dowry deaths and "bride burning" in Indian cultures, a mother-in-law may encourage or support her son's torture and killing of his wife. She may even participate in the murder herself (Johnson and Johnson, 2001). According to Sev'er (1997), these mothers-in-law may see no other option, as they are also trapped in a patriarchal and oppressive system in which they must serve and obey the wishes of their husbands and sons. They themselves often "lead horrible lives in which they are second class citizens, oppressed, controlled, dominated, and undervalued by their fathers, husbands and sons" (Johnson and Johnson, 2001, p. 1062). It is still gender violence when women participate in or collude with men in violence that targets women (McWilliams, 1998). The gender of perpetrators is irrelevant, but understanding the reason why women perpetrate violence against other women is essential in order to identify solutions that will reduce the risks to women's lives.

METHODOLOGICAL PERSPECTIVES

There has been a general acceptance of and support for the use of qualitative methods to seek new understanding of women's lives and the contextual frameworks that encompass them (Brayton, 1997; Brodsky, 2003; Maynard, 1994). Feminism is about challenging gender inequities and the factors responsible for and results of those inequities. The use of women's voices as the centerpiece of research stands within a feminist framework. When so many of the justifications for violence are due to the subordination of women, institutional patriarchy, misogyny, and gender inequality, it follows that women's voices create the emergent theoretical foundations for an examination of violence directed toward them.

The stories that are reported through human rights agencies are often graphic, personal, and compelling. They describe circumstances of torture, violence, and oppression. They may be shared with the intent and purpose of compelling the reader to action. But, as Olesen argues, "rage is not enough" (2000). Scholarship and careful inquiry should not be dismissed. The contextualized, lived experience of individuals and the meaningfulness that results is central to understanding the human experience. Social inquiry is always value-laden, even politicized. Therefore, when human rights organizations collect the testimonies of women who have been victimized, even traumatized, the stories are a testament to the context and reality of the inquiry. While the testimonies may not meet traditional research criteria of validity, they do meet interpretive criteria of meaningfulness and credibility as well as the feminist criteria of action.

Methodologists have long challenged testimonials and narratives as valid research practice. How does the reader know whether the stories are true? What are the political or social agendas of the organizations that collect the data? Testimonials have routinely been the voices of those "who have been silenced, excluded and marginalized by their societies" (Tierney, 2000). Because personal narratives illuminate the oppressive conditions that exist for women (conditions that have yet to be fully realized or understood), the task is to acknowledge the circumstances in which the stories emerged and fully account for those conditions. They need not be an end to the study; it is our contention that they should be a beginning. But because the conditions may not support further study, the imperative at hand is to document, listen, accept, and act. The task of recording the stories that describe the violent conditions and placing them in a historical, social, and political context must ultimately lead to social movements that will improve those conditions. Aggregated numbers do little to motivate action. Stories and personal accounts provide what is necessary for understanding individual and collective pain. RAWA has a popular expression: *"Having my own experience,"* meant to convey the importance of firsthand experience in an individual's empowerment process (Brodsky, 2003). Women's stories make an important contribution to this book; they are its centerpiece. When the victims themselves are brave enough to step forward, there may be greater likelihood of attention. The survivor's words are the "counter-narratives" (Cooke, 1996) to what may be otherwise reported. Without women's voices, what is reported becomes incidence data, merely numbers, rather than an understanding of the human experience.

There are several points that support this argument. Women's personal stories illuminate the distinction between victimization on a personal level or a political level. In other words, the stories connect the justifications to one person's perspective or to culturally sanctioned violence. The stories provide a context for the violence and identify cultural issues that support it. Context is a key factor to understanding behavior. The stories provide information about the presence or lack of safety mechanisms for women within a culture. Women's experiences more often than not define the assumptions about women and men and the roles they play in a culture. Women's experiences connect the commonalities of women's status and subordination worldwide. Without individual experiences highlighted, it would be impossible to "connect-the-dots" between cultures. Numbers provide no foundation for generalizations of experience. Finally, the stories already available confirm that the world remains a dangerous place for women.

Individual narratives have value over aggregated numbers because the information derived from the narratives is information from the true experts. In some cases, those experts have experienced the violence first-hand and are already successfully working to overcome and change their lives and their environments. These inside "experts" can help us to understand the types of interventions that work naturally in this setting and others like it, informing the design of any effective interventions offered from the outside (Brodsky, 2003).

Furthermore, stories humanize the events. Many of the women whose stories are published are named. When human rights organizations reported a story about a Nigerian woman sentenced to be stoned to death as a result of an accusation of having had an affair outside of marriage, the world was concerned. When the world learned that her name was Amina Lawal, her story became riveting. Human rights activists began "Free Amina" campaigns to challenge the court sentence. E-mails circulated worldwide with "Free Amina" in the subject line. Her name humanized the circumstances she faced. As a result, there were letter writing campaigns from human rights and women's groups from around the world, and the Nigerian government was pressured to intervene. Naming became the social change agent. Lawal's sentence was overturned in 2003, no doubt due partially to political lobbying and to public outcry against what many felt was an unjust punishment.

The experiences highlighted in this book provide a context for understanding the violence. The brave women who speak of their experiences to human rights workers and others interested in their experiences often take risks by doing so. Although documented through the lenses of those who experienced the atrocities, the stories speak volumes. At the very least, they are compelling enough to warrant the attention of groups and individuals concerned with women's rights, human rights, and violence. "In this sense, the *testimonio* might be seen as a kind of speech act that sets up special ethical and epistemological demands. When we are addressed directly by an actual person, in such a way as to make a demand on our attention and capacity for judgment, we are under an obligation to respond in some way or other; we can act or not on that obligation, but we cannot ignore it" (Beverley, 2000, p. 558). The stories implore us to action and commitment.

THEORETICAL PERSPECTIVES APPLIED
TO GENDER VIOLENCE

Because violence against women takes multiple forms, exists within diverse contexts, and is committed by diverse perpetrators, no one theory adequately explains gender violence. There are many ways to theorize this issue. There have been biological arguments that attempt to explain and legitimize male violence against women, but they have proven shortsighted and most theorists interested in gender violence take a historical and cultural view (Wiesner-Hanks, 2001). The sociological perspectives applied to violent behavior are varied and sometimes focus on individual behavior. Ahuja's (1987) social bond theory explains violence against women in terms of the offender's social adjustment, values, and beliefs where social structural conditions contribute to perpetrators experiencing feelings of insecurity and anxiety due to inappropriate upbringing, abnormal childhood development, and abnormal life events (Natarajan, 1995). Social learning theory postulates that individuals learn how to behave through experience and early exposure to violence (Bandura, 1978; Skinner, 1953). Theories that examine the use of power within frameworks identify the role that power plays as a mechanism of control (Lukes, 1980; Yodanis, 2004). The social/cultural lens considers violence a response to structural norms within the social environment, cultural norms, and power differentials. For example, people uprooted from their home and culture may feel segregated and isolated and experience hostility and discrimination. This often results in clinging strongly to the familiar values and practices of their home culture in a fundamentalist way (Moghissi and Goodman, 1999; Sanday, 1981). If women were expected to be subservient in their culture of origin but begin to assimilate some of the more egalitarian values of a new culture, men may commit violence as a way to enforce the dominant patriarchal values of the home culture to assure their legitimized power.

In addition to these, there are a significant number of theories applicable to this issue and a review of them all is beyond the scope of this chapter. It is our contention that the more viable theories challenge existing power frameworks and call for a complete reorder of the race, class, and gendered norms that exist. They also consider the many different cultural and social norms in place. Therefore, of particular note, is the feminist theoretical framework that establishes socially constructed male dominance and female subordination as the primary cause of violence against women. The more traditional the gender roles and male dominance over women, the more likely violence against women is observed and condoned (Yodanis, 2004; Herzog, 2004). There is strong evidence to suggest that cultures with more traditional, patriarchal attitudes and more extreme conditions of subordination of women generate more severe and frequent violence against women (Sanday, 1990; Bui and Morash, 1999; Song, 1996; Yodanis, 2004). Furthermore, fear plays a significant role in dominating women. "Not every man must be violent toward every woman in order for violence to control women's behavior. Rather, knowing that some women are victims of horrific violence is enough to control the behavior and limit the movement of all women in society. The creation of a culture of fear secures men's status over women" (Yodanis, 2004, p. 658).

In contrast, cultures with greater equality between genders may generate less gender violence. Peggy Sanday reported on the connection between women's status and rape incidence in tribal cultures. She found that the cultures that could be distinguished as "rape-free" were more egalitarian. Although a division of labor existed within the cultures, the roles that men and women each had were respected, integrated, and interdependent (Sanday, 1981).

Feminist theories appropriately challenge the existing social order to reconstruct a new vision in which the division of labor, capital distribution, race and class distinctions, normalized heterosexuality, and gender conformity are reworked into a more equitable system. Only then will the power differentials, fear factor, and individual and group norms mitigate violence perpetrated against women.

In order to fully understand the magnitude of the violence, and the experience of it by those victimized, cultural differences within the institutions of marriage, gender roles, employment, and so on must be inspected. An examination of the varied forms of violence perpetrated against women worldwide and the context in which it occurs makes it possible to more fully comprehend the social and structural institutions that forsake women and fail to provide for them. Finding the common threads between the forms of violence may lead to a better understanding of the issue and provide discourse on the effects that the violence has on the social order as a whole.

The application of theories must be fluid, and in fact, change as the cultural circumstances evolve. Political unrest, immigration, economic challenges, natural disasters, and other major transformations impact the incidence, type, and justification for violence against women within a given culture. It is our contention that understanding violence against women requires an interdisciplinary approach. Explanations for the violence do not fall within the context of any one theory because it is so complex and multifaceted. However, by establishing a feminist theoretical foundation from which context, experience, and social order are juxtaposed, a deeper understanding of the violence perpetrated against women will evolve.

CONCLUSION

Violence against women is increasingly becoming an issue of international magnitude and debate. Effective action discrediting the patriarchal underpinnings of violence against women only began in the 1970s, mostly in North America and the United Kingdom (Rhode, 1989; Brownmiller, 1975; Sev'er, Dawson, and Johnson, 2004). Global efforts to stop violence against women are beginning, but the pace is slow. The United Nations has taken steps to end violence against women by ratifying the Conventions and Declarations on the Elimination and Violence against Women and the UN Convention on the Elimination of All Forms of Discrimination against Women (CEDAW) to which 174 countries have ratified or signed successions (Sev'er, Dawson, and Johnson, 2004). Naming and identifying the atrocities that women endure worldwide will expose all of us to the complexities and terrible consequences of these forms of violence.

Once the phenomenon of violence against women is understood within the cultural justification that supports it, it can be challenged. Ultimately, this can lead to the creation of effective policies on the international, national, state, cultural, and community levels that account for racial, sexual, and class disparities. Hearing women's voices is a step toward creating safer conditions worldwide for women and girls. The consequences to waiting are, essentially, lost lives.

We have included discussions of violence against women in more than eighty countries. While this is not easy reading, it is necessary reading. To understand the plight of millions of women worldwide is to better realize the human rights atrocities that must be abolished. It is a first step.

2

THE SOCIOPOLITICAL CONDITIONS THAT PREDISPOSE WOMEN TO VIOLENCE

There is a deplorable trend towards the organised humiliation of women, including the crime of mass hate.

(Boutros-Ghali, 1995)

Violence against women does not occur in a vacuum. Education, religion, cultural values, family structure, socioeconomic status, traditional beliefs, myths, geography, economics, government policies, criminal statutes, political unrest, and natural disasters all affect the violence and in many cases, contribute to it. It is these factors that are explored in this chapter. While the influences identified may operate as individual forces, they also often become integrated to support a cultural ideology that perpetuates the violence and suppresses forces that may stand in opposition. There is little debate that institutionalized male superiority and the cultural male dominance that stems from it are at the core of the violence perpetrated against women worldwide.

Some violence resulting from male entitlement is strikingly overt. For example, in December 1989, Marc Lepine killed fourteen women at Montreal's Ecole Polytechnique engineering school. He entered an engineering classroom with a gun drawn and told the men to leave before he opened fire on the women. Lepine wounded another nine women and four men before he fatally shot himself. He had been rejected by Polytechnique's engineering school, where thirteen of the women were students (the other victim worked as a clerk). In his suicide note he blamed feminists for spoiling his life (Came, Burke, Ferzoco, O'Farreli, and Wallace, 1989). "A police search of his room yielded a list of nineteen prominent Quebec women he also intended to kill. Lepine was acting out the violent rage against losing male privilege" (Kome, 2002).

Less overt forms of violence can be more complex, manipulated by cultural values and norms that are not static. Values and practices are manufactured, reconstructed, and reinforced by culture (Moghissi and Goodman, 1999). Values and norms can be altered by many factors such as law, war, religion, or natural disasters (e.g., drought causing famine). For example, violence against women has been a serious problem in many areas of the world where political troubles, such as civil wars and land disputes (e.g., South Africa, Northern Ireland) occupy the majority of the country's energy and attention. In these cases, because so much energy is spent trying to win political freedom and human rights, there is little attention paid to assuring the rights of one distinct group: abused women. In these troubled areas there is little agreement that human rights must focus on women living with violence.

This chapter provides a sampling of examples of the interplay of sociocultural norms and values and types of violence perpetrated against women. It outlines how specific cultural circumstances and values increase risks to women's safety both within and outside of the family. The institutionalization of male superiority in most cultures has resulted in violence against women "as a natural expression of male dominance" (Fox, 2002). To an even greater extent, male dominance has subordinated women through discriminatory practices of the most fundamental social experiences. These experiences can be divided into microlevel vulnerability and macrolevel vulnerability. However, there is considerable overlap in these two areas. Many situations that are family-based result from community cultural norms.

MICROLEVEL VULNERABILITY

As global stability fluctuates, changing family conditions appear to increase women's vulnerability to violence. Political and social upheaval, changing environmental conditions, and exposure to changes in family roles may affect women's safety in the home, aside from any culturally sanctioned forms of violence that may coexist. The context in which the violence occurs is closely connected to changes within the social, economic, and personal realms. It lessens or becomes more severe, depending on what other conditions are present.

Political Instability

Political instability impacts people on the national and international levels, and it also has serious implications for women, the family, and the community. When countries are faced with political turmoil, the cultural instability is reflected by what happens within the family structure. Women's safety within a community may be determined by what that community is facing in a political context.

Uzbekistan attained independence in 1991 with the dissolution of the former Soviet Union. It is a good example of a country struggling to impose laws and citizens' rights after political turmoil in the post-Soviet era. While the Uzbek government has attempted to legislate rights for women, Human Rights Watch reports that the reality for women living in violent homes is bleak.

According to Human Rights Watch, women in Uzbekistan are still in subordinate roles to men and are blamed if they are victims of violence. There are no laws that specifically address domestic violence, although a perpetrator could be prosecuted under the criminal statutes that address general violent behavior. While the government does not keep statistics on domestic violence, it is understood that domestic violence is commonplace in Uzbek society. Furthermore, it is deemed a "normal situation" by the women living there (Human Rights Watch, 2001f).

Contributing factors to domestic violence in Uzbekistan are the high rates of poverty, alcohol and/or other drug use, and the age of the couple involved. Contrary to what was intended after independence, the average marriage age for girls has declined since 1991. This limits access to education and employment for the brides (called kelins). It also means that the decisions about the kelin's life will be primarily made by her mother- and father-in-law. They can decide whether she works outside the home, who she will be friends with, how often she will see her family of origin, and so on. The new bride's life is fully controlled. In some ways, the in-laws can also control the violence a new bride is exposed to within the home.

Uzbek custom holds that the young bride must fulfill her obligations to the older generation. Much depends on the attitude of the young bride who must give way to the older generation. If relations with the older generation are good, then the mother- and father-in-law will not allow the husband to beat his wife (Human Rights Watch, 2001f).

Human Rights Watch estimates that a large number of suicides by women in Uzbekistan is attributable to domestic violence in the family.

*M*y stepsister was beaten by her husband because she gave birth only to girls. She hanged herself, leaving four daughters. They were together for sixteen years. She was sixteen when she married and had only finished the eighth grade. She was in the hospital many times [for beatings]. One year before

*she hanged herself she tried to poison herself. They saved her life that time. . . .
Over sixteen years of marriage she had four concussions. She never told anyone,
but the neighbors could hear everything. She never went to anyone. Her relatives wanted to call the police but she would not let them. She sent the children
outside to play and hanged herself in the bathroom. The children found her. . . .
The police came; they did an investigation and did not find any signs of violence. There was no criminal case opened.* (Human Rights Watch [HRW],
2001f, p. 41)

Divorce is available to women in Uzbekistan but there are many legal,
religious, and administrative barriers. There is a great deal of stigma attached
to divorce, particularly in a society that blames women for abuse. A judge
can impose a six-month waiting period before hearing a case again, in an
attempt to get the couple to reconcile.

Other forms of violence against women are not considered criminal in
Uzbekistan. While rape is illegal and the criminal code does not specify anything related to a woman's marital status, it is basically assumed that sexual
relations is part of the marriage contract. A women's crisis center adminis-
trator in Tashkent said, "The police would laugh if a married woman tried
to report a rape case" (HRW, 2001f, p. 39).

It is estimated that the incidence of domestic violence in Russia is four
to five times that of domestic violence in the West. An estimated fourteen
thousand women a year are killed by their partners in Russia (Horne, 1999).
Even more striking is the concern that the numbers of murders of women
in Russia are on the increase. However, because reporting these crimes was
a difficult thing for women in the Soviet Union, the supposed increase may
simply be a reflection of more accurate reporting in Russia now. Studies
about violence against women in Russia have focused on the more severe
forms; therefore it is questionable whether the lesser forms of abuse are even
being taken into account in newer studies on the problem. Furthermore,
most of the studies have as their foundation interviews or surveys with perpetrators which does not account for a victim's experience.

There are few resources in Russia for women who want to leave. As
of 1999, there were only two cities in the entire country with shelters: St.
Petersburg and Langepas. The first crisis hotline in the country was opened
in 1992 in Moscow (Horne, 1999).

Domestic violence has always been prevalent in Russia, supported by
historical stories that made women out to be magical and possess evil powers. Women have always been portrayed as dangerous and in need of control. Historically, Russia has held legal double standards for women that
made them more accountable for crimes than men. "For example, in the

mid-seventeenth century, there was no penalty for the husband's murder of his wife, but a wife who killed her husband was to be buried up to her neck and left to perish" (Horne, 1999). A custom of marriage in the 1800s was for a bride's father to pass a whip to her new husband. Myths continue to contribute to violence against women in Russia. Beliefs such as "if he beats you, he loves you" remain prevalent. "A common joke in which a wife is asking her husband why he is beating her and he replies: If I could think of a reason, I would kill you" (Horne, 1999, p. 58).

Although Russian woman are purported to be independent, pressure remains to be a traditional wife in the home and rely on the husband for financial support. For abused women, this means that even if there were resources for them to leave an abusive home, they will likely not be able to find employment to support themselves or their children. Housing in Russia is limited, and many extended families live together so the option to leave an abusive home and go live with relatives is not available for most women. Stringent sex role socialization contributes to the problem because women are expected to take care of home and family issues and men are responsible for decision-making. Because domestic violence is seen as a "family" problem, it remains a victim's problem. Therefore women are responsible for stopping domestic violence in the home, which assures the belief that women provoke the abuse.

In 1999, the United States Agency for International Development (USAID) reported that a Romanian edition of *Playboy* magazine published an article "How to Beat Your Wife without Leaving Prints." In the article were descriptions of the kinds of tools to use (e.g., sticks and washing machine drive belts) and how best to hold the woman down to make the beating easier. "The author, who remained unidentified, advised that any screams of pain would be bogus and that the wife would want to be beaten again. The article closed by wishing the reader a harmonious marriage." (Loue, 2001, p. 26). While women's groups in Romania objected, their complaints were dismissed. Proponents argued that the article was a joke, and the women were taking the issue too seriously.

There is little documentation about woman abuse in Romania. Its history is one in which dictators, patriarchy, and a poor economy have each played a role to oppress women and thwart attempts to prevent woman abuse. Nicolae Ceausescu ruled Romania from 1965 to 1989 where the people lived in fear of his guards and police. Family members were often convinced to "rat" on family members or neighbors who were dissenters and no one knew whom to trust. Ceausescu imposed restrictions on women's reproductive freedoms in the name of pronatalism and socialism. He changed the abortion rights laws that made abortion nearly impossible to obtain, outlawed contraception, and essentially his "marriage between demographic concerns and nationalist policies, turned women's bodies into instruments to be used in the service of the State" (Loue, 2001, pp. 54–55). As a result, women's lives became less important to the greater social good. Violence perpetrated against women was dismissed as unimportant.

Violence is an integral part of Romanian society today. One study conducted in two regions, Bucharest and Iasi, found that two-thirds of the women interviewed had been victims of violence, and a third of them had been victimized by their intimate partner. This study reported that approximately 85 percent of the women interviewed had witnessed violence perpetrated by another, including between intimate partners and parents and children (Loue, 2001). Spouses who beat their partners will not be prosecuted for a crime if the injury to the partner does not cause the loss of a major organ or death.

As in many other countries that have suffered from despot regimes, Ceausescu's rule obliterated the social support networks for the individuals living in the country and shattered the church's influence. Therefore, there are no mechanisms, charities, legal remedies, or shelters in place for women seeking asylum from abusive relationships. On both an individual level and a social level, there are few remedies to woman-battering in Romania.

Refugee Status

Women in refugee camps appear to be at particular risk of violence. The level of domestic violence in refugee camps is reportedly high due to housing and food shortages, and lack of security (Human Rights Watch, 2000b). Women in refugee camps have no access to legal support and have limited medical care after an assault.

In 1998 and 1999, the Human Rights Watch found that Burundian women refugees in the Tanzanian camps were victimized at high rates. Most were members of the Hutu ethnic groups who fled to Tanzania between 1993 and 1996 to escape their country's civil war. However, the Tanzanians were not welcoming of the influx of Burundians, having taken in refugees from Rwanda and the Republic of the Congo as well. The Tanzanians found the refugees to be a drain on the country's resources. Human Rights Watch reported that the Burundian women were being victimized both by their male partners as well as Tanzanian nationals.

As is the case in most countries, Burundian women are subordinate to men in their society. They have little or no access to education and are dependent on their husbands or male relatives for support. Decisions within the family are made by the males, including how the family's limited resources will be used and when the couple will have marital sexual relations. If the male decides that the limited food provided by humanitarian aid in the refugee camps should be sold for meager financial gain, rather than feed the children, the wife has no recourse. Women are responsible for childcare, preparing the food for the family, and taking care of the home. It is accepted that women may be punished physically if their husbands are dissatisfied. Other pressures in the refugee camps that contributed to the violence were the poverty, lack of employment or other time-consuming tasks, feelings of displacement, and emotional and behavioral scars from fleeing a war-torn country. One Burundian refugee woman summed up the situation to Human Rights Watch: "A wife is just like a child in Burundi. She is not supposed to question her husband's decision" (Human Rights Watch, 2000b, p. 18).

Some of the injuries sustained by women in the camp were so severe that the women had to be hospitalized. Women were beaten with fists, bottles, sticks, and machetes (pangas). Many women had visible scarring, broken limbs, cuts, and other abrasions. Many had contracted a sexually transmitted infection, presumably from husbands who were sexually active with women other than their wives, and some were raped by their husbands. Furthermore, while men taking multiple wives is illegal in Burundi, some men who fled the country married other women in the refugee camps, only to then find their Burundi wives escape to the same refugee camp. Some Burundi men openly took new wives and started new families in the refugee camps.

Domestic violence was not seen as a crime by the Tanzanian authorities. The general approach to this type of violence was counseling. In many cases, the women were intimidated by their husbands into not reporting the incidents. In general, the failure of the Tanzanian police to respond to domestic violence reports by refugee women only allowed the violence to continue and the perpetrators to go unpunished. In one documented case, a thirty-nine-year-old woman with a bruised upper lip and swollen eye reported:

> *My husband beat me and insulted me using vulgar and obscene language about my body. He compared my body to other women's whom he had before, and this was in the presence of our children. After beating me, he forced me to have sex with him. I did not report this case to the police because, in the past, they have not arrested him after I reported similar incidents.* (HRW, 2000b, p. 29)

There were additional threats to the women in the Tanzanian camp. Some of the women were likely to be attacked while doing routine daily chores: collecting firewood, gardening, getting water, and so on. For example, women are responsible for growing crops that will feed the family. However, the areas where women can grow food are often away from the main areas of the camp, thereby increasing women's vulnerability to violence and attacks.

Immigration Status

Immigrant women often find themselves living in two worlds. They bring their traditional cultures with them to the new country but are also exposed to different social orders in the new community. Acculturation as a result of the adaptation of new cultural norms may conflict with the traditional norms and be a source of stress for the families that have resettled. This stress may exacerbate violence in the home.

Immigrant women living in the United States may be influenced by both their traditional home culture and American culture. As a result, research suggests that they are more vulnerable to abuse by intimate partners than nonimmigrant women. There may be language barriers, and the immigrants may be unfamiliar with the legal and social systems in the United States. Cultural perspectives may prohibit women from seeking help from outsiders when living with an abuser or may have them accept the violence as a disciplinary tool. The language barriers, inability to find gainful employment, and lack of education may keep immigrant women from fully integrating into American society and make them more likely to "fall through the cracks" when they are victimized by violence (Bui and Morash, 1999; Raj and Silverman, 2002).

In the last few decades large numbers of people from other countries have journeyed to America to work in the growing U.S. computer industry. As foreign computer professionals immigrate to the United States, they sometimes bring with them spouses, and stories have emerged regarding domestic violence in these households.

Wives, who enter the United States with visas that tie their status to their husbands' work visas, are unable to leave the home or divorce abusive husbands without threat of deportation or poverty. For many immigrant women, even the thought of divorce would bring shame upon her family in her home country. So these women stay in abusive, sometimes life-threatening conditions, uncertain of their future because their legal right to stay in the United States is contingent upon their husbands' jobs.

Research on Latina, South Asian, and Korean women living in the United States reveals that 30 to 50 percent of the women have been abused physically or sexually by their intimate partners (Raj and Silverman, 2002). As women become more acculturated, they may challenge the prescribed gender roles of their home countries. Their behaviors may change, and they may not be willing to conform to traditional roles within the home. Abuse is the male's way to control the changing roles. One woman from India who arrived in Silicon Valley in California with her husband confided "He would humiliate me every day, call me names, slap me, pull my hair. I would just sit there and cry all the time. Every day felt so long" (Chaudhry, 2000).

Raj and Silverman refer to "immigration-related abuse" as that connected to a woman's status as a noncitizen. Because immigrant women may be socially isolated, batterers may find ways to keep women from their families, cutting off any e-mails or letters to them. Abusers may keep women from establishing relationships with anyone outside the home, refusing to let them enroll in language classes or travel unaccompanied. This will increase the woman's inability to function in the United States, and abusers will use this knowledge to further demean them and keep women from establishing any independence. If the women have a less protected immigration status than their husbands, the abusers may threaten the women with deportation if they do not act as the abuser demands.

All of these conditions create a more vulnerable circumstance for women who are not born in the United States. Immigrant women are least likely to seek outside help for battering. Cultural norms, unfamiliarity with American social network systems, economic dependence on the abuser, fear of losing their children, and language barriers make it impossible for some women to find the help and safety they need. Bui and Morash (1999) confirmed that class, culture, patriarchal beliefs, and the changing norms between husbands and wives due to acculturation all affected Vietnamese women's experience of violence perpetrated by husbands.

While there are some agencies trying to reach out to immigrant women in the United States, until recently there has been little research to address violence within the immigrant community. Even less research has been conducted on immigrant women living in other countries that face the same conditions but have fewer resources. Although women who live in countries where the laws against domestic violence are inadequate may be able to rely on other, less formal networks for safety such as tribal councils or religious supports, all immigrant women are in a precarious circumstance when married to their abusers.

Regional Conflicts

Areas of the world experiencing conflict may have an entirely different constellation of factors that contributes to women's vulnerability. The following examples illustrate the dynamics that put women at risk.

THE MIDDLE EAST

World events that have recently focused on the Middle East region have shed light on the status of women living in those countries. Ongoing war between Israel and the Palestinians, Iraq and the United States, and other regional disputes have provided some dramatic accounts of living conditions there. However, while the world witnesses the more overt dangers faced by citizens living in threatened or war zones, violence perpetrated against women by intimate partners gets little attention. Domestic violence in the Middle East is not well documented.

There is wide diversity within Middle Eastern culture; but because wife battering may be acceptable under particular circumstances in the traditional patriarchal structure of a Middle Eastern family, there is an enforced code that separates what happens behind closed doors from public scrutiny. In many Middle Eastern countries, it is up to the male family members to maintain the family honor. Should a woman bring dishonor to the family, beatings are acceptable punishment in many cultures. Extreme forms of punishment include honor killings (see chapter 9 on honor killing). Some women turn to the illegal practice of hymen reconstruction to avoid the wrath of their families should their hymens not be intact on their wedding night (Frank et al., 1999).

Lebanon has suffered for years from civil war, and this stress, coupled with poverty, housing shortages, and crowded living conditions (with extended family members often sharing the same living quarters), has been identified as contributing to domestic violence in that country. When in-laws share living arrangements, husbands have to deal with a wife in the home and the demands of a mother who requires respect and care. Husbands unable to balance the demands and conflict, reportedly lash out at the wife in violent ways. A study of low-income Lebanese Muslim and Christian Armenian women identified three main reasons for women being abused: "Unmet marital role expectations, conflicts with in-laws, and substance abuse [by the husband]" (Keenan, El-Hadad, and Bailan, 1998). One Armenian woman reported, "He came home after work and the meal was not ready and he beat me. He has become very nervous since the war. My children are not doing well in school. He holds me responsible, so he beats me." Another woman reported, "My husband drinks daily. Three days after my youngest child was born, it was hot and I was sleeping with the baby on the balcony. He wanted to have sex on the balcony. I refused and he threw me out into the street after the beating" (Keenan, El-Hadad, and Bailan, 1998, p. 359).

NORTHERN IRELAND

A Northern Ireland police report from the year 2000 reported that approximately 88 percent of all domestic violence calls in Northern Ireland were from women, and over one-half of the calls reported physical and/or sexual assault (Northern Ireland Human Rights Commission, 2001). According to the Royal Ulster Constabulary figures, one woman suffers a serious assault every day in Northern Ireland (Northern Ireland Women's Aid Federation, 2004). There are many reasons for the high incidence of domestic violence and sexual assault in Northern Ireland. For many years serious violence and killings have been part of everyday life in Northern Ireland. There has been a strongly entrenched paramilitary presence there, with men trained in guerrilla warfare and personal protection skills. In addition, weapons are easily available in many homes. Men may be very angry over the killing, imprisonment, and mistreatment of their compatriots. Men are accustomed to using their fists and violence to solve problems.

The Irish culture is one in which young men have been socialized to be strong and violent (McWilliams, 1998). Many have been arrested and have spent many years in prison, sustaining beatings for their beliefs. Within the National/Republican group (usually Catholics who oppose Protestant and British rule) they have traditionally relied on the informal justice of the "Punishment Squads" to mete out punishment for violations of social norms. "Knee capping" was one type of punishment which involves breaking the knees or shooting the knees (before the decommissioning of illegal weapons as a result of the cease-fire of the Good Friday Agreements of 1994). Egregious offenders may suffer a "six pack" which is shooting or breaking both knees, wrists, and ankles for violating social rules.

Many children may have grown up in houses where they watched one or both of their parents taken away in handcuffs, and there are regular riots in their communities, with grenades and petrol firebombs being thrown into their neighborhoods; windows of the houses closest to the border of the Republic and Loyalist areas are boarded up or covered with bars and wire mesh to keep grenades out of their homes. With this type of violence as a backdrop in their lives, violence in the home does not seem very different from life outside the home.

Because of the political "troubles," members of the police and security forces are permitted to keep their weapons at home, which makes them easily available. These weapons do not have to be used to shoot women in order to terrorize them. "One woman reported how her partner would recall episodes from the *Deer Hunter,* in which the Russian roulette scene was evocative of a man living on "the edge": "It was both mental and physical. You know I am thinking of times when he would put a gun to my head (and play Russian roulette with me) . . . but there was not physical harm done then" (McWilliams, 1998, p. 131).

Alcohol and drinking in pubs is part of life in Northern Ireland. The "lads" often gather to drown their sorrows or for camaraderie or to plan strategies over a few beers. Alcohol is also frequently a precursor to violence committed against women and may be used as a "mitigating factor" when sentencing an offender. If a man was drunk, he is likely to get a lighter sentence (Shanahan, 1992).

Ironically, because of the political troubles in Northern Ireland, some women from Great Britain or the Republic of Ireland have resettled in Northern Ireland after leaving their husbands, hoping that their husbands won't follow them into a potentially dangerous area (McWilliams and McKiernan, 1993).

Catholic women in Northern Ireland have historically been reluctant to ask the police for help because they feared greater reprisal by the nationalists if the woman were to do so. The police may not respond to her call, fearing an ambush. If they do respond, it may be much later, and they may arrive with many reinforcements. If her partner is arrested, the battering charge may be dismissed if he will turn informer on those instigating the political troubles. He is then free to harm her again.

"In this area [Northern Ireland] the police are not people that you normally go to. . . . We look after ourselves. . . . When we look for help, the police are never included. They are always seen as the harasser" (McWilliams and McKiernan, 1993, p. 56). This sentiment is still heard today in Northern Ireland.

For millions of women, intimate partner violence is a daily experience, condoned as a private family matter. For others, this type of violence erupts and/or is exacerbated as a result of social, economic, and political forces. Intimate partner violence is found in chaotic cultures, but it is also found in stable cultures. A discussion of additional factors that contribute to domestic violence in stable cultures follows.

MACROLEVEL VULNERABILITY

While conditions in the home may trigger violence, there are social issues that create conditions in which women's safety is increasingly jeopardized. Communities that establish social norms where women are subjugated and discriminated against provide the backdrop to violence perpetrated against them. Education, religion, cultural values, and policies all influence how members of a community are treated.

Education

The ability to read is one of the most fundamental skills to social order. Furthermore, education provides new perspectives and open dialogues about ideas and concepts that may challenge traditional authority (Flake, 2005). Without education, women's rate of participation in development is reduced significantly. Women are deeply affected by the lack of access to education or the shortage of it, which results in high rates of illiteracy for women (Ballara, 1993). Education for women who are denied it represents a pathway to social freedom; it represents autonomy, independence, and the ability to understand potential new ways of life. As a representative of the Revolutionary Association of Women of Afghanistan (RAWA) explained when asked about challenging the Taliban's denial of education to women and girls:

> *We always thought deeper than just giving women education. We thought the purpose was giving women a consciousness—political, social, cultural—giving them that consciousness meant a revolution. We obviously had to start with basic education but couldn't stop at that because just giving that education wasn't enough to break the chains in the family and society, and that was the goal, to liberate women.* (Brodsky, 2003)

A woman without education is fully dependent on others, usually her husband, to read to her (newspapers, legal documents, etc.), and to inform her of the law or policies relevant to her culture. If she cannot read, only low-level jobs will be open to her, and the meager wages associated with low-level employment may not be sufficient to support herself and her family. In turn, women's poverty levels become disproportionate to men's. Women who cannot find work that pays enough will be less able to leave a dissatisfying, abusive, or dangerous relationship. They are completely dependent upon others for accurate information including availability of social, financial, and legal resources.

It is estimated that 95 percent of illiterate adults live in nonindustrialized nations, and a disproportionate number of those who are illiterate are women and girls (Ballara, 1993; Women's International Network, 2000). In the early 1990s, approximately 64 percent of African women were unable to read and/or write (Ballara, 1993). India is reported to have one of the lowest female literacy rates in Asia with over 60 percent of the female population illiterate (Caleekal, 2001). After seven years of Taliban rule in Afghanistan, the ban on female education in that country contributed to a high rate of illiteracy and dependence (Morris, 1996). In Paraguay, the percentage of illiterate women is much higher than the rates for men (Women's International Network, 2000). In the United States, illiteracy contributes to poverty, single parenthood, and displaced homemakers. An American child's success in school was most affected by her mother's literacy rate (Commission on the Status of Women, 1993). Most importantly, educational attainment of women has been one of the markers identified that reduces the risk of violence perpetrated against them (Flake, 2005).

In many parts of the world, educational and employment opportunities are being lost because social conventions relegate women and girls to second- or third-class citizens. Educating girls and women leads to increased participation in development and democracy-building efforts and economic productivity resulting in reduced childbearing. Women's educational advancement also helps future generations. Educated mothers are more likely to send their children to school. Educated girls are more likely to seek high-paying employment opportunities outside of the home (Speth, 2000). The more options for earning their own living a women has, the less trapped she may feel in a dangerous or violent relationship. If she can support herself and her children, a possibility exists that she can leave her abuser and will be better able to secure safe housing and perhaps travel far from the community where the abuser lives.

Religion

Of the many religions practiced by people worldwide, some have specific links to violence against women. Strict religious teachings may be the result of cultural interpretations, and sometimes vary from the actual teachings or writings of the faith. For example, the Qur'an does not require female circumcision, although it is sometimes cited as the reason for committing the practice.

Religions have been responsible for condoning or generating a variety of forms of violence against women in the past century (i.e., the Magdalen Asylums in Ireland and the Trokosi system in Ghana). Many religions do not permit sex outside of marriage, and women have been whipped or put to death for premarital or extramarital sexual relations based on religious decree (i.e., Sharia in Islam). Homosexuality is also a punishable offense in some religions. Because same-sex marriage is prohibited, individuals who engage in sexual acts with members of their same gender are often accused of either premarital or extramarital relations (Schild, 1991).

Women who are married to men who are abusive may want to divorce or leave them, but since many religions discourage it, women stay in dangerous relationships. The Catholic Church has encouraged women to try to work through a troubled marriage and salvage it if possible. Some religions don't allow a woman to divorce her husband but do allow for husbands to divorce their wives. In some religious traditions, it is much easier for a man to divorce a woman than the other way around. Some religions also allow for a husband to kill his wife if she is discovered or suspected to be in an adulterous relationship, although the reverse is not true. Such was the 1987 Iranian case of Soraya M. whose husband wanted to marry another woman but reportedly had no grounds for divorce against Soraya. Therefore he accused Soraya of adultery and Soraya, innocent but now disgraced, was stoned to death by the villagers (including her husband, father, sons, and the religious mullah) of the town in which she lived. The stoning purportedly brought back honor to the village "in the name of God the compassionate, the merciful" (Sahebjam, 1994, p. xiii).

Cultural Values

In addition to discriminatory practices that may lead to violence, there is a wide array of cultural distinctions that undermine women's safety in the home and community. We have listed here a few that affect women's safety.

UNDERVALUED FEMALES

The devalued female effect is demonstrated by the high rate of female feticide and infanticide in India, Pakistan, and China, for example. Girls, who are sometimes considered expendable, may be sold by their families into slavery or prostitution to provide money to support the impoverished family. Pakistan and India are most often identified as two of the countries with a serious sex ratio imbalance. In India, a traditional blessing on a woman is to say "May you be the mother of 100 sons." Pakistan has been reported to have an even lower percentage of females than India; only nine hundred females for every one thousand men (Sen, 1992), resulting from infanticide or feticide. (See chapter 3, "Femicide.")

In the 1990s, an estimated sixty to one hundred million women from around the world were "missing" (Sen, 1992; Coale, 1991; Cohen, 2000;

Visaria, 1963; Das Gupta, 1987; Coale and Bannister, 1994). These are women who were unaccounted for: born and then "disappeared." They were kidnapped, sold by their parents, given away as sexual slaves, forced to repay the debts of their ancestors, systematically neglected to death, hidden, murdered, or tricked into believing that they are going to a legitimate job in another country. Once they are in the commercial sex market, they are likely to contract diseases and almost never escape. Many die there. By 2000, an estimated two million girls worldwide (between ages five and fifteen) were forced into the commercial sex market annually (United Nations Population Fund, 2000a).

According to "the rule (Article 258, Qisas) enforced by Islamists, the value of a woman's life, calculated as blood money (dieh) payable to the family of a victim for a wrongful death is just half that charged for the death of a man" (Moghissi and Goodman, 1999, p. 306).

"SOCIALLY DESIRABLE" FEMALE PHYSICAL CHARACTERISTICS

Gender conformity is illustrated in most cultures by strict adherence to dress and fashion. Individuals who challenge the stereotypical assumptions of how they should look may be in danger of punishment ranging from harassment, beatings, whippings, or even death. During the Taliban's rule of Afghanistan from 1996 to 2001, groups of men (the religious police) who found women outside their homes who were deemed "improperly dressed" (which ranged from lack of a burka covering all but their eyes to women who appeared to have white socks on under the veil) were severely beaten in the streets.

Footbinding of young girls in China has been illegal for almost a century, but the practice continued in many rural parts of China well into the twentieth century. Bound feet were believed to make a girl much more sexually desirable and marriageable. Once their feet had been successfully bound, the growth stopped, and the foot deformed, it was not possible to restore normal function or skeletal structure even if the feet were unbound later in life. Walking was always painful, and most women whose feet were bound were never able to do more than hobble. As of 1997, up to one-third of women in Beijing over the age of eighty still suffer from the effects of having their feet bound as children (Cummings et al., 1997).

The importance of women's physical beauty as a means to social acceptance cannot be overstated. Reports of acid attacks as a means of retaliation by rejected suitors demonstrate the importance of physical beauty in women's social acceptance. In Bangladesh between 1996 and 1998 there was a fourfold increase in reported acid attacks from forty-seven to more than two hundred (Bellamy, 2000). Acid attacks have been reported in Egypt, England, India, Italy, Jamaica, Malaysia, Nigeria, and Vietnam (Welch, 1999).

Dano, a teenage boy, had a crush on Bina's cousin, who did not return his affection. One night, while Bina and her cousin were asleep in a shared bed, Dano and a few friends entered their room with battery acid to punish Bina's cousin for rejecting him. Bina, to protect her cousin, jumped in front of Dano. At first, Bina thought the burning liquid thrown in her face was boiling water (Welch, 1999).

In Kashmir, acid was thrown into a bus and three women were burned. Such attacks are a part of a campaign to enforce an Islamic dress code among women (Hussain, 2001). In India, some women have been attacked by acid after refusing the advances or rejecting arranged marriage proposals or because the dowry a woman brings to a marriage is not large enough. When desire and sex are the motivating factor, acid is thrown at the genitals and the breasts as well as the women's face. In Cambodia, women have been burned by battery acid by the wives of men with whom they had illicit sexual encounters as a means of punishment, retaliation, revenge, or making the woman sexually unattractive (Mydans, 2001). The targets of attempts at disfiguration are usually young, beautiful women (Welch, 1999).

Nargis, fourteen, refused to become her neighbor's second wife. The rejected man sprayed her genitals with acid while she was in the bathroom that she and her brother shared with the neighbor's family (Welch, 1999).

This practice of disfiguring women who have rejected men is not limited to Asia. In 1986 two men slashed American model, Marla Hanson, in the face. Her landlord, Steven Roth, a television makeup artist whose overtures Hanson had rejected, orchestrated the attack after Hanson broke her lease early and demanded the return of her rent deposit (Welch, 1999).

Women's Chastity

Female virginity is so highly valued that in countries where a bridal price is paid, it is often much larger if the father can assure the groom that his daughter is a virgin. Cultural attitudes form the backdrop for behavior expectations and gender role conformity. There have been several cases of women being sentenced to serious punishment for premarital and extramarital sex in primarily Islamic countries. Sharia, or Islamic Law which governs social behavior, imposes the penalty of one hundred lashes for premarital sex, eighty lashes for falsely accusing another of a sexual offense, and death by stoning for adultery.

Farzana, age twenty-five, was publicly lashed one hundred times for premarital sex in Kabul in 1999 based on Sharia law in Afghanistan. Her mother also received thirty-nine lashes for "immoral behavior" because she knew of her daughter's relationship but did not report it to the authorities. (Associated Press, 1999b).

Two Nigerian women who claimed they were raped feared pressing charges because of the low probability of a conviction. They each became pregnant as a result of the rapes, had to carry around the evidence of "their fornication," and were punished according to the law for "their" crimes (Cunliffe-Jones, 2001). The raping of women has been used as a systematic way to punish and demoralize husbands, fathers, sons, and brothers of the women who are raped. These women are seen as the property of men, while the physical, social, emotional, and economic impact that the rape will have on the women themselves is often disregarded.

In 2000 in Nigeria, a seventeen-year-old woman named three of her father's friends as her assailants. None of them was "proven" to have been the father of her baby, because Sharia requires four male Muslim witnesses of good standing to the illicit sex or a confession by the offender in order to determine guilt. Because there were not four male witnesses, and none of the men confessed, the girl was sentenced to 180 lashes, 100 for premarital sex, and 80 for falsely accusing the men. Her guilt was obvious because she was pregnant and unmarried (Cunliffe-Jones, 2001).

In some cultures, women's desired virginity supports female genital mutilation (FGM) in some cultures. If a girl has undergone FGM and her vaginal opening is completely fused over by scar tissue, her husband can be assured that she is still a virgin. Although the practice has been outlawed in some countries, many proceed with the custom. In France, a man was convicted after his infant daughter died of an infection resulting from her female circumcision. The procedure had been performed on the baby at home. In the United States and Canada, fear of being forced to undergo circumcision can be grounds for asylum. A Nigerian woman was granted refugee status in Canada because she felt that she might be persecuted in her home country because of her refusal to inflict genital mutilation on her baby daughter (WomenAid International, 2000). A woman from Togo was granted refugee status in the United States to avoid the procedure herself (Kassindja and Bashir, 1998).

MACHISMO

Machismo is an overt form of cultural male dominance. In countries where machismo is the prevailing male attitude, male control is illustrated by more extreme forms of "maleness" which puts women in a subservient role and often at risk. For example, in places where machismo is present, men believe that they have to demonstrate their virility with early and frequent sex with multiple partners (Parker, 1996). A married man who has several extramarital affairs increases his chances of bringing home a sexually transmitted disease, including HIV. Women in Brazil, where machismo is present, have been beaten for refusing sex or for asking their partners to wear a condom. Therefore, a woman in those circumstances maintains little control over her own body and perhaps faces potential disease, lethal harm, or physical abuse from her husband's wrath should she attempt to protect herself with a condom. Machismo in Peru is represented by extreme masculinity reflected in sexual aggressiveness, alcohol consumption, and strength over women. In contrast, "marianismo" describes the female role as demonstrated by the Virgin Mary's behaviors, capable of withstanding great torment and suffering (Flake, 2005).

HOMOPHOBIA

Same sex intimacy is illegal in many places and may be punishable by death in some countries including Mauritania, Sudan, Afghanistan, Pakistan, Chechen Republic, Iran, Saudi Arabia, United Arab Emirates, and Yemen (Amnesty International, 1999). In countries where it is not illegal, many people still believe it is wrong and "punish" gay men and lesbians for their behavior. Homophobia, in its less severe form, is expressed by exclusion of gay people, name calling, and employment, medical, and housing discrimination. Homophobia's most heinous manifestation includes "gay bashing" (taunting, threats, physical assault) and murder.

In 1988 Claudia Brenner and her partner Rebecca Wright were camping on the Appalachian Trail in Pennsylvania (in the United States) when they were shot multiple times by an individual who, while spying on them, observed them engaged in a romantic encounter. The man shot at them with a hunting rifle, mortally wounding Rebecca who died at the campsite. Claudia was shot six times, including in the head. She managed to hike through the woods, walking for three hours to reach a highway where she was picked up by a motorist and taken to the hospital. After a long rehabilitation process, Claudia survived (Brenner and Ashley, 1995).

The murderer's attorney tried to minimize what he did and connect it to the same-sex relationship as provocation. During opening arguments, attorney Michael George said "We are to present testimony that Stephen Carr has been sexually abused as he was growing up by a neighbor of his and by a male in the prison system down in Florida and that his mother was in a lesbian relationship [and] because of his lifestyle growing up, [he had] been ridiculed through the school system. We are prepared to present testimony that every attempt he ever had to carry on a relationship with a woman has been refused and in effect has resulted in him being termed a freak or similar adjectives. We are prepared to present evidence that what happened on the afternoon of May 13, 1988 affected Steve's ability and pushed him over the edge and provoked him in effect, to do the act which he is alleged of doing should the court find that is what occurred. One fact which I want the court to take into consideration is that the women were engaged in a lesbian act at the time the incident occurred" (Brenner and Ashley, 1995, pp. 174-75).

After local media contributed to the homophobic reaction to the case, Brenner responded "In bold, banner, one-inch type, the *Ithaca Journal* had headlined the story about the hearing, WOMEN TEASE ME, MOUNTAIN MAN TESTIFIES. The Associated Press article under it used the words *sex, sex acts, lesbian,* and *taunted* repeatedly. It referred to me [Claudia] as Rebecca's Ithaca lover. The sensationalism was bad enough. Besides that, it was flatly wrong. He hadn't testified. We hadn't teased him. And the press never refers to a partner in a heterosexual couple as a *lover*—it's always *companion* or *wife* or possibly, *boyfriend*. Unless it is the *National Enquirer* reporting on the affair, the sexuality in a straight relationship is a nonissue. But here our sexuality was in the lead paragraph, splashed all over my home town in a lurid headline" (Brenner and Ashley, 1995, p. 146).

VICTIM BLAMING

The most common thread that connects the many forms of violence perpetrated against women worldwide is the overriding attribution of blame to those victimized. The very act of being female in a male dominant world assumes "difference-as-inferior" (Fox, 2002). Women who are victimized by male dominance are blamed for the violence perpetrated against them.

The right of a husband to beat or physically intimidate his wife is culturally ingrained in many societies (United Nations Population Fund, 2000a; 2000b). In parts of South Asia, Western Asia, and Africa, men have the right to discipline their wives as they see fit. Women in these cultures also believe that a certain amount of physical abuse is justified under some circumstances. Eighty percent of women surveyed in rural Egypt reported that beatings were commonplace and even justified, particularly if the woman refused her partner sex (El-Zanaty et al., 1996).

In many cultures, men and women ascribe to rape myths that allow men to rape without compunction and for rape to go unreported because the victim believes that she caused the rape or deserved it (Burt, 1991). "Estimates of the proportion of rapes reported to authorities vary, from less than 3 percent in South Africa to about 16 percent in the United States" (United Nations Population Fund, 2000a).

Rape myths in the United States are common. In the United States, women who dress seductively, who have "loose" reputations, or who don't fight their assailants are less likely to be believed if they claim they have been raped. Many believe that when women say "no" to sex, they really mean "maybe" or "yes." If a man spends a lot of money on a date, he frequently believes that his date "owes" him sex.

When Malamuth (1981) studied U.S. college-age men and asked them if they would force a woman to have sex if they could get away with it, half said "yes." He also asked them if they would rape a woman if they were sure they wouldn't get caught. More than one-third anonymously admitted that, under certain circumstances, they would commit rape if they believed they could get away with it. Chiroro, Bohner, Viki, and Jarvis (2004) reported that an examination of three studies on the relationship between rape myth acceptance and proclivity to rape found that men who believe in sexual dominance over women have been found to have a higher inclination to rape. According to Mary Koss and colleagues (1988), one in twelve U.S. men admitted to committing acts that met the legal definitions of rape, and more than three-quarters of men who committed rape did not label it as rape. In another study by Rapaport and Posey (1991), they found that almost half of U.S. college-aged men admitted to using coercive behavior to have sex, including ignoring a woman's protest, using physical aggression, and forcing intercourse. These responses support the notion that many men within the United States believe that forcing a woman to have sex is acceptable and that men do not always equate forced sex with rape. Many people believe that a weapon must be used or the victim must be beaten or worse for forced penetration to be rape (Frese, Moya, and Megius, 2004; Abrahms et al., 2003).

In some parts of Asia and the Middle East, rape is not viewed as a violation of the female as much as it is a violation of her male protector; rape of a female is an acceptable way to punish her entire family; if a woman does not defend her honor and resist, she deserves to marry her assailant or die to preserve the family's honor.

In Hong Kong, Taiwan, and the People's Republic of China, if a woman is raped, she is viewed as no longer chaste. Since there is an extremely high premium on marital fidelity and premarital chastity, women who are raped have disgraced the family, and they are no longer considered "respectable women" (Tang, Wong, and Cheung, 2002). In China "unmarried women who were raped by acquaintances chose to marry their rapists rather than file charges against them, because they believed that no other man would marry women with such experiences" (Tang, Wong, and Cheung, 2002, p. 977). Several women in the People's Republic of China drowned themselves after their husbands and parents reviled them for having allowed themselves to be raped (Honig and Hershatter, 1988). These are examples of how women have been sacrificed to preserve the harmony and honor of the family (Gilmartin, 1990; Honig and Hershatter, 1988).

Policies

Policies can be social, religious, and legislative, by decree or legal mandate. They are influenced by the cultural attitudes prevalent in the region and are created in different ways. In some countries, the laws are based on religious principles, in others they are decreed by a monarch or ruler, and in yet others, they are created by a body of elected officials. However, just because something is a legal policy does not mean that it is honored and respected. Social policies and customs, which have developed over centuries of tradition, are often much more important than laws, especially if the laws are selectively enforced.

In some countries where clitoridectomy/FGM has been a ritual for centuries but is now illegal, the practice still continues and few or no arrests have been made for violation of the law. Rape and wife battering are illegal in the United States, but both of these crimes are common. Dowry in India has been illegal since 1961, yet is still a practice in India today. Since the 1980s, dowry deaths have increased fifteenfold. The law alone has not been effective in reducing the problem (Pratap, 1995). The following section provides some examples of religious, social, and legal policies in places that do little to protect women from cultural violence.

RELIGIOUS POLICIES

Sharia is just one example of a religious policy that may dominate cultural norms and influence what could be described as discrimination against women. Sharia is based on the teaching in the Qur'an and is carried out in some countries as the legal law of the land. Aspects of Sharia which impact women's freedoms include imposition of Islamic dress code, the veil (Hejab) on women, sexual segregation of public life, and the right of the father or male guardian to treat his child (of any age) in any way he sees fit, permitting him even to kill his child (Article 220 of Qisas, the Islamic Criminal Code) (Moghissi and Goodman, 1999). Although both men and women are expected to adhere to Sharia, women's punishment seems to be more frequent and more severe for comparable violations of Sharia. For example, pregnancy can be the evidence of a woman's infidelity, but not a man's. Under Sharia, if eyewitness testimony is accepted to convict someone of extramarital sex or rape, four men are required as eyewitnesses or eight women. Since there are rarely four male Muslim eyewitnesses, men are much less likely to be punished than women, since if a woman becomes pregnant and her husband was not present during the time period the woman became pregnant, the developing pregnancy is obvious evidence that she had extramarital sex, even if it was rape. If she can't prove rape, she could be stoned to death for having sexual relations outside of her marriage.

Of course there are other religious beliefs that establish themselves as social policies. Others are found in the violent practice descriptions in part II.

SOCIAL POLICIES

In many parts of the world women are expected to be virgins at marriage and remain sexually faithful to their husbands throughout marriage. In the Middle East, historically it has been the role of the father, brother, uncle, grandfather, or husband to protect the honor of the family by ensuring that the women of the family do not engage in premarital or extramarital sex. If the woman does have premarital or extramarital sex, or if someone *believes* that she has, the family's honor is seriously tarnished. Often, the only way to restore the honor to the family is to eliminate the offending member. This is typically done by one of the men of the family publicly killing the transgressor. In many Middle Eastern countries, the penalty for murder is death. However, in cases of "honor" the penalty is much lighter. In fact, if a minor kills the woman (usually his sister or cousin) he is given a very short sentence (often under two years), and is viewed as a hero by the family for restoring their honor. Chapter 9 discusses honor killing more thoroughly.

Dowries are illegal in India because many brides were killed for providing insufficient dowries. Although illegal since 1961, dowry is quite common today and actually increases when the country is experiencing prosperity. It is one of the reasons there is such high feticide or female infanticide in India. If a family can't provide sufficient dowry, they may not be able to marry off their daughter. It is considered shameful in India to have an unmarried daughter.

Child brides are promised in forced marriages in many parts of the world. It is a socially condoned practice. For example, in Pakistan, marriages are often arranged to help the bride's family gain status, improve their economic conditions, settle a debt, settle a blood feud, or regain the family's honor. Although arranged marriage in and of itself is not violence or brutalization, it can be oppressive when the girls have no say in whom they will spend the majority of their lives with and who will have control within the marriage. If the husband and/or his family are cruel, a girl may have to endure decades of torture at their hands. Violence can and does result in these situations in the form of forced sex on demand, beating, bride-burning, and acid attacks. In many cases, wives cannot leave an arranged marriage, and if they do, their families of origin will not take them back. She usually cannot take her children with her because they are legally the property of the husband. In the most egregious situations, these wives sometimes commit suicide as the only way to avoid further abuse.

In Abba Khel, Pakistan in 2002, after Hussain Kahn killed two other men in the Noor family by mistake, Hussain was convicted of murder and sentenced to death. The Noor family demanded eight million rupees and eight of the condemned man's daughters in marriage. The girls ranged in age from two to seventeen. They were included in the deal just to humiliate the condemned man further. The deal was agreed to so their father would not be hanged, and the two oldest girls (fourteen and seventeen) were married to men aged fifty-five and eighty-three. Human rights activists became involved and made the facts of this case public. The president of Pakistan intervened and stopped the forced marriages once he was made aware of the case (Moreau, 2002).

In some Islamic cultures women are expected to preserve their modesty by covering their entire bodies in a chador (fabric that falls from the top of the head to the ankles, fastened under the chin) and burka (face mask worn by women) (Brooks, 1995) so that none of their skin, hair, or figure are visible. This is sometimes referred to as "the veil." This "Islamic resurgence" has been increasing since the late 1970s and has had a profound impact on religion, politics, and society within the Islamic world (Brenner, 1996). There has been resistance to this practice in some primarily Islamic countries, such as Indonesia where those who oppose the veil believe that it is not Islamic, but Arab (Brenner, 1996). They argue that the Qur'an requires the veil for prayer only and that it is excessive and impractical for daily wear especially in extremely hot and humid locations. However, the expectation for women to cover themselves may be severe.

A woman arrived at a Kabul hospital with burns over 80 percent of her body. An official of the Taliban, the fundamentalist group ruling most of Afghanistan from 1996–2001, prohibited the doctor from undressing her. The doctor explained that she would die if he did not treat her. "Many Taliban die on the battlefield," replied the official. The woman, untreated, died (Physicians for Human Rights, 1998).

A mother watched her daughter writhe with stomach pain for days. But she did not take her to a free clinic because she could not afford the head-to-toe burka that Afghanistan's Taliban religious leaders insisted women and girls shroud themselves in when they venture out in public (Behind the Veil of Oppression, 2001).

Rasekh, a fluent Farsi speaker trained in public health, interviewed the woman whose daughter died for want of a burka. In another interview, a woman described how her eight-year-old sister had been caught outside without a burka and was beaten by religious police. The girl was so traumatized she would no longer leave the house.

The "three obediences" in China require a woman to be obedient to her father when she is a child, to her husband when she is married, and to her son when she is widowed. Violation of these obediences is seen as justification to punish the woman with beatings (Tang, Cheung, Chen, and Sun, 2002).

The "four virtues" are tidiness, fidelity, propriety in speech, and commitment to needlework (Tang, Wong, and Cheung, 2002). Failure to satisfy these four virtues is grounds for discipline, including beating. Women in China almost never report domestic battering because it is attributed to their failure to be a good child, wife, or mother. Even if they do report the battering, Chinese tend to assume that the woman must have violated the four virtues or the three obediences (Tang, Wong, and Cheung, 2002). Newspapers in China often depict battered women as being unfaithful to their husbands, being unable to produce a son, or being unable to please their husbands (Chen, 1999; Meng, 1999; Wang, 1999).

Bride kidnapping still exists in parts of the world today and is a direct result of cultural norms, traditions, and patriarchal social attitudes. It has been reported recently in Kyrgyzstan, Turkmenistan, Turkey, China, Japan, Ethiopia, and among the Asian Hmong (Werner, 1997; Kleinbach and Amsler, 1999). A recent case in Ethiopia garnered international attention when a woman was acquitted for killing a man who kidnapped and raped her (Metcalf, 1999). Among some of these cultures the practice is illegal, but still prevalent, due to its traditional roots (Criminal Code, Kyrgyzstan, 1994). In Kyrgyzstan it is described as a national tradition by many, rather than a crime (Kleinbach and Amsler, 1999). A passage from *Being Stolen*

(Bishkek International School of Management and Business and the United Nations Development Programme, 1995) describes this attitude toward bride kidnapping:

> *A* *fter some time, she fell in love with him too. Now they have four children. They never fight, they live in peace. They have now been living happily together for twenty years. They respect each other, which is very important. . . . The practice of the older generation has shown that such marriages are stable. Our government does not allow stealing. But in spite of that stealing is still common here.* (p. 49)

Bride kidnapping ranges from women who help arrange their own "kidnappings" to nonconsensual, forcible abduction and rape. Kleinbach and Amsler (1999) report that many of these kidnappings are nonconsensual resulting in the abducted woman being forced to marry against her will. There is an element of coercion that occurs resulting in women "choosing" to stay because in Kyrgyzstan, if a woman refuses to marry her kidnapper, she is often considered a "spoiled" postmarriage woman (even if she is still a virgin), and it is possible that because of that, no man would marry her (Kleinbach and Amsler, 1999). In a recent study of kidnapped women in Kyrgyzstan, most were taken by force or deception, nearly one-fifth did not even know their future husbands, and one-fifth or more were forced to have sex by their kidnappers before they were married (Kleinbach and Amsler, 1999).

> They steal women because they don't consider the woman's feelings. Men are used to assum[ing] that the woman is destined to settle down when she is brought to [. . . his home]" (Kleinbach and Amsler, 1999)

LEGAL POLICIES

The "one child family" policy in China has been in effect since 1979. The Chinese government created this policy with good intentions—to reduce the population rate in China so the entire population wouldn't starve by the twenty-first century. Because boys are preferred in China, many female babies were killed at birth or given away for adoption in orphanages. Many of these babies were adopted by Western couples and left China. With the advent of ultrasound, female feticide replaced female infanticide. Because of these practices, there is now a gender imbalance among young people of marriageable age, with far too few women. A recent development in China to remedy this situation is the kidnapping of young mothers to be taken to other parts of China to be married to young men. The trafficking of women from other parts of Asia also profits from the imbalance (Rosenthal, 2001).

Some women don't adhere to the one child policy and try to have a second child. Once the pregnancy is detected, the woman is usually coerced into having an abortion or fined heavily for the birth of the second child. Forced sterilization often follows the abortion of women who try to violate the policy. For additional information on this policy see chapter 3, "Femicide."

Puerto Rican women, living both on the island of Puerto Rico and in New York City, have some of the highest rates of sterilization compared to women in other parts of the world and women of other ethnicities living in New York City. By the 1980s, Puerto Rico was experiencing the highest female sterilization rate in the world (Garcia, 1985); one-third of Puerto Rican women living on the island had been sterilized (Lopez, 1997, p. 3). Additionally, throughout the 1970s, the rate of female sterilizations performed by hospitals in Puerto Rican neighborhoods in New York City increased by 180 percent—a much greater increase than was experienced by hospitals in predominately black or white neighborhoods (Sterilization Safeguards, 1975). The high number of sterilizations performed on Puerto Rican women was motivated not by an educated choice for personal and sexual freedom but rather by the patriarchal and capitalistic ideologies of Puerto Rican culture and United States federal policies.

Historically, the U.S. government had a vested interest in controlling the growing numbers of poor Puerto Ricans. U.S. corporate profits were dependent on Puerto Rican land for factory sites as well as cheap labor to staff the factories. The sterilization of Puerto Rican women was deemed appropriate in that it both curbed population growth and preserved a cheap labor force of women because Puerto Rican women would no longer require maternity leave or benefits (Garcia, 1985).

The population control policies of the United States would not have been so successful in Puerto Rico had it not been for the patriarchal ideology already held on the island. Sterilization efforts to curb the growth of poor populations, in both Puerto Rico and New York City, have only focused on the sterilization of women, not the sterilization of men. Legislation cut the amount of federal assistance a woman received if she continued having children or if she did not get sterilized (Thomas, 1998). Some women were sterilized without their knowledge during surgery for a different purpose, and many were not aware of the permanency of sterilization when they consented to it (Lopez, 1997). In addition to such misinformation women received about sterilization, many were not presented with alternative methods of contraception, and it was not uncommon for health-care providers to sterilize their patients because they felt that the poor "did not have sufficient initiative or responsibility for controlling their fertility" (Lopez, 1997, p. 12). Although legal, these policies resulted in the unethical abusive treatment of women.

CONCLUSION

Worldwide, the growing "feminization" of poverty results from war and civil conflicts, environmental degradation, and rapid urbanization, all of which take a disproportionate toll on women. However, with education and economic opportunities, women can advance from a situation where they are triply disadvantaged—being poor, being female, being unmarried—to one where they work in society at large, and in the development of the next generation (Speth, 2000).

In many parts of the world, women are seen as the property of their husbands and fathers and may be sold, beaten, or killed at the whim of the patriarch. The origin of the Western cultural tradition of the father giving his daughter away in marriage stems from the belief that the daughter belongs to the father until she is given to the husband by the father. Depending on the culture, these practices are justified by social, legal, and religious policies.

The role of women within each culture is perceived in very different ways. Cultures have developed various practices as a means of maintaining social control. These practices are often based on perceived social needs. Understanding the purpose they serve within a culture and finding an acceptable alternative social or cultural practice in an effort to reduce violence against women may be difficult.

Sociopolitical issues pose complex obstacles that prevent many women from living in safety. The impact is not only on the individual herself but on her entire family and community. The cost of violence, oppression, and brutalization of women is enormous and creates generations as well as cultures of hate. Proposing legal, social, and political remedies to the violence requires understanding of cultural practices as well as the historical underpinnings that drive the violence.

II

VIOLENT PRACTICES

3

FEMICIDE: INFANTICIDE
AND FETICIDE

For fulfillment, many sons; for the sake of beauty, one daughter.

(Hedge, 1999)

This chapter examines the disproportionate killing of female fetuses (feticide) and infant girls (infanticide) that results in a significant gender imbalance in favor of males. These practices are not the only factors that account for such a gender imbalance in countries where it is practiced; trafficking, wife and intimate partner murder, sexual slavery, and the selling of female children also contribute to the significantly fewer girls and women in the population.

Infanticide and feticide have been used as the means to eliminate unwanted children throughout history, however these practices have been and still are disproportionately applied to females. The justifications, mechanisms, and consequences of these practices will be addressed as well as the social, cultural, and economic factors associated with killing girls. In some instances laws have been used to encourage feticide, and in others they have been created with the hope of eliminating it. Successful attempts to eliminate femicide are reviewed as well. Female infanticide and feticide most commonly occur in Asia; as such, China and India are a focus of this chapter. Although there are many countries with sex ratios in infancy favoring males, only those with the most serious imbalances will be covered in this chapter.

SCOPE OF THE PROBLEM

Males tend to be most highly prized in countries where females leave their parents and move into their husbands' homes with the husbands' parents when they marry. The circumstances then make married women unavailable to care for their parents as they age, and the parents of only girls face old age without caretakers. The bride's labor and availability are transferred to her husband's family upon marriage, leaving her parents with limited or no assistance. This system is present in both India and China.

Sons are preferred because in addition to being wage earners, they can also bring other economic assets to the extended family in the form of dowry or the unpaid labor of the wife. There are many societies in which only males can carry out religious, social, familial, or cultural responsibilities. Not only are females unable to do most of these things, they are also often a financial burden on a family as in the case of dowry, where girls are expected to marry and provide substantial sums of money and gifts to her husband's family.

Motherhood has been exalted and venerated, but in many parts of the world this is contingent upon whether the mother gives birth to sons (Chandrasekhar, 1994); women are often viewed as nothing more than wombs to bear sons (Hedge, 1999). In India, for example, only sons carry on the family name, and according to Hindu tradition, only a son can light his parents funeral pyre thereby assuring their safe passage to the afterlife (Glenn, 2004). A son is believed to be more of an economic asset through wage earning and by attracting a substantial dowry (Hedge, 1999). This attitude "manifests itself in the systematic neglect of girl children when it comes to breast feeding, nurturing, food intake, health care, personality development, property rights, and in extreme cases female infanticide" (Patel, 1997, p. 19). One of the long-term consequences of infanticide and feticide is a shortage of brides for men of marrying age. In South Korea the difference between males and females of reproductive age is projected to be 940,000 (Chuan, 1995). Projecting further to the year 2020, in China there will be 35 million more males than females; in India, 25 million; and in Pakistan, 4 million (Sex-selective Abortion and Infanticide, 2004).

I lay on my bed weak after childbirth. My mother-in-law picked up the baby and started feeding her milk. I knew what she was doing. I cried and tried to stop her. But she had already given her milk laced with yerakkam paal [the poisonous juice of the oleander plant]. Within minutes, "the baby turned blue and died," Karuppayee says matter-of-factly. (Aravamudan, 2001)

In 1994, 117 boys were born for every 100 girls in China (WHO, 1997). By 2002, that ratio was 109 boys for every 100 girls (Central Intelligence Agency, 2002). Some governmental and cultural attempts to stop the femicide have been showing promise. However, relying primarily on laws has only reduced the problem, not eliminated it. The cultural norms that drive these practices must also be addressed and challenged. In China, as well as other countries where males are more highly valued, the ratio of males to females is significantly higher (Cohen, 2000), especially if couples are permitted only one child (Farah, 1997). The phenomenon of missing girls in China in the 1980s was documented to have been related to the government's population policies, such as the one-child policy (Johansson and Nygren, 1991). In Korea in 1995, the male to female sex ratio under the age of five was 108.5, with higher ratios of males in large cities such as Taegu and Pusan (Cho, 1995). As of 2002 in South Korea there were 111 boys per 100 girls and in India, 105 boys to every 100 girls born. In India, by adulthood, the ratio shifts to 107 males for every 100 females (Central Intelligence Agency, 2002). Because sex-selective abortions and prenatal diagnostic tests for sex determination are illegal and under tight surveillance in India, some mothers who might have aborted their fetuses are carrying them to term. However, when unwanted girls are born, systemic neglect of health and nutrition of females and high rates of maternal mortality and abuse in adulthood continue to decrease the numbers of girls and women (Cohen, 2000; Sewell, 2000). With natural disasters such as the 2004 tsunami when food and clean water are scarce, one wonders if the limited resources will be distributed equally to male and female children. If male children are disproportionately given access to the resources, this may lead to an even greater gender imbalance in the areas affected by natural disasters.

TYPES OF FEMICIDE

The two mechanisms typically employed to support cultural male preference are infanticide and feticide. There are other manifestations of this preference, such as neglect or lack of medical treatment of older female children. However, sex-selective killing of females on the largest scale occurs before or shortly after birth. While most countries have a sex ratio of approximately 104 boy babies born to every 100 girl babies, the countries highlighted in this chapter have sex ratios at birth of 110 to 100 (Central Intelligence Agency, 2002). In other countries where infanticide is the primary method of femicide, the ratio at birth is similar to the worldwide average but changes in favor of males shortly after. In the normal course of events, the ratio ultimately increases in favor of females due to a variety of reasons: males die younger and more often due to injuries, wars, and so on.

Infanticide

Infanticide is the deliberate killing of a child in its infancy, including death through neglect (Hom, 1992). Historically it has been practiced on every continent (Williamson, 1978; Jeeva, Gandhimathi, and Phavalam, 1998), and the gender of the infant killed is almost always preferentially female, especially in periods of famine and poverty (Hom, 1992). Female infanticide has been practiced in such diverse cultures as Ancient Rome, among the Yanomami Indians of Brazil, and in Arabian tribes (Mitra, 1993).

The countries currently with a sex ratio imbalance due to infanticide or sex selective abortions include India, China, Guam, Pakistan, Taiwan, Hong Kong, and the Republic of South Korea. In some instances infanticide and feticide are employed; in others where there are no restrictions on the number of children, parents may continue to produce children until they have fewer daughters than sons. In large and diverse countries such as China and India, these practices are not universally employed but tend to be more common in the rural regions. The inner-land provinces of China are, in general, more isolated from outside influences and are subject to greater poverty, have greater need in physical labors, and preserve more traditional gendered ideologies compared with the coastal areas.

Because there are almost no examples of groups engaging in preferential male infanticide as a universal social practice, infanticide is a reflection of the deadly consequences for females of the cultural domination of patriarchal cultural values (Hom, 2001). This practice represents a crime of gender in the form of persistent and extreme abuse and devaluation of females (Hom, 2001) and reflects the authoritarian and hierarchal assumption that the male engendered version of the "natural order" of the world is legitimate (Hom, 1992). Justifications for infanticide are economic, familial, and societal (Williamson, 1978). Medical testing for sex selection, though officially outlawed, has become a booming business in China, India, and the Republic of Korea. Though no reliable infanticide statistics are available because many, perhaps most, cases are unreported, substantial disparities in gender population figures in these areas remain (Bellamy, 2000). "The killing of infant girls is a form of violence against the infant herself, the mother, and all women in the society in which the practice occurs. Female infanticide is a gender-based discriminatory judgment about who will survive" (Hom, 2001, p. 141).

Because women are blamed for the sex of their children, women who have given birth to girls . . . "have been poisoned, strangled, bludgeoned, and socially ostracized . . . [some have been driven] to suicide, others into mental institutions. . . . The pressure on women is so great that many openly weep on learning that they have given birth to a girl" (Chang, cited in

Weisskopf, 1985, p. A1). Women who are abused in India frequently experience this violence because they have given birth to a girl or for failing to give birth to a boy (Jeeva et al., 1998). This attitude is misguided. Because the male's sperm determines the sex of the fetus, to prevent women from being blamed for giving birth to daughters, one strategy may be to clarify and emphasize the father's role in determining the sex of the child (Sharma, 2003). When mothers make the decision to kill their babies, one wonders if they do so for themselves, their babies, or both. African women onboard slave ships crossing the Atlantic during the sixteenth and seventeenth centuries killed their children because they were demoralized and desperate about being enslaved and wanted their child to be in a better place (Bolles, 2002). Slave women in the United States were driven to infanticide, often after they were raped, to save their infant girls from the lives of misery that they themselves were forced to endure (Bolles, 2002). Women who kill their infant girls sometimes do so to keep them from experiencing the torture that they believe awaits their daughters within their culture: harassment, battering, alcoholism of their husbands, sexual abuse, shame, humiliation, and loss of dignity (Jeeva et al., 1998).

Feticide

In some countries, such as China, infanticide is being replaced by feticide (abortion of female fetuses), now that ultrasound can determine the sex of a fetus with a high degree of certainty (Garel et al., 2003). High tech medical tests to visualize the fetus in utero (ultrasound scans) or to determine the gender of the fetus through genetic testing early in pregnancy, such as amniocentesis and chorionic villi biopsies (CVB), are being used to support the elimination of unwanted female fetuses (Patel, 1997). These medical techniques are more readily accessible because of improved mobility between rural and urban areas (Sharma, 2003). Amniocentesis can be extremely accurate for determining sex at about sixteen weeks, while CVB is reliable at approximately twelve weeks (Patel, 1997). Some parents are choosing sex determination and abortion over infanticide for which they are less likely to be arrested. Because feticide is the interruption of development of a fetus that parents haven't seen, it may be less traumatic than killing a newborn baby.

Ultrasound is used most frequently in India and China because it is the more accessible and the least invasive and expensive of the three. Ultrasound is also less definitive than the other two and often will not yield the necessary information as early as the more invasive tests. A sex determination (SD) ultrasound scan can cost more than 300 rupees in India. The ultrasound and an abortion may cost as much as 7,000 rupees. But many families can't afford ultrasound and abortion. Although infanticide is illegal, while abortion is not, it is cheaper to kill a baby girl after it is born. Among the Bihari in India, a common sentiment is that "it is better to be aborted than burned by one's mother-in-law after marriage for insufficient dowry" (Krishna, 2002). Bride burning, which often results in death, occurs when the bride's dowry is considered insufficient by her in-laws.

Health care practitioners in India are engaged in debate over the appropriateness of SD tests. Some support SD as a population control measure. Others respect the choice of the couple and perform the test to help the woman prevent beatings by her husband and other family members for producing a daughter. A third point of view supports SD tests to identify fetal abnormalities only. Some oppose SD tests because they are opposed to abortion (Patel, 1997).

SELECTED EXAMPLES

India and China have the largest populations in the world; both have over one billion people. They are also countries in which infanticide has historically been practiced. Since these two countries account for approximately one-third of the world's population, their practice of femicide impacts millions of women.

China

As early as 2000 BC female infanticide was documented in China. A Chinese poem in "The Book of Songs" (believed to date from 1000–700 BC) offers the following advice to new parents:

> When a son is born
> Let him sleep on the bed,
> Clothe him with fine clothes,
> And Give him jade to play with. . . .
>
> When a daughter is born,
> Let her sleep on the ground,
> Wrap her in common wrappings,
> And give her broken tiles for playthings.
>
> (Glenn, 2004)

According to the World Health Organization, as of 1997 more than fifty million women were estimated to be "missing" in China. This situation resulted from the institutionalized killing and neglect of girls due to Beijing's population control program started in 1979, that limits families to only one child (Farah, 1997).

Methods of infanticide included suffocation, drowning, abandonment, exposure, crushing the infant's skull with forceps upon delivery, or injecting formaldehyde into the soft spot of the infant's head (Chang, 1988; Hom, 2001). Infanticide has now been replaced by feticide (Chowdhry, 1991). Many female fetuses are currently aborted, victims of ultrasound technology that revealed the baby's sex. Others are starved to death after birth or are victims of violence, and some go untreated when ill (Jones, 2000).

China's one-child policy has drastically slowed population growth which has accounted for approximately three hundred million fewer births in one ten-year period (Slavic Center for Law and Justice, 2002). China has not only limited families to only one child (except in very rare circumstances), but women are encouraged by the government to use birth control, have abortions, become sterilized, delay marriage, and seek permission from the government regarding the timing of pregnancy. Extremely low population growth rate is critical if China is to survive. By 2002 the one-child policy became law in China. There are a few exceptions permitted for women to have a second child. Ethnic minorities or rural couples can try for a boy if their first child is a girl. Twins are permitted. In some provinces couples who marry after age twenty-four or twenty-five, couples who wait until after five years of marriage to have their first child, people who remarry, and coal miners can have a second child (Sanger, 2003). Otherwise, couples who have more than one child must pay exorbitant fines and face loss of residency rights and their homes. Additional children are often barred from attending public schools.

In some parts of rural China "illegal" children are sometimes born in "secret," their births never officially registered (Rosenthal, 2001). Babies are supposed to be registered in home communities but when women move around the country to work in different regions, they can avoid registering the birth of a daughter (Allison and McCurry, 2004). Unannounced spot checks by the State Statistics Bureau have discovered up to 40 percent of girls in some villages were unregistered (Rosenthal, 2001).

Even if millions of Chinese infant girls are unregistered rather than murdered, the pattern of discrimination they face is one that will severely reduce their opportunities. If a parent fails to register a girl, her birth will be hidden from the government and therefore she will not legally exist. She may be denied medical attention, school attendance, and access to other government services (Porras, 1996). Female children who do survive may be victims of neglect. Mothers are generally more likely to take their boys to medical centers or to private physicians, and they are likely to be treated at an earlier stage of disease than girls (Farah, 1997).

The vast majority of babies in Chinese orphanages are able-bodied girls. In most cases, boys found in orphanages are mentally or physically disabled. Although the children are called orphans, many of them do have parents who don't want them because they are girls. Up to a million baby girls are deserted in China every year as a result of the one-child policy and its traditional preference for sons (Blewett and Woods, 1995).

My name is Ma Dongfang. I came to the United States in 1998. In 1991, I became pregnant with what would have been my second child. I was already married with one legal child, and to become pregnant again was a violation of China's one child policy. I was forced to abort this child, as many women are who become pregnant with second children. The incredible heartbreak of losing my second baby was followed with even more despair. After this abortion, the doctors inserted an IUD device into my uterus without either my knowledge or permission. I soon became very ill as a result of the IUD and endured months of horrible pain and discomfort. Excessive bleeding, weight loss, insomnia, and fatigue nearly cost me my job. I begged the doctors to remove the device, but if they had removed it, they themselves would be breaking the law. Still, my body could not tolerate the device, so instead they inserted Norplant into my arm. The Norplant proved to be no less distressing. The Norplant gave me night sweats, anxiety, and depression. Again, I begged the doctors to remove the Norplant, not because I intended to have another child, but because I was suffering so greatly. Bound by Chinese law and fearful of the consequences, the doctors refused. Had I found a way to remove the device myself, I would have lost my job and possibly undergone a forced sterilization or reinsertion. When I arrived in the United States, an American doctor removed the device that was causing such harm to my health. I received asylum here, and I now live peacefully with my husband and child as permanent residents. I found a job with Radio Free Asia where I now work to help promote freedom and democracy to those suffering as I had in China." (Dongfang, 2002)

In 1990, official Chinese census data suggested that 5 percent of all Chinese girls are unaccounted for (Kristof, 1991). A study by the Chinese Academy of Social Sciences, reported that millions of men in China cannot find a wife (Manthorpe, 1999). As a result, the kidnapping and slave trading of women in China has increased. According to official Chinese figures, since 1990, approximately eight thousand women a year have been rescued by authorities from forced "marriages." To provide more brides in China, slave trader gangs abduct women from other Asian countries, such as northern Vietnam, to supply the demand for wives in China (Manthorpe, 1999). The gender imbalance is much greater in rural China, where the boy-to-girl imbalance is estimated to be as high as 130 to 100 (Allison and McCurry, 2004). If this trend continues, males between the ages of fifteen to forty-four will outnumber females in China by 19.6 million. There will be a drastic shortage in the numbers of available women for romantic pursuits. The suicide rate for women in the rural areas is reportedly the highest in the world for females, in part because of the pressure on women to bear a male child (Vess, 1998).

In an attempt to reduce female infanticide and sex-selective abortion, there are a number of laws that prohibit femicide in China. The Chinese government has passed many laws since 1986 to reduce the incidence of feticide and sex-selection abortion, but the sex ratio imbalance is still extreme. When China's population reached 1.3 billion, Zhang Weiqing, Minister of China's National Population and Family Planning Commission, said that the Chinese government intended to even out the gender imbalance at birth by the year 2010 (Freymond, 2005). To accomplish this they are proposing yet another law to outlaw sex-selective abortion. To date, China's laws have done little to stop female infanticide or feticide. The laws are well intentioned but not effective. This is likely due to many layers of contentious interests between central and local political agendas, the stronghold of traditional cultural values, changing socioeconomic structures, and improved social welfare policies. A more successful approach to challenge this cultural norm must be developed, including efforts to shift perspectives that value boys' worth to a high degree while discriminating against girls.

India

There are signs for reproductive clinics in India that read "Pay 500 rupees now and save 50,000 rupees later," (Rohtak, 2003) meaning that if the fetus is a girl, it is less expensive to pay for the ultrasound and abort the baby now than to pay to raise a girl and pay much more for her eventual dowry later. In U.S. dollars, this would equate to $35 to $45 for an abortion rather than $3,500 to $4,000 on a dowry. Women in India have ultrasounds ostensibly to determine if the baby is healthy but may bribe the doctor to reveal the sex of the fetus. Prenatal sex-selection tests are performed with two motivations: parental preference for sons and increased income for practitioners (Patel, 1997). Men have much greater earning potential because they are stronger and more likely to be educated than girls, so they can get better, higher paying jobs. In addition, a son will bring a great deal of wealth into an Indian family when he marries and his wife brings a dowry. Some states, such as Punjab, Haryana, and Gujarat, which are the most affluent states of India, have very low female-to-male sex ratios (Priyadarshini, 2005). In affluent areas where people can afford sex determination tests and sex-selective abortion, feticide is more of a problem. In poorer areas where the sex ratio is imbalanced in favor of males, infanticide is more common.

Female infanticide occurs in every caste, community, and socioeconomic group in India. In Dharmapuri, one of the worst affected areas, an average of 105 baby girls were killed every month in 1997. Evidence supporting this was collected from the records of the primary health centers operating in these areas. Of these, 260 deaths occurred in Pennagaram, where female literacy was very low (31.3 percent), well below the state average of 41.8 percent. In the three years between 1994 and 1997, almost 3,000 infant girls died in Pennagaram (Aravamudan, 2001). According to the 2001 census, the Salem district of Tamil Nadu reported 826 girls for every 1,000 males (Athreya, 2001). Between the 1991 and 2001 census in the 0 to 6 year age category, the number of girls to every 1,000 boys in India fell from 945 to 927, with only 770 girls per every 1,000 boys in the Kurukshetra district of the state of Haryana (Sharma, 2003). More than one-third of infant deaths per year are due to female infanticide (Sabu, Rajaratnam, and Miller, 1998). As of 1999, more than 22 million females were missing in India (Hedge, 1999). Because of this, the male to female ratio has increased from 103 to 100 in 1972 to 111 to 100 in 2000 (Sarvate, 2000).

> *I have given birth to six daughters. Rani, Sita, then . . . one died, then another died; then came Deepa, John, and my last girl Fatima, the baby. . . . I killed my third and fourth child. . . . One drop of Errukulam milk, that's all. . . . If I had the money my babies would be alive today. They were beautiful babies.* (Pechi, cited in Hedge, 1999)

Some parents perceive the birth of a daughter as not only an economic burden but also the cause of diminishing their families' prestige and honor (Krishna, 2002). Why expose daughters to a future of neglect and abuse and force impossible financial burdens on the family. "The logical and simple solution is to set daughters free" (Hedge, 1999) by killing them.

> *In the last forty years I have grown up seeing girl babies being killed all around me—by my grandmother, mother, sister, aunt, and neighbors. So it does not strike me as something wrong.* (Krishnakumar, 2002)

There are many methods used today in India to dispose of infant girls. "Traditionally, unwanted girl children are fed milk laced with either yerak- kam paal or paddy husk as soon as they are born. The husk method is more cruel; it slits the tender gullet with its sharp sides as it slides down the tiny throat. The more 'modern' families use pesticides or sleeping pills. Some- times, they just suffocate the infant with a pillow" (Aravamudan, 2001). Parents also put powdered grain into the formula of infant girls, which kills them, without leaving evidence of purposeful killing (Anandhi, 2001). A baby girl may be left bleeding to death after her umbilical cord is cut, or harmful substances are applied to the wound to cause infection and subse- quent death (Krishna, 1999). Some female infants are put into sand bags and throttled to death (Sharma, 2003). "A spoonful of steaming hot curry . . . or a pinch of snuff; . . . the infant dies with no name, invisible in her birth and death . . . a baby of the burial pit" (Hedge, 1999).

In 1999, Palaniamma described how her mother-in-law had just killed her sister-in-law's third daughter. "My husband's mother wrapped the new- born girl in a wet towel. She threw it on the ground and pushed it with her toe. 'Who wants this?' she said and went out of the room. All of us stood there, afraid to pick the baby up. My sister-in-law, who was weak after the delivery, just wept. A few hours later, the child died. They got a doctor's certificate to say it had pneumonia" (Aravamudan, 2001).

If a case of suspected infanticide is registered with authorities, the body is exhumed, and the "old" methods of killing can be detected. However, newer methods are harder to detect. An infant can be deliberately weakened and dehydrated by its own parents. This is accomplished by wrapping the baby in a wet towel or dipping it in cold water soon after delivery or as soon as it comes home from the hospital. If she is still alive after a few hours, she can be taken to a doctor who will diagnose pneumonia and prescribe medicines. The prescription is carefully preserved, but the medicines are never purchased. When the child finally dies, the parents have a medical certificate to prove pneumonia. The villagers also cremate the little bodies to leave no "evidence" to exhume. Avoiding detection has become as important as the killing itself, especially as even cremation arouses suspicion, burial being the usual practice (Aravamudan, 2001).

Female infanticide is best documented in Tamil Nadu. In parts of Gujarat, mothers have been known to drown newborn infant girls in milk. In Rajasthan, there are entire villages where no girl has been born for de- cades (Aravamudan, 2001). Infanticide has also been documented in north India. It is common in some parts of Bihar, Uttar Pradesh, Rajasthan, Gujarat, and Madhya Pradesh (Sudha and Raja, 1998). In Bihar, infanticide is carried out primarily by traditional birth attendants or midwives (Priyadarshini, 2005). However, in some parts of India the elder brother of the father kills the girl child. A mother is not allowed to touch her husband's elder brother due to the purdah system. Mothers may want to resist infanticide, but if the child is in the lap of her husband's elder brother, she cannot retrieve it because she is not permitted to touch her husband's brother (Priyadarshini, 2005).

> *I gave away one daughter for adoption to the agency. . . . It was the sixth borne I gave away. I lost one when she was months old, another was stillborn . . . God is really testing me. . . . This is my seventh child. . . . I did not see her until one in the morning. . . . I was so sure this one was a boy. . . .* (Shelvi, cited in Hedge, 1999, p. 515)

Sex selection, followed by selective abortion can only be viewed as a free choice if women have other viable options. Women will lose status within the family, be subjected to taunts and abuses, and even be physically thrown out of the house as a consequence of not producing a son. The lyrics of a traditional Indian song exemplify this attitude: "The daughter in-law has produced a daughter. Throw her cot out of the house. The father-in-law should be informed that a girl has been born into the family so that he can remove his turban" [an indication of humiliation and misfortune] (Krishna, 2002). A traditional Indian blessing that reinforces this notion is "May you . . . be the mother of one hundred sons" (Ramanamma, 1991, p. 74; Pandey, 1969).

> *What do you think this girl will face? She can't run around with a pair of shorts like a boy can, she has to cover herself. I have to protect her. I have to manufacture her dowry from God knows where. And when she dies her brother needs to pour the water before her funeral pyre is lit. And she does not have a brother. She has nothing but suffering ahead of her. . . . It's not going to change. So tell me, am I mad, or what is wrong with my killing this child?* (Hedge, 1999)

SUCCESS STORIES AND PROMISING PRACTICES

There have been attempts by both nongovernmental organizations (NGOs) and governments to reduce femicide and the problems caused by the practice. Some are proactive, some reactive. Mother Teresa's Sister's of Charity Orphanage provides care to many Indian children, mostly unwanted female babies. The Indian and Pakastani governments have taken steps to address the problem by placing bassinets outside of police stations, hospitals, or charity organizations to receive unwanted girl babies. These babies then usually go to orphanages.

In Pakistan, between 1998 and 2003, 113 infant girls were found dead, but in most instances, the authorities did not thoroughly investigate or perform an autopsy (Mansoor, 2003). A sign outside of Pakistan's largest charity organization reads "Do not murder. Lay them here" (Armughal, 2004). For every one baby that was found in the cradle, at least one hundred "disappeared" shortly after birth (Aravamudan, 2001).

In Tamil Nadu, India in 1992 the Cradle Baby Scheme was initiated, and cradles were placed outside of government health centers for parents to dispose of unwanted babies, who were almost exclusively girls. An additional element of the initiative begun by Tamil Nadu's Chief Minister Jayalalitha in 1992 was to provide money to poor families with one or more girls (Sabu, Rajaratnam, and Miller, 1998). In the four years following the inception of the program, 136 girls were received by the center. In 2000, however, 1,218 cases of female infanticide were brought to the attention of the authorities (Radhakrishnan, 2002). The program was not considered successful, so it was abandoned. It was reinstated in 2001, but it was then administered on the district level, and the reception centers were in districts. In the district of Dharmapuri, 461 babies were received between April 2003 and June 2004 (Sridhar, 2004). The infant cradle scheme in Pakistan now results in between twenty-five and thirty baby girls per month deposited in the cradles (Mansoor, 2003). Due to these types of efforts, female infanticide in Pakistan is decreasing. In 1998, 391 infant girls in Pakistan were found dead, 68 in 1999, 59 in 2000, 52 in 2001, and 39 in 2002 (Mansoor, 2003).

By convincing expectant mothers to deliver their children in hospitals, officials hope to have a better chance of rescuing unwanted infant girls. In India, there have been a variety of legislative attempts to make female infanticide illegal, but the practice still continues. Clearly, the legislative approach does not work by itself. These practices are not likely to decrease until women have other options.

In India, some villages have instituted monitoring committees to identify pregnant women and counsel high risk couples (who already have daughters) to consider sterilization once they have given birth (Hindu, 2003). Some attempts are focused on improving literacy because, the lower the female literacy rate, the less women are valued; the less females are valued, the more disposable they are. Between 1991 and 2001, the literacy rate for females increased in Tamil Nadu from 51 to 65 percent and this has helped women better understand their rights and reproductive choices (Athreya, 2001).

Illiteracy is one of the major contributors to violence against women in India. As literacy increases, women are more likely to be self-sufficient with more employment options. This allows for alternatives to abusive marriages or the burden imposed by giving birth to a daughter. One specific program focuses on reducing illiteracy, and therefore infant deaths, in the Kerala literacy program in India. Kerala, one of the poorest states in India, has a physical quality of life index that resembles some Western cultures (Kesselman and William, 2000), because Kerala's literacy mission has improved the status of women with a 90 percent literacy rate (Kerala State Literacy Mission, 2003).

Prior to 1957, violence against women in Kerala was a serious problem, including dowry death, infanticide, feticide, physical and psychological victimization of women, early marriage and childbirth, and forced marriages. In 1990 the state of Kerala inaugurated the Total Literacy Program, which aimed for 100 percent literacy of all, including people in all castes. Each district within the state designed a literacy program to meet their specific needs. As a result of these changes, the status of women in that state has changed. The first female Indian Supreme Court justice, the first female head of the stock market, the first female state chief engineer, the first female surgeon, and the first Indian female internationally recognized as a literacy expert were all from Kerala. Other positive events have occurred as a result of increased literacy: infant survival rate has improved (especially among female babies) (Kerala, The Facts, 1993), life expectancy for women has increased, childcare has improved, and women's overall health is better. There is a direct positive relationship between an Indian woman's ability to read and a greater survival rate of her children (Hill, 1986). Prior to 1990, the infant mortality rate in Kerala was 120 per 1,000; in 2003, it was 19 per 1,000. The sex ratio in Kerala is 1,058 females per 1,000 males (as compared to an average sex ratio nationally of approximately 950 females to 1,000 males in the rest of India) (Census, 2001). It appears that many fewer children are dying and that females are surviving at a much higher rate than males.

A further outcome of this program is that there has been an increase in domestic violence reporting (New Internationalist, 1993). This may be because there may be an increase in violence due to a backlash by men resentful of women's improved status or because more women are now willing to report and better understand the options to report.

CONCLUSION

Most laws to stop female infanticide criminalize women responsible for the killing, usually the mother, grandmother, or midwife. But cultural discrimination and individual-directed blame create an environment that forces women to perpetrate these crimes. Women are blamed for giving birth to girls and are punished for it as well. To avoid the blame and punishment, they are under unimaginable pressure to sacrifice their daughters. It is the equivalent of social infanticide. Understanding that this is social, rather than individual infanticide, policymakers and leaders at the institutional and ideological levels have a responsibility to challenge the underlying assumptions that allow infanticide to be an available option to women oppressed by the conditions in which they live (Hom, 2001). Because of the double bind women are in, laws that target the individual woman who kills her daughter will not stop infanticide. Social reform is essential if there is to be any meaningful reduction in the practice.

The cultural scripts a woman lives with, combined with the obligations to her family, and socialization to subordinate her own needs to the men in her life all contribute to infanticide and feticide (Gil and Anderson, 1999). Although many women live with poverty, neglect, and subordination, they are held accountable for the violence in their lives. Objectified, with the main purpose of creating more males, they are declared murderers when the system forces them to carry out patriarchal and misogynistic ideals (Hedge, 1999). In addition to other forms of oppression, such as race and class, female infanticide constitutes a deadly denial of women's rights to life and liberty on a large scale (Bunch, 1990). It is one of the more insidious of the many manifestations of violence against women.

They are not butchers, they are helpless.

Woman doctor speaking of women who kill their infant daughters in India.

(Hedge, 1999)

4

FEMALE GENITAL CUTTING: CLITORIDECTOMY, FEMALE CIRCUMCISION, FEMALE GENITAL MUTILATION, OR RITE OF PASSAGE

Every summer a group of girls would go off [with the circumcision performer]. And every year, at least one girl would not come back. We all knew why.

Sierra Leone woman (Retlaff, 1999)

The terms in the chapter title are all used to describe a "surgical" procedure experienced by approximately two million girls and women worldwide each year, fifty-five thousand each day (Cook, Dickens, and Fathalla, 2002). The practice dates back to 4000 BC (Hellsten, 2004). The type of procedure varies, as does the motivation for it. Sometimes there are several terms used to describe the same event, depending on one's political ideology, culture, and experience. These terms may be used interchangeably depending on motivation or perspective. The term "female genital mutilation" (FGM generally refers to the dysfunctional disfiguring of a woman's genitals, whereas "female genital cutting" (FGC) may be used to refer to the same practice while respecting its cultural significance. "Clitoridectomy" usually is used to mean the removal of part or all of the clitoris and the clitoral hood. Both "female circumcision" and FGM are often used interchangeably to refer to any form of the procedure. Any of these practices can be performed as a rite of passage or initiation rite.

The practice of surgically removing part of the vulva in women and girls has been occurring worldwide, and with people migrating from one continent to another taking their practices with them, can now be found on most continents in varying degrees. It is viewed differently in different parts of the world and takes many forms, from a slight nick of the clitoral hood to complete surgical removal of most of the vulva and clitoris. The form of the procedure and motivation for it differ from place to place. Historically, Western doctors used clitoridectomy to cure epilepsy, kleptomania, and melancholy (Hellsten, 2004; Lightfoot-Klein, 1989). Clitoridectomy was performed by Dr. Isaac Baker Brown, a British gynecologist, as a cure for female mental disorders and masturbation in the mid-1800s (British Medical Journal, 1867). This practice was introduced in the United States in the 1860s and continued in some form until at least 1937 (Barker-Benfield, 1975).

FGC is a cultural practice, rather than a religious one, and as such, it is performed by members of many different religious groups. This chapter will focus on the political, religious, and cultural justifications for as well as the common techniques of FGC. Complications of the procedures and legal approaches to eliminate it are discussed. Programs from a number of countries that have been successful in reducing the incidence and severity of FGC will be highlighted.

> *It was on a Saturday night when my Mum called me and she said, "my daughter, come" in a low voice.*
>
> *I went quietly. Suddenly my mum said: "My daughter, tomorrow is your D-day."*
>
> *I was shocked to hear that but I was not expected to say anything.*
>
> *In the morning I was dragged and pinned on the ground.*
>
> *When three women sat and crucified me on the floor.*
>
> *I cried until I had no voice.*
>
> *The only thing I said was "Mum, where are you?"*
>
> *And the only answer I got was "quiet, quiet, girl."*
>
> *The pain I had experienced was one which I will never forget for the rest of my life.*
>
> *And I would not wish the same to happen to my friends.*
>
> *That night I had a sleepless night.*
>
> *I could see an old lady with many blades doing it again and again and again.*
>
> *I screamed, and my Mum came running to check on me.*
>
> *My loving parents, is this what I really deserved?*
>
> *I'm asking all of you, is this what I really deserved?*
>
> (Fouzia from Kenya Macharia, 2003)

The poem above was written as an assignment for school by Fouzia Hassan Osman from Kenya when she was ten years old. She wants to become a doctor, so she can help others who become sick from "the cut." Fouzia says that she will forgive her mother only on the condition that she will not permit circumcision for her younger sister (Macharia, 2003).

SCOPE OF THE PROBLEM

Worldwide, an estimated 130 million girls and women have undergone female circumcision, clitoridectomy, genital cutting, or female genital mutilation, and at least two million more a year are at risk of undergoing the procedure (Center for Reproductive Law and Policy [CRLP], 1999). Although this practice is prevalent in over twenty-seven countries in Africa (Toubia, 1995; WHO, 1999; Hellsten, 2004), Asia, and the Middle East, its consequences are being felt worldwide as people from the areas that practice the ritual travel to and reside in other parts of the globe. There are women living in Europe, Canada, Australia, Belgium, Denmark, Sweden, New Zealand, and the United States who have undergone genital cutting (WHO, 1999; Lockhart, 2004). In the United Kingdom, between three to four thousand new cases are believed to take place every year among the immigrant population from Eritrea, Ethiopia, Somalia, and Yemen (Bosch, 2001). Geographically, female circumcision is practiced in a band of countries that crosses sub-Saharan Africa north of the equator. The practice is not evident in Southern Africa nor in the Arabic-speaking countries in North Africa, with the exception of Egypt (Toubia, 1995). The following countries have an estimated prevalence rate of genital cutting of at least 50 percent in certain regions of the country: Benin, Burkina Faso, Chad, Cote d'Ivoire, Djibouti, Egypt, Eritrea, Ethiopia, Gambia, Guinea, Guinea-Bissau, Kenya, Liberia, Mali, Nigeria, Sierra Leone, Somalia, Sudan (common in the north), and Togo (98 percent among the Tchama but absent among the Adja Ewe) (Shell-Duncan and Hernlund, 2000; WHO, 1996; Izett and Toubia, 1999; Lockhart, 2004; Hellsten, 2004).

Female circumcision is performed in the United States and Europe in surprisingly high numbers (Davis et al., 1999). It is estimated that at least ten thousand children in the United States are at risk of being subjected to female circumcision (Jackson, 1991) because their parents want to carry out traditional cultural practices to assure their daughters' marriageability should they return home. Reports of female circumcision being practiced among African and Asian immigrants to western countries have led to a variety of legislative and legal responses (Davis et al., 1999). These responses will be discussed at length in the section on Success Stories.

As a result of FGC, medical practitioners worldwide are having to pro-

vide care for circumcised women and deal with requests by families to circumcise their daughters. However, as women become more independent in
cultures where female genital cutting is commonplace, some women are
leaving their homelands to avoid it and seek political asylum in other parts of
the world. Therefore, female genital mutilation is not just a psychological,
emotional, and economic issue, but also a political one.

Common Techniques of Female Circumcision

The term "female circumcision" refers to traditional practices that
consist of the removal of all or part of the external female genital organs. In
the rural areas, female circumcision is performed primarily by midwives or
elderly women of a village, and the technique is passed from generation to
generation (Davis et al., 1999). There are regional and individual variations
to the techniques used, but there are five general classifications.

(1) Pharaonic or Total Infibulation (Type III)—The Pharaonic
method reportedly came from Egypt via the Sudan. This is the
most severe and mutilating technique, consisting of the removal of
the clitoris and hood as well as the labia minora and most of the
labia majora. The sides of the vulva are often joined by thorns of
the acacia bush. Occasionally, silk sutures are used. The vaginal
opening is tightly closed except for a small opening to allow the
exit of urine and menstrual blood. Complete closure of the opening is prevented by the insertion of a small sliver of wood or a
match stick (Davis et al., 1999; Adebajo, 1992; CRLP, 1999;
WHO, 1999; Toubia, 1995).

(2) Modified Infibulation—a milder form of infibulation, which
involves the same amount of cutting, but only the front two-thirds
of the labia majora are stitched, leaving a larger opening (Toubia,
1995).

(3) Clitoridectomy or Excision (Type II)—Removal of the clitoral
hood, the glans of the clitoris, and the labia minora (Adebajo,
1992). The vaginal opening is partially closed with acacia thorns.
This technique retains the labia majora and allows a larger vaginal
opening than the Pharaonic method (Toubia, 1995; Davis et al.,
1999; CRLP, 1999; WHO, 1999; Lockhart, 2004).

(4) Sunna Circumcision (Type I)—The clitoral hood is removed
while the glans and the body of the clitoris remain (Toubia, 1995;
Adebajo, 1992; CRLP, 1999; WHO, 1999; Lockhart, 2004).

(5) Unclassified—all other procedures that include total or partial

removal of the external female genitalia or damage to female genital organs for nontherapeutic reasons. These procedures include pricking, piercing, incising, stretching, or cauterizing by burning the clitoris and/or labia and/or surrounding tissue; introduction of corrosive substances or herbs into the vagina to cause it to bleed for the purpose of tightening or narrowing it (CRLP, 1999; WHO, 1997; Snow et al., 2002; Lockhart, 2004).

Some girls are circumcised at birth, but procedures performed at one month of age or older are more likely. To signify the rites of passage, the vast majority of female circumcisions are done before puberty (Davis et al., 1999). In some communities women are circumcised and married on the same day, while others may have their previous circumcisions opened before first intercourse within marriage (Burns et al., 1997). In Bendel State in Nigeria, female circumcision may be performed on women who are seven months pregnant because a commonly held belief in that culture is that the baby will die if its head comes in contact with the clitoris during

Normal Female Genital Anatomy

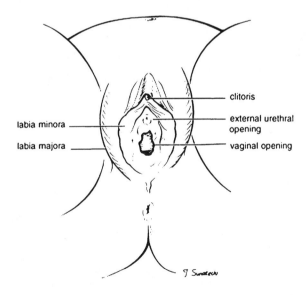

Normal Female Genital Anatomy. Reproduced with permission from *Pediatrics* 102, no. 1: 154, 155. Copyright © 1998 by the American Academy of Pediatrics.

Type I Female Genital Mutilation

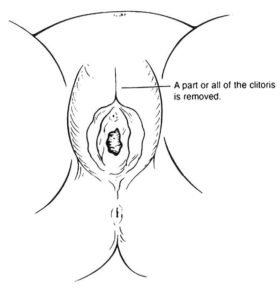

A part or all of the clitoris is removed.

Type I Female Genital Mutilation. Reproduced with permission from *Pediatrics* 102, no. 1: 154, 155. Copyright © 1998 by the American Academy of Pediatrics.

childbirth (Adebajo, 1992). Other reasons for female circumcision include prevention of promiscuity, cosmetic (the clitoris and the labia are perceived to be ugly unless "trimmed"), removal of evil spirits (women harbor evil spirits), uncircumcised women are considered unclean and should therefore be avoided, preservation of virginity (particularly with infibulation, since the hole that is left after stitching only allows for menstrual flow), and income or status for the practitioners (Adebajo, 1992). Infibulation not only increases a woman's value and power, it also provides her with an almost impenetrable armor that can help protect her from rape (Lightfoot-Klein, 1989). Various instruments, including kitchen knives, razor blades, or pieces of glass, scissors, sharp stones, and even teeth are used to perform the operation (Dierie, 1998; Davis et al., 1999). In Gambia, fingernails have been used especially on young girls (Dorkenoo, 1994).

In rural areas, anesthetics are never used. Instead, children are restrained by women who hold down their arms and legs with their own (Davis et al., 1999). One Gambian mother remembers "the screams (of the girls) calling for mercy, gasping for breath, pleading that those parts of their bodies that it pleases God. . . . I remember the fearful look in their eyes when I led them to the toilet, *"I want to, but I can't. Why Mum? Why did*

Type II Female Genital Mutilation

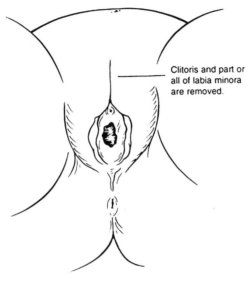

Clitoris and part or all of labia minora are removed.

Type II Female Genital Mutilation. Reproduced with permission from *Pediatrics* 102, no. 1: 154, 155. Copyright © 1998 by the American Academy of Pediatrics.

you let them do this to me?'' Those words continue to haunt me. My blood runs cold whenever the memory comes back" (CRLP, 1999, p. 2). Herbal mixtures, earth, cow dung, or ashes are rubbed on the wound to stop bleeding. The newly circumcised females have their wounds and their entire pelvis bound tightly for forty days (Davis et al., 1999).

In the Nandi ritual (Kenya) of female circumcision, after the circumciser cuts off the clitoris with a curved knife, she then pours traditional herbs on the wound that cause excruciating pain. The girls are supposed to endure the pain in silence as proof of their adulthood. There is not supposed to be any pain at this point because the sex organ is supposed to be numb as a result of the application of stinging nettles prior to the procedure. There is usually considerable bleeding, which sometimes results in hemorrhage and death. These deaths are not discussed, and the parents of the girl and the initiators bury the corpse discreetly (Nyangweso, 2002).

Reasons for Female Genital Cutting (FGC)

Women who have been circumcised tend to support continuing the practice (Nwajei and Otiono, 2003). Those who favor the continuation of

Type III Female Genital Mutilation

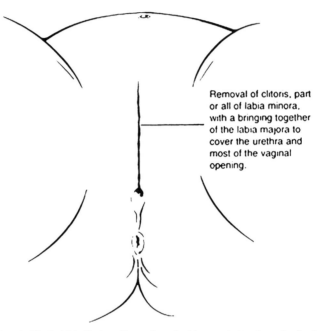

Removal of clitoris, part or all of labia minora, with a bringing together of the labia majora to cover the urethra and most of the vaginal opening.

Type III Female Genital Mutilation. Reproduced with permission from *Pediatrics* 102, no. 1: 154, 155. Copyright © 1998 by the American Academy of Pediatrics.

female circumcision appear to do so primarily because of tradition or cultural conformity. Because circumcision practices are ubiquitous within the limited sphere of some rural dwellers, these women cannot compare their conditions with those of uncircumcised women. Women in places where FGM is common accept the long-term health consequences of being circumcised as simply a woman's burden (Davis, Ellis, Hibbert, Perez, and Zimbelman, 1999).

In some parts of Africa, and elsewhere in the world, female circumcision is a sign of a woman's sexual purity and is required for her to be married. Uncircumcised women are often viewed as unclean, not marriageable, and disloyal to their cultures (Moschovis, 2002). Therefore, female midwives and a girl's own female relatives are among the strongest proponents of the practice (Hosken, 1993). Women may push their daughters to be circumcised in order to ensure that they can be married off, a process which includes the payment of a dowry or bride price to the parents; if the girl is not circumcised, bride price or marriage are unlikely. The payment of bride price in some communities is of great significance as an economic element of survival (Kiiti, 2005).

Often, a woman who never marries is shunned and has no means to provide for herself if only males are permitted gainful employment outside of the home. In some cultures a woman cannot own property or inherit wealth even if she is employed, unless she is circumcised or married. An uncircumcised woman is frequently likened to a loose women or prostitute. In some communities, offspring of uncircumcised women may be killed (Lightfoot-Klein, 1989). In these patriarchal cultures the need for economic survival pressures women to be circumcised and to circumcise their daughters (Gunning, 1992). To do otherwise would almost assuredly lead to an isolated life and an untimely death. Uncircumcised girls will also suffer greatly without inheritance or acceptance.

Performing circumcisions is a lucrative way for a woman to support herself. A woman is often compensated much better for her circumcision services than for her midwifery or nursing services (Lightfoot-Klein, 1989). In the Sudan, 89 percent of married women have undergone FGM (WHO, 2001). As women with exceptional power and influence, Sudanese grandmothers and midwives may perform the procedure.

Some women view their circumcisions with pride. It is usually carried out in the context of an elaborate ceremony, which is part of the initiation to womanhood. This may be viewed as the most important day of a girl's life (Lightfoot-Klein, 1989). Girls will be accepted as adult members of the community once they have undergone this "rite of passage." During this celebration that may last several days, newly circumcised women may receive many gifts and a great deal of attention (Gruenbaum, 1988). Surrounded by women in their community who have undergone the procedure, they are unlikely to question their own circumcisions or those that will be performed on their daughters (Davis et al., 1999). Female circumcision is often seen as a "fact of life," as all of the female role models in one's life have undergone the procedure. Many believe that this procedure will confer health benefits on the woman. Increased fertility and producing a greater number of healthy children are believed to be two of the benefits of female circumcision, though often the opposite is true.

After Mende Nazer's infibulation (the most severe type of female genital cutting) in her hut in the Sudan at the age of eleven, which she describes as pain worse than anything she could have imagined (Nazar and Lewis, 2003), she asked her mother why she held her down and allowed this to happen to her. Her mother kept saying "I'm sorry, I'm sorry, I'm sorry" (p. 79) with tears in her eyes. . . . She later told her "It will make you healthy. It will make you clean. It will keep you a virgin" (Nazar and Lewis, 2003, p. 81). In a culture where bearing children is one of the few things women have some control over, a procedure which is thought to increase this capability is desirable (Lightfoot-Klein, 1989).

My aunts said . . . "That's not fair. We're leaving Aman out by doing the other two. It's not good for our name—our brother's name, and besides, she's the oldest and it's shameful to do the younger ones and not her."

They invited everybody. They killed one bull, two goats, and a sheep, and cooked the whole night. They asked me if I wanted to be circumcised. . . . I told them yes, I wanted to. All the girls my age wanted to because it's shame not to . . .

There was a big woman there who holds the girls while they are being circumcised—a strong woman. I told her "You don't have to grab me hard, I'm not going to run." I said . . . "I'm not going to cry either . . . You don't have to tie me, I want everyone to be proud of me." If she had tied me it would have seemed as though I was frightened. . . . She said "It's not a big thing, it's not that painful. . . . Don't let your family down. Don't let yourself down. The children will laugh at you tomorrow if you cry today." I told her I wouldn't cry—I was going to be strong. And I was.

She was getting out her knives and all the other equipment and wiping them to make them clean. Then she took some of the charcoal powder between her thumb and forefinger and started playing with my clitoris, pulling on it so that it would become bigger. . . . She cut everything—she didn't cut the big lips, but she sliced off my clitoris and the two black little lips which were haram *(impure). . . . I thought I was going to die.*

Oh God. . . . It had only just started. I looked around to see if someone would help, but I just saw smiling faces. . . . I opened my mouth and pretended I was laughing, but I was dying inside. She sliced off the top of my big lips, and then she took thorns like needles and put them in crossways, across my vagina to close it up. She put in seven thorns, and each time she put one in, she tightened them together with string. When she was finished she put on some black paste to stop the bleeding and make the wound dry up fast. And then some egg yolk to make it feel cool.

I was so proud. They did it because they love me. (Aman from Somalia in Barnes and Boddy, 1994, pp. 53–57)

Sometimes FGC is agreed to by the girl as a form of barter in order to obtain something she wants, like a secure future, a better husband, or an education.

Kakenya Ntaiya, a Masai, was engaged through an arranged marriage agreement at the age of five. Most of the girls she knew were married by the time they were fourteen. "I decided that I wanted an education, and it was not an easy thing because I had to actually struggle and go against the traditions that I should get married between age twelve or fourteen. That was a big challenge for me to actually convince my father and my community and my elders that I wanted an education. In my community they do female genital mutilation, and I had to go through that when I was sixteen. So I talked to my dad, and I told him, "I can only do this if you'll allow me to go to school." And I told him I didn't want his support financially because I will work on a farm and get my own school fees. (Sheridan, 2004)

Some girls undergo circumcision because they fear what will happen if they don't. During the Nandi initiation ceremony in Kenya, teenage girls are warned of the dangers of having an intact clitoris: if the clitoris is not removed, it will grow large and develop branches; it is dangerous for the health of the baby for if the baby's head touches the clitoris, the baby will die or become abnormal; husbands will become impotent if their penis touches the clitoris; it can make the girl insane; or she will be ostracized by the entire community and will never marry (Nyangweso, 2002). Peer pressure is also a significant motivating factor. One highly educated woman in north Sudan insisted that her parents take her for circumcision in her teens because she hated being different from her friends and being laughed at—she now greatly regrets it (Kiiti, 2005).

In some areas the practice of female circumcision is being modernized but not abandoned. More often in the larger cities, many people are choosing to have their daughters circumcised by physicians in a hospital under local or general anesthesia to decrease pain and the risk of infection.

Educational campaigns by the World Health Organization (WHO) and the Women's International Network have increased awareness of the social, medical, and psychological consequences of these procedures. The WHO influence, however, is primarily in and around urban centers. One of the most important factors affecting the attitude toward female circumcision in the rural provinces is the opinion of national rulers (Davis et al. 1999). In provinces in which the ruler disapproves of the custom, the prevalence of female circumcision is decreasing. However, the majority of the rulers are not unhappy with female circumcision (Davis et al., 1999).

Religious and Political Justifications for FGC

This custom is practiced in developed as well as developing nations throughout the world. It is commonly associated with Muslim cultures (Davis et al., 1999), however the prophet Mohammad gave guidelines for female circumcision that included leaving the clitoris intact (Ogiamien, 1988). Traditional Islamic scholars have posited that female circumcision is not required by the Qur'an, and if it is performed that it should be slight as the clitoris contributes to the woman's sexual enjoyment, from which both she and her husband benefit (Winkel, 1995). Some Christians living in the Middle East and Africa also adhere to this cultural practice (Jehl, 1999). Although it is a practice that is more common in parts of Africa, it is also commonly carried out in the Middle East, India, and Sri Lanka (CRLP, 1999). FGC is practiced by members of many religions (Lax, 2000). In Arabic, Tahara is the word used to refer to FGC, which means "to purify" (Lax, 2000). Since removing the clitoris makes it more difficult for a woman to enjoy sex, it decreases the likelihood that she will have sex outside of marriage. In addition, removing the clitoris is seen in some cultures as removing the masculine part of the woman's body, the part that becomes erect during sexual excitement in the same way the penis does.

In 1946, female circumcision was banned in Africa by British occupational forces and made punishable by imprisonment, but the practice remained commonplace among the indigenous populations (Ogiamien, 1988). Genital cutting has also been used as a symbol of normalcy to celebrate the end of civil unrest (Moniaga, 2002). In 1997, as a means of showing the country's solidarity after the civil war in Sierra Leone, approximately six hundred women underwent FGC as part of the celebration (French, 1997).

According to Davis et al. (1999) recent social and political changes in Africa have not always resulted in changes in the practice of female circumcision. Economic changes associated with development actually increased women's economic dependence on men, causing them to focus on maintaining their marriageability and to prevent divorce by keeping husbands sexually and reproductively satisfied (Davis et al., 1999). The resulting economic insecurity made it unlikely that parents would risk leaving their daughters uncircumcised (Gruenbaum, 1982).

FGC is often prevalent in patriarchal societies, where men seek to curb, and at times, even eradicate women's sexuality (Lax, 2000). Major decision-makers regarding FGC are heads of families, religious leaders, and village chiefs. Community members defend FGC as a means of continuing cultural traditions, fulfilling religious obligations, preparing girls for marriage, and controlling female sexuality (Population Council, 2002). Psychoanalytic analysis of FGM suggests that it stems from men's unconscious fear of women's sexuality (Lax, 2000). One could argue that this is misguided since women are the ones actually performing the cutting. However, mothers who have themselves undergone this experience, and have lived with the consequences, would probably be less willing to force this on their daughters if men within the culture would be willing to accept a noncircumcised wife. In places where literacy rates for girls are increasing, the incidence of FGM is decreasing (Igwegbe and Egbuonu, 2000; Adongo et al., 1998; Mbacke et al., 1998). In Egypt, girls are less likely to undergo genital cutting if either of their parents (but particularly the mothers) achieved higher educational levels (Egyptian Fertility Care Society, 1996).

SHORT-TERM COMPLICATIONS OF FGC

The passage which follows is the account of Waris Dierie, an international supermodel, and United Nations special ambassador, who underwent the most severe form of female circumcision/female genital mutilation at the age of five in the desert of Somalia. She described her ordeal and her flight from a forced arranged marriage in her book *Desert Flower* (Dierie, 1998).

After the gypsy sewed me up, the only opening left for urine and menstrual blood was a minuscule hole the diameter of a match stick. This brilliant strategy ensured that I could never have sex until I was married, and my husband would be guaranteed he was getting a virgin. . . . My genitals became infected, and I ran a high fever. I faded in and out of consciousness. Feverish, bored, and listless, I could do nothing but wonder: Why? What was it all for? At that age I didn't understand anything about sex. What did I know about being a woman? Although I didn't realize it at the time, I knew a lot about being an African woman: I knew how to live quietly with suffering in the passive, helpless manner of a child. For over a month my legs were tied together so my wound would heal. . . . My genitals were sealed up like a brick wall that no man would be able to penetrate until my wedding night, when my husband would either cut me open with a knife or force his way in. (Dierie, 1998, pp. 43–45)

The aftermath of these procedures can include the immediate complications of shock, infection, damage to the urethra or anus, scar formation, tetanus, bladder infections, septicemia, HIV, and hepatitis B (Davis et al., 1999; Dierie, 1998; Odoi, Brody, and Elkins, 1997; Shell-Duncan and Hernlund, 2000; Boyle, 2002; Lockhart, 2004).

LONG-TERM COMPLICATIONS OF FGM

My periods began one day when I was alone out tending my sheep and goats. The day was unbearably hot, and I sat weakly under a tree, feeling even more uncomfortable because my stomach hurt. I wondered, What is this pain? . . . About an hour later I went to pee and saw blood. I thought I was dying. . . .

Looking for something that would bring me relief, I went back into the desert and started digging a hole under a tree. The motion felt good and gave me something to take my mind off my pain. I dug and dug with a stick until I had a spot deep enough to bury the bottom half of my body. Then I climbed in, packing the dirt in around me; the underground hole was cooler, sort of like an ice pack, and I would rest there during the heat of the day. (Dierie, 1998, pp. 141–42)

While she was in Somalia, Waris would regularly dig a hole in the cool ground as a means to cope with the pain associated with menstruation. When she left Africa, after years of enduring this pain on her own, she sought the help of a physician, and only then did she discover that not all women had this excruciating experience with menstruation.

Long-term complications include chronic and recurrent urinary and pelvic infections that can lead to sterility, cysts and abscesses around the vulva, nerve pain, difficult urination, painful periods, the pooling of menstrual blood in the abdomen, difficulty with labor and delivery (Arrowsmith, 1996), sexual dysfunction, depression (Elchalal, 1997); and death (Davis et al., 1999; Dierie, 1998; Odjujinrin, Akitoye, and Oyediran, 1989; Shell-Duncan and Hernlund, 2000; Odoi, Brody, and Elkins 1997; Boyle, 2002; Lockhart, 2004).

Menstrual blood backed . . . the same way the urine did. . . . The pressure . . . was excruciating. The blood came out one drop at a time . . . my periods were very bad, I started passing out. The pain paralyzed me, and I didn't know what to do about it. . . . I still thought what happened to me happened to all girls. (Dierie, 1998, p. 143)

Her mother believed that this was the experience of all women because all the women she had ever known had the same type of menstrual history following FGC. They simply thought that this was part of being a woman.

Bleeding and hemorrhage are not only concerns at the time of the initial procedure. Some women experience heavy bleeding, excruciating pain, and infection at the time of initial sexual intercourse (Odujinrin, Akitoye, and Oyediran, 1989). The scar must be torn or cut open to allow for a penis to enter. This can result in a woman bleeding to death or future fear of sexual relations. Aman describes what happened when she was "devirginized" . . .

I will never forget the pain. I remember having my circumcision ripped open with the sound like the tearing of a piece of cloth and feeling at the same time the most awful pain. Then I became unconscious. When I opened my eyes . . . there was blood, pee, and dirt. I was in so much pain that I couldn't move my legs. It was as though I was paralyzed. And the blood wouldn't stop flowing. (Aman from Somalia, Barnes and Boddy, 1994, p. 179)

While women suffer considerably during and following FGC, their male partners also suffer as a result of their wives circumcision. Men report negative physical, psychological, and economic experiences as a result (Almroth et al., 2001). Physical problems include difficulty with penetration, penis wounds, and inflammation and bleeding. Decreased sexual desire and enjoyment and a desire to hurt their partners and make them suffer are the psychological concerns men experience. There are also additional medical care expenditures that men must pay resulting from their wives FGC. Because of the negative experiences that women who have been circumcised and their partners live with, efforts are underway to reduce both the severity and incidence of FGC worldwide.

FGC AS A JUSTIFICATION FOR POLITICAL ASYLUM

In both the United States and France, women from Mali, Somalia, Togo, and Nigeria have requested political asylum to avoid forced circumcision for themselves or their daughters (Reynolds, 1994). The following case describes one woman's attempt to be granted U.S. political asylum from FGM. Fauziya Kassindja's ordeal is described in her book *Do They Hear You When You Cry?* (1998).

In 1993 Fauziya Kassindja was living a happy life as a teenager from Togo. She lived with her parents and siblings in the city of Kpalime, and attended school in Ghana, the country bordering Togo. She and her family were devout Muslims, who did not believe in the custom of female circumcision. Her older sisters had been married and had not been circumcised. After the untimely death of her father, her mother was evicted from her family home by her uncle, who then became her guardian. Her uncle and aunt decided that she should stop attending school, get married, and become circumcised. Fauziya was then forced into an arranged marriage to a man she didn't know as his fourth wife by her uncle, the patriarch of the family. Within days of the marriage she was to undergo female circumcision, which she dreaded. So much so, that on the eve of her circumcision, and with the aid of her older married sister Ayisha, she fled the country in the dark of night with a stranger to Germany with only the clothes on her back. She had never been on a plane before, did not speak German, and didn't know anything about Germany, or anyone there. She was terrified of leaving her loving sister and mother, and beloved country, however she was even more terrified of the arranged marriage which awaited her and her impending circumcision.

After a long and difficult period in Germany, Fauziya was advised by a friend in Germany to come to America with forged documents to request political asylum. When she arrived at Newark International Airport in New Jersey on December 1994, female genital mutilation was not considered a legitimate justification for political asylum. She was sent to several detention facilities where she spent many unbearable months as an inmate. Her case was championed by Laylia Miller Bashir, an attorney. While in prison, she was caught in a riot and beaten. Finally, after more than a year in several detention facilities, she was granted political asylum on June 13, 1996. (Kassindja and Bashir, 1998)

There have been some recent developments as a result of Fauziya's struggle for political asylum within the United States. . . . "There has been some progress in recognizing that gender-specific harms, such as FGM, should qualify a woman asylum seeker for protection. Not all judges and INS trial attorneys enthusiastically embrace the principle, but many do, and the Board of Immigration Appeals' decision established binding precedent, upon which other cases may rely" (Kassindja and Bashir, 1998, p. 507).

It is unlikely that a woman seeking asylum will speak freely of such private things in an interview which is to take place within hours or days of arriving in the United States (Kassindja and Bashir, 1998). "Fauziya's case provides a good example of the way in which humiliation and a sense of personal privacy may limit the information that an asylum seeker will tell strangers. When Fauziya was questioned by an INS official at Newark Airport, she told them that her reason for seeking asylum was to flee a forced marriage. She was too embarrassed to talk about the impending genital mutilation she had fled" (Kassindja and Bashir, 1998, pp. 508–9). Unfortunately asylum does not solve this problem and creates different types of problems—scores of women seeking refuge without sufficient social services available to provide for their needs in the host country.

In September 1996, the U.S. Congress passed (PL104 140) a law that recognizes FGM as a felony and allocates money to educate the immigrant population about the practice (Kassindja and Bashir, 1998; Federal Prohibition of Female Genital Mutilation Act of 1996). On an international level, in 1994, the United Nations Commission of Human Rights and its subcommission on the prevention of discrimination and protection of minorities identified female circumcision and FGM as having serious health and other consequences for both women and children (United Nations Committee on the Elimination and Discrimination against Women [CEDAW], 1994). FGM is also banned in an increasing number of countries, including Sweden, Belgium, Norway, and the United Kingdom (Bosch, 2001). As of 2002, over 190 countries agreed that health-care services must provide basic human rights and fundamental freedoms that would prevent FGM (Edwards, 2002). According to the Center for Reproductive Law and Policy (CRLP), by 1999 nine countries where FGM has been common have passed laws criminalizing the practice. These countries are Burkina Faso, Central African Republic, Djibouti, Ghana, Guinea, Senegal, Tanzania, Egypt, and Togo. Penalties range from six months to life in prison, and by January 1999 there had already been prosecutions in Ghana, Egypt, and Burkina Faso (CRLP, 1999). There are a number of countries that are making progress on the legislative front; however, implementation of the laws requires significant change of cultural attitudes within the legal system.

SUCCESS STORIES AND PROMISING PRACTICES

A variety of justifications have been offered to stop the practice of FGC: rights of children, rights of women, freedom from torture, and the right to health and bodily integrity (Shell-Duncan and Hernlund, 2000).

Some women and girls in cultures where FGC is commonly practiced are defying their families and cultures to reject the practice or request a modified version for themselves or their daughters. In some places "mock ceremonies" are being carried out where the rite of passage ceremony takes place but where no genital cutting occurs (Lightfoot-Klein, 1989). There are vocal indigenous African feminists who are working with health care professionals and activists within the international community to hold conferences exploring the ramifications of the surgeries and possible ways to stop them (Gunning, 1992).

Various approaches have been attempted to reduce the incidence and severity of FGC. For example, Nigerian authorities announced that they will observe International Day for Zero Tolerance to Female Genital Mutilation on February 6 each year (*Afrol News*, 2004). There have been a number of countries that have reduced the incidence of FGC within the last decade in Africa. Four countries highlighted in this section are Senegal,

Kenya, Uganda, and Burkina Faso. These programs have all been successful because they examined the reasons for genital cutting in the culture. In some instances, the severity of the procedure was reduced, in others, the incidence decreased. However, because of their successes, other villages and countries are following their lead.

Senegal

FGM has been decreasing in Senegal since 1998. In 1991, a UNICEF-sponsored education program was initiated called Tostan, meaning "breaking out of the egg" in the language spoken by most Senegalese people. This is an eighteen-month long educational program primarily for the rural women of Senegal. This program began by emphasizing literacy, health, and hygiene education (World Bank, 1998). It has been successful, in large part, because the program was offered in the mother tongue of the people of Senegal, rather than English or French.

People in the village of Malicounda-Bambara determined that they should discuss FGM after completing their sexual health and literacy programs when it became clear to them that FGM was associated with many of the medical problems faced by the women of the village. They began to challenge the traditional practice and discuss their options (World Bank, 1998). No FGM procedures were performed that year in Malicounda-Bambara (World Bank, 1998). News of this grassroots movement spread to other villages and was met with mixed reactions. However, some villages followed suit, and after women from Malicounda-Bambara talked to more people, and with the assistance of Tostan's educational program and the suggestions of the religious leader Imam Ker Simbara, the Malicounda-Bambara story was presented to even more villages. Hearing of the new approach, villagers were encouraged to tell their own stories and draw their own conclusions. By 1998, thirteen communities had joined together and created the "Diabougou Declaration" which announced that FGM would no longer be practiced among the more than eight thousand members of those thirteen communities. President Abdou Diouf proposed a national resolution to ban FGM, and in 1999 the resolution passed. Violators of the ban will face a five-year prison term (U.S. Department of State, 2004). Although FGM has not stopped completely in Senegal, it has been drastically reduced (Mackie, 2000). By June 2002, 285 villages in the Kolda region pledged to abandon the practice. By March 2003, 108 villages in the Tambacounda region voted to abolish the practice as well.

Burkina Faso

In 1996 Burkina Faso passed laws to prohibit FGM. FGM in Burkina Faso was usually associated with an initiation rite when Mossi young girls were traditionally secluded during the cutting ceremony and taught to be good young wives and mothers. Following the seclusion, there was a community celebration with dancing and drinking. However, FGM is also practiced in the belief that it will strengthen a woman's ability to bear children. In addition, they believe that childbirth is dangerous for an infant if it comes in contact with the clitoris during childbirth (Hosken, 1999). Approximately two-thirds of women in Burkina Faso have undergone this procedure (World Bank, 1998). It provides older women with a way to make a reasonable living. They earn US$2 to $3 per patient. The per capita income in Burkina Faso is US$210 (World Bank, 1998).

More than two decades prior to the 1996 legislation, missionaries began the fight against FGM in Burkina Faso. Early attempts to eradicate the practice helped to create a dialogue on the subject (U.S. Department of State, 2004). Articles 380, 381, and 382 went into effect in February 1997. Article 380 established fines and prison sentences for both family members and practitioners who request or promote the practice. The prison term of ten years can be given if the victim dies as a result of the procedure. Article 381 establishes severe consequences for medical practitioners who perform FGM. Article 382 establishes fines for those who know of a case of FGM without informing the authorities. As a result of these articles, the percentage of girls undergoing excision in Burkina Faso dropped from 70 percent to 66 percent between 1997 and 1999 (Hosken, 1999). Between 1997 and 2000 there were sixty convictions of both excisors and accomplices, resulting in sentences and prison fines (U.S. Department of State, 2004). The sentences for those convicted have increased from three days to ten months with the passage of Article 380. Between 1997 and 1999 there were approximately 250 meetings, conferences, and presentations made in the country as well as numerous radio and television programs on FGM (Hosken, 1999).

Kenya

"Circumcision through words" is an alternate rite of passage in some parts of Kenya that has replaced genital cutting. Sunna, excision, and infibulation are all practiced in Kenya. The type of procedure done depends on the local custom in an area, although infibulation is least common. Overall in Kenya, 38 percent of women between the ages of fifteen to forty-nine have undergone FGC. The incidence in some districts is quite high (Population Council, 2002). In some tribes of Kenya, the proportion of girls circumcised can be as high as 95 percent: Kisii (97 percent), Massai (89 percent), Kalenjin (62 percent), Taita Taveta (59 percent), and Meru/Embu (54 percent) (United Nations, 2003). Bride price is often dependent upon having been circumcised.

Traditionally, female initiation has included weeks of seclusion, instruction on the responsibilities of wives and mothers, the FGM procedure, and a ceremony to recognize the "new women." There have been attempts through governmental policies, legislation, and the media to improve the status of women in Kenya, so that bride price won't be tied to FGM.

In 1982 and 1989 a presidential decree banned the practice of FGM. The government prohibited government hospitals and medical clinics from performing FGM. In 1999 the Ministry of Health, with support from the World Health Organization, launched a national plan of action to reduce the proportion of girls and women undergoing FGC, increase the number of communities supporting elimination of FGC, increase the number of health care facilities that provide follow-up care to girls who have undergone FGC, and to increase the technical and advocacy capacity of organizations and communities involved in FGC elimination programs (Ministry of Health, 1999). In 2001 Parliament passed the "Children's Act" to outlaw FGM for girls under seventeen. These actions were not successful in achieving a significant reduction in FGM in Kenya. Research was conducted to determine what strategies would likely be successful. A series of workshops were developed by MYWO (Maendeleo ya Wanawake—a Kenyan women's organization), and PATH (the U.S.-based Program for Appropriate Technology in Health in developing nations) and supported by a number of women's organizations and communities (Chege, Askew, and Liku, 2001). These workshops provide songs, skits, poems, and information to educate women about alternatives to FGM. In discussing the importance of stopping the practice, the pejorative term "mutilation" is not used, rather the more neutral term "circumcision" is used. The use of the word circumcision in southern Africa fits the way people see and understand the procedure. In their words "no women would take their child for "mutilation" (Kiiti, 2005).

The alternate initiation rite includes all of the culturally important aspects, without the actual cutting. For example, the seclusion, education about being a wife and mother, presentation of social and cultural norms, and ceremony to present the "new women" to the community are still present. However, the genital cutting has been replaced by information about reproductive anatomy and physiology. Community-wide sensitization is also an important element of the new approach (Izett and Toubia, 1999).

The pilot project started with thirty girls in Tharaka Nithi in the Meru district of Kenya in 1996 and by December 2002, 1,500 girls had participated in the ritual (PATH, 1997). Many of the women who used to perform the circumcisions now actively condemn the practice. In December 2000, in a highly publicized case, two sisters took their father to court to avoid being forcibly circumcised. The social acceptance of this change is so wide that an uncircumcised girl is now referred to as "manyanga" (Kiswahili to mean y*oung, new*), while a circumcised girl is described as "mitumba" (meaning *secondhand, used*) (PATH, 2003).

Uganda

The Sabiny people of Uganda have historically practiced female circumcision, and they are very protective of their cultural practices. In their culture, female circumcision has been required for a woman to be married and even to gather grain (Metcalf, 1996). In some cultures, uncircumcised women cannot touch or prepare food.

Initial attempts in 1992 to end FGM among the Sabiny people actually resulted in an increase of the practice due to insensitivity on the part of the reformers. A film of a gory mass circumcision of a group of girls was shown to the residents of the village to convince them to stop genital cutting. The local people were outraged and shocked that their cultural custom was portrayed as barbaric and backward. As a result of backlash to the film, two years later, twice as many girls chose to be circumcised as a means of proudly defending their traditional practice (WomenAid International, 2003).

Several years later, there was a radical change in attitude about female circumcision due to the efforts of the UN Population Fund program REACH. Both the Sabiny clan elders and the girls themselves now work together to stop FGM. In a respectful and nonjudgmental way the Sabiny people are encouraged to be proud of their culture, but they are asked to critically evaluate the value of some of their rituals. A ceremony to mark a girl's passage into womanhood is culturally valid even without FGM. REACH presents a nonjudgmental message without using the phrase "genital mutilation," which may carry an implicit criticism. They discussed the harmful effects of FGM, including excessive bleeding, urinary problems, infections, the risk of HIV from contaminated tools, the formation of scar tissue that can interfere with childbirth, severe debilitating pain, and psychological trauma.

Because this is a patriarchal society men must condone change for it to be effective. Presentations are made to men on the potential dangers to their sisters, daughters, and wives—and how the practice can inhibit the healthy birth of potential sons. REACH also provides the teenage girls with important information and sends them into their schools to educate others about the dangers of FGM (Mbugua, 1997). REACH works with other nongovernmental organizations (NGOs) to enhance physicians' skills in treating complications from FGM. REACH volunteers also visit local hospitals to talk to patients about the dangers and complications associated with FGM.

In addition, a new holiday was created, a cultural day that celebrates community and establishes new and venerable roles for women who were previously performing female circumcision. During this day, girls undergo a symbolic rite of passage within their communities. After a feast, gifts, and a ceremony, the girls are considered women (United Nations Population Fund, 2003)

CONCLUSION

The FGC described in this chapter is not the only type of surgical alteration of the genitals. There is a recent trend in Western countries for women to undergo plastic surgery to make their labia more pleasing to themselves and to men. Women whose genitals do not look like those seen in pornographic images are reportedly selecting surgical remedies to achieve what they perceive as a cultural standard of desirability. While some women seek reconstructive surgery to restore the hymen before their wedding night to assure blood that is an indication of virginity (see chapter 9 on honor killing), some Western women are undergoing hymenoplasty in an attempt to rekindle a marriage. The *Wall Street Journal* reported that one woman did it to surprise her husband as a honeymoon gift. Another woman reported "It's the ultimate gift for the man who has everything" (Chozick, 2005).

If a practice is labeled negatively by those outside the cultures that engage in it, the response is likely to be hostility and backlash. FGC is physically painful and harmful, but it also serves an important cultural role, which makes it meaningful to both the girls and their communities. "FGM is a practice which is deeply rooted in the traditions of a number of societies . . . it requires a careful and sensitive approach . . . that respects the primacy of the role of grassroots actors in its eradication" (Amnesty International, 1997).

The term used to describe this custom is not as important as understanding why it continues. The impacts of the practice, the cultural reasons for it, the meanings it conveys, and the values people place on it are important. It is a physically harmful practice, but socially and culturally a significant tradition. This is an extremely complex issue, with individual, familial, community, religious, and national implications and entanglements. In addition, FGC has medical, social, cultural, and economic consequences. This issue is so divisive because it derives from or impacts women's rights, the meaning of family, state obligations, human sexuality, gender inequality, race, Western ethnocentrism, postmodern colonialism, and cultural autonomy (Boyle, 2002; Sibley, 1997; Gunning, 1992).

Government bans are not usually effective unless they are initiated in conjunction with community willingness to change. Governments that institute bans in response to pressure exerted by powerful wealthy nations are seen as "selling out" by their people, and the result may be an increase in the practice. In some countries where policy and laws make FGC illegal, if there is not widespread cultural condemnation of the practice, FGC does not stop, it is driven underground, with a decrease in the number of people seeking medical help in the event of a botched procedure (Amnesty International, 2004a).

Trying to eliminate it without replacing it with community-driven alternatives that convey the same meaning will not be successful. In the 1970s, a group of Western Peace Corps nurses went to Liberia to provide medical care to people in rural villages. They initially provided help by fighting infections and hemorrhages of young girls following their initiation rites but then missionary nurses attempted to eliminate the practice of FGC altogether. The response of the local people was to continue the practice of FGC, but they no longer brought their girls for critical medical care following the initiation rites (Hales, 1981). In an attempt to stop what they viewed as a dangerous practice through their own cultural lenses, the nurses actually decreased their effectiveness by not taking into consideration the importance of the culture and the meaning of the FGC. Many women in cultures where FGC is practiced are afraid to denounce the practice because conventional wisdom in their communities suggests that females who are noncircumcised are unclean, impure, and of lower social status. These women fear that the decision to not have their daughters circumcised will put the daughters' futures in jeopardy (Ben-Ari, 2003). A multifaceted approach, taking into consideration the cultural factors that drive the practice, is the best way to reduce the incidence and severity of FGC worldwide.

5

SEXUAL VIOLENCE

The boys never meant any harm against the girls. They just wanted
to rape.

(Green, 1999, p. 69)

S exual violence occurs within different contexts and relationships. The
victims are overwhelmingly female although perpetrators may be anyone: strangers, partners, husbands, relatives, friends, teachers, dates, religious
leaders, bosses, employees, police officers, military commanders, and so on.
This chapter reports on the contextual variables of sexual violence and
describes circumstances that increase women's vulnerability to assault and
rape. Highlighted are incidents reported from Bosnia, Rwanda, South
Africa, Sudan, and the United States. However, many other countries are
referenced as sexual violence appears to be pervasive in its many manifestations. Attempts to reduce sexual violence are often thwarted because the
underlying cause of women's sexual victimization is due to deeply rooted
gender divisions and varied cultural expectations that overwhelm proposed
solutions. However, two completely different but promising approaches are
described at the end of the chapter.

THE SCOPE OF THE PROBLEM

There is a vast body of data from Westernized countries describing and
examining rape and other forms of sexual assault. Its occurrence is less documented in countries where political and social structures do not support the
criminalization of sexual assault, where victims have no recourse or ability
to disclose events, or where culturally established norms further devalue
women's experiences to such a degree that the lines between men's dominant sexual rights and women's subordinated ones are entrenched. Worldwide, women's vulnerability to sex crimes is dependent upon class, caste,

93

religion, race, sexual identity, and other forms of discrimination that may diminish women's safety. The variety of contexts in which sexual violence occurs underscores the enormity of the problem. "The many possible combinations of location and relationship mean that sexual violence can be in private or public locations and may be opportunistic or organized and in some instances 'ritualized'" (Kelly and Radford, 1998, p. 58).

In industrialized countries, it is estimated that as many as one out of five women are raped at least once in their lives. The 2003 U.S. Department of Justice statistics from the National Crime Victimization Survey reported that there were over three hundred thousand reported rapes, attempted rapes, and sexual assaults annually. Friends or acquaintances committed over half of these (Catalano, 2004). Nevertheless, it is generally understood that these estimates are not a reflection of the actual number of occurrences due to the stigma, fear, and confusion that keeps many women from reporting these experiences. Other forms of sexual assault such as forced sodomy and unwanted touching are reported even less frequently. However, a U.S. study suggested that the younger a woman reports her first intercourse, the more likely it is that force was used (Watts and Zimmerman, 2002).

Overall, rape and other forms of violence against women are understood to be universally underreported. It is not hard to understand why. In 1680, Matthew Hale wrote: "It is true rape is a most detestable crime . . . but it must be remembered that it is an accusation easily to be made and hard to be proved . . ." (Solomon, 1991). This perspective has changed little over the centuries and continues to influence the credibility of women who suffer from these crimes. Therefore it is not uncommon for women not to report their experiences of sexual violence. Rape myths are still prevalent, discouraging women to report the incidents while simultaneously protecting men's interests. This keeps women believing that they are somehow responsible for the attack or that they did something wrong and deserve what happened.

A victim's rape experience may vary due to sociocultural attitudes, but universally women fear disclosure of the incident because of the stigma it brings. For example, in societies where loss of virginity brings shame on the family as well as the individual, a woman may keep her victimization secret and fear its disclosure, sublimating her individual needs for those of the community to which she belongs. Disclosure of the attacks may bring greater danger to a woman who is considered shamed and disgraced; she may be beaten because of what has happened to her (Luo, 2000).

Generally, women do not trust police or other authorities or believe that they have her best interest in mind. In countries where cases may go to court, cases may last months and the victim's personal life is called into question, seriously damaging her social standing or respectability, as well as that of her family's. Accused rapists are often treated relatively well, with legal counsel and rights ensured, while the victim's credibility is repeatedly challenged. Furthermore, rapist convictions are universally rare, and even when it occurs, there is little compensation or satisfaction that results. So-called justice does not necessarily make the aftereffects of the crime easier to cope with or shorten the duration of the victim's recovery. If the accused goes to jail or is punished, the victim remains afraid and her safety may be jeopardized if the perpetrator is released. Reimbursement for expenses generated by health care for the victim, legal consultation, unplanned pregnancy, moving expenses to ensure safety, and so on is most likely nonexistent (Davies, 1994; Khodyreva, 1996; Rozee, 1993).

With so many countries politically rooted in patriarchy, rape, and/or sexual assault is most often viewed as "a man's perogative." In cultures with conservative sexual mores, rape has many consequences. Rather than a direct violation of the woman, some cultures view rape as a crime against the family of which the woman is a member. For example, many Asian and Middle Eastern cultures equate a woman's worth with her sexual purity. A Cambodian woman who has been raped may bring shame upon her family should her victimization become at all public (Lykes et al., 1993). A Taiwanese woman who is raped by someone she knows may be encouraged to marry the rapist to maintain her reputation and her family's (Luo, 2000). A Zimbabwean sexual assault victim's reputation may suffer, or worse, she may be beaten for having been vulnerable and exposed (Itano, 2003). In some cases, the humiliation is too much to bear, and a victimized woman may see suicide as the only way out of an agonizing life after victimization (Heise, 1993).

The Context of Sexual Violence

The threat of rape by strangers confines women's liberty as women spend their lives considering ways to stay safe and employ crime reduction strategies into their routines, such as not walking alone after dark, not speaking to strangers, keeping doors and windows locked, and so on. Thirty years ago rape was described as a form of gender "terrorism" because of the restrictions women feel imposed by the threat (Griffin, 1975). That has not changed. Because attackers can be virtually anyone, women's safety is compromised everywhere, including the home and community most familiar to her.

RAPE AS A MEANS OF POWER AND CONTROL

The victims of rape range from the very young to the very old because sexual attractiveness, provocation, promiscuity, and sexual interest have nothing to do with this crime. One of the earliest books that documented the history of rape was *Against Our Will* by Susan Brownmiller (1975). It included testimonies that described victim's experiences and raised awareness that rape can happen to anyone.

> *I am seventy-three years old, and I was raped when I was sixty-seven. A young fellow followed me into the elevator of my apartment building. He was wearing a green uniform. . . . He had a wrench in his hand. He shoved me against the wall and started hitting my head. Later I had to have five stitches. He told me not to make a sound. . . . He told me to get on the bed. He pulled off my underthings, and then he tore into me.* (Brownmiller, 1975)

The definitions of rape vary; some follow legal statutes, some follow cultural mandates. A typical definition follows: "A man commits rape when he engages in intercourse with a woman not his wife; by force or threat of force, against her will and without her consent" (Estrich, 1987). While this definition may capture the essence of rape in many countries (see variations in sections below), it does not speak to whether the crime is condemned accordingly. Women's testimonies about their personal experience of being sexually attacked by strangers at random, acquaintances from social circles or work, men they have dated, friends, and others such as clergy, bosses, neighbors, and roommates have exposed the wide variety of circumstances and contexts in which rape occurs. However, responses to rape victims usually critique the victim's culpability but rarely ask why men rape and why so many perpetrators are excused.

MARITAL RAPE

Marital rape, wife rape, and spousal rape are all terms used to describe sexual assaults when the perpetrator is a woman's husband or ex-husband. Many countries do not exempt husbands from rape charges. In others, marital rape is condoned while other circumstances of rape are not. In this case, "rape from a woman's point of view, is not prohibited, it is regulated" (Rozee, 1993, p. 505). However, the frequency with which husbands commit rape against their wives is largely undetermined. Sometimes the sexual violence is an integral part of other violence that occurs in the family. Sometimes, sexual violence stands alone as the husband's way to attempt to maintain control over his wife. Sometimes, marital rape is a condoned aspect of marital relations.

In the United States, several studies found rates of marital rape reports between 8 and 10 percent (Bennice and Resnick, 2003). Of the 930 women in the United States interviewed by Diana Russell, 14 percent reported having been raped by a husband or ex-husband (Russell, 1990). However, because rape by a husband is less likely to be labeled as such, it is estimated that these percentages are low. Ten percent of the women in Russell's study reported being victims of both wife rape and beatings (Russell, 1990).

Marital rape often coexists with other violent forms of control in marriage. Beatings, torture, sexual abuse, and psychological control may be present as well. It is now generally understood that marital rape will be found more often in relationships that are also physically abusive (Bennice and Resnick, 2003).

My husband was a very violent man, and he used sex as another means of hurting and degrading me. He would order me to do things and if I refused or gave any sign of being unwilling, he would hit me until I obeyed and then hit me for getting it wrong or being too slow. Subsequently he would just walk in, order me to strip, and then rape me. (Russell, 1990, p. 351)

While cultures may not recognize marital rape per se, familial relationships within certain cultures may sanction, condone, or accept sexual violence against women under the guise of normal and legitimate marital relationships. In Zambia, a husband is exempt from criminal prosecution if his wife refuses to have sex with him and he forces her (Green, 1999). A Gusii man in Kenya is considered "a 'real man' when the bride is unable to walk after her wedding night." New husbands "are expected to boast of their ability to make the bride cry" (Green, 1999, p. 35). In Central America, as many as one-half of women in abusive relationships reported that they were also raped by their husbands (Davies, 1994). Because unrestricted sexual relations between man and wife are universally considered part of the marital contract, rape within marriage is a severely underresearched area.

GANG RAPE

Worldwide, the circumstances and context of gang rape incidents vary. Sometimes gang rape is attributed to racism, ethnic hatred, war conditions, human rights atrocities, or gang initiation. Within certain cultures, gang rape is sanctioned, as a form of "punishment" for women deemed dishonorable. South Asian women appear to be more vulnerable to this form of punishment, particularly because of the impoverishment many women suffer and the strict social or caste systems in place. In some cases, such as the United States, gang rapes occur as a result of peer pressure gone awry or organized gang activity. Gang rape may be a ritualized form of controlling women's sexuality and power or may simply be more prevalent than other forms of rape in a culture. In Russia, one report estimated that three-quarters of attackers did not act alone during a rape (Khodyreva, 1996).

More often than not, media attention brings incidents to the forefront because the authorities were notified. It is difficult to estimate how many cases go without any legal intervention because victims are afraid, ashamed, or silenced in their reporting efforts. There have been several prominent cases of gang attacks reported in the United States. The cases all involved young men attacking young women. The perpetrators had more in common than those they chose to victimize. The power and control that underlies the assaults were the common threads through all of these crimes.

In 1989, boys from Glenridge, New Jersey, sexually assaulted a mentally handicapped girl with a broom handle and baseball bat after enticing her into a basement with the promise of a date. As many as thirteen boys were present. When they realized what was happening, most left, although none tried to stop the attack. Four boys were accused of crimes involved in the case. The young woman, who was seventeen years old at the time (the same age as the assailants) had an IQ of 64, admired the boys, and considered them her friends. She agreed to go to the basement with them because she trusted that they would not harm her (Lefkowitz, 1997).

In 1991, three St. John's University student athletes were accused of forcibly sodomizing and sexually abusing a fellow female student. The alleged abuse lasted five hours during which time the accused were said to have forced the woman to perform oral sex, thrust their penises against her face and fondled the woman's breasts. The defense attorneys argued that the sexual "activity" was consensual. The jury believed the defense argument and the three defendants were acquitted (Solomon, 1991).

In 1993, nine teenage boys were arrested in Lakewood, California. They called themselves the "Spur Posse." The boys were accused of raping and sexually assaulting girls in order to collect "points" in a competition they had devised. Some of the girls who were molested were as young as ten years old. Some of the individual boys claimed they had collected as many as sixty points (which would equal sixty assaults). While the media coverage helped to raise questions about the practice, the parents of the accused defended their boys' actions. One parent suggested that their son did nothing that any other American boy wouldn't do.

In India, the caste system keeps groups separate, even within a single village. Dalits, or "untouchables" are often separated from others in the village in which they reside. Upper-class caste members may try to take advantage of Dalits. One brutal example involved Ram Chandra who, with his wife, Ramvathi, owned a parcel of land in Hassanganj. Upper-caste villagers wanted the land, and Ram Chandra refused to relinquish it. In September 1998, Ramvathi was reportedly gang-raped by five men of an upper caste from the village as punishment for refusing to give up the land. Because of the stigma associated with rape, it was difficult for them to report the assault. When they did, the police refused to take the report, which resulted in allegations that the police had been paid off by the accused. Determined to reclaim their property, Ram Chandra and Ramvathi returned to the village on January 1999 where they were attacked by approximately seventeen men from the village armed with sticks and axes.

> *They attacked my wife with a stick; she fell down then and there. After that my wife came to me and laid over my body to save me, then they had beaten my wife with sticks and axes. She got deep injuries on the head and shoulder and her right hand and leg broken. One of the attackers put off all the clothes of my wife, raped, and inserted and pushed the stick in her private part.* (Amnesty International, 2001)

In July 1999, Amnesty International reported that a Dalit woman was gang-raped and then murdered in front of villagers in Bhavanipur in the district of Uttar Pradesh, India. A girl of a different caste had eloped with the woman's son. The girl's father had gone to the mother's house where the mother was reportedly held, then gang-raped, tortured, and burnt alive (Amnesty International, 2001).

In South Africa, there is a type of gang rape known as "jack rolling." It is reportedly common and targets young schoolgirls. Sometimes, the rapes end in the girl's death. "If they know you, they will kill you after raping you because if they don't, they know you will reveal their names. So, if they know you and they rape you, you are fortunate if they don't kill you" (Green, 1999, p. 71).

Reports of gangs that prey on France's immigrant neighborhood girls emerged in 2003. Hughes LaGrange, a sociologist with the Center for Scientific Research in Paris, estimated that gang rapes have dramatically increased in France over the last twenty years. Some of this perceived increase (there are no firm statistics) may be due to the victim's willingness to report the violent incidents. However, the increase may also be due to more gang initiation rites where an individual's manhood must be proven through the rape of girls (Sciolino, 2003).

In one case, the *New York Times* reported that seventeen men were on trial for repeatedly raping two thirteen-year-old girls in a housing district primarily built for France's immigrants. After their victimization was rumored in their school, the director called the police. But the universal blame placed upon victims remains strong in this case. Questions about why the girls were out alone and what they were doing with boys lingered. And the assailants were exonerated with comments like "The boys have needs" (Sciolino, 2003).

CHILD RAPE AND ASSAULT

There is an enormous body of literature on child sexual abuse and rape. Because of the breadth of research available, it is beyond the scope of this book to cover it, but it is important to note that child sexual abuse has been documented worldwide (Pitcher and Bowley, 2002). One study from twenty countries estimated a range of 7 to 36 percent of girls (and 3 to 29 percent of boys) have experienced sexual abuse during childhood (Watts and Zimmerman, 2002). Some rates of child rape may be higher in certain countries than others due to the cultural norms, civil unrest, war conditions, and other contexts that increase children's vulnerability. Overall, it is estimated that the rates for girls worldwide is 1.5 to 3 times greater than for boys. Perpetrators of these crimes are similar in characteristic to those who commit sexual assault against adults. Perpetrators of child sexual abuse are most frequently male, known to the victim, and most commonly a close relative (such as father or another male family member), although teachers, religious leaders, family friends, caregivers, and so on, are also perpetrators (Watts and Zimmerman, 2002). The lifelong consequences of child sexual abuse have been well documented in the literature.

There are parts of the world where no research has been conducted on child sexual abuse or where other conditions or human rights crimes dominate any one subtext of violence perpetrated. Of recent concern are reports that child and youth rapes are on the rise in some countries. For example, in Zimbabwe, the rate of reported rapes has increased over the last decade and shown that the majority of victims are under fourteen years of age (Green, 1999). In 1991, seventy-one girls aged fourteen to eighteen, were raped by male classmates in northern Kenya. Additionally, nineteen girls died when the chaos that erupted collapsed the iron bunk beds that they were hiding under. Reports from the boys involved in the rampage stated that they were angry when one of their soccer games was cancelled, and they decided to take it out on the girls nearby. The schools vice principal, reportedly responded "The boys never meant any harm against the girls. They just wanted to rape" (Green, 1999).

It has been stated that South Africa has one of the highest per capita reported rape rates in the world (Jewkes, 2004; Peacock, 2002), although this often reported fact has recently been challenged (Vetten, 2004). Contributing factors to the reportedly high rate of rape include the country's recent history of apartheid, high unemployment rate, poverty, and the AIDS epidemic. Although rape crisis organizations have been around in South Africa since the 1970s, like in other countries, the cultural and political circumstances of South Africa alter the nature of the crime. Anne Mayne, attributed with starting the first rape crisis organization in South Africa, shortly after the 1975 UN International Year of the Woman Conference in Mexico City wrote: "The police take rape very lightly, especially in black areas. They repeatedly let even the most violent men out on bail. Some rapists attempt to rape the same woman again to intimidate her into dropping charges against them. The police don't even withdraw the bail in such circumstances" (Russell, 1989, p. 227).

In 2002, several highly publicized cases brought attention to child rape in South Africa (Peacock, 2002), although some believe the accuracy of these reports has been greatly exaggerated (Jewkes, 2004). The reports explained the reason for the apparent increase in recent rapes of children was due to a popular South African myth that if you have sex with a virgin, you will be cured of AIDS. The "virgin myth" in rural South Africa was fueled by the belief that a girl's intact hymen prevents HIV from contaminating her blood. Sexual intercourse with a virgin will allow men to receive this clean blood, which will cleanse their own infected body (Leclerc-Madlala, 2002; Pitcher and Bowley, 2002). Other reasons for the apparent surge may have been due to increased reporting of the crimes, increased willingness by the police to respond to reports of rape and an increased willingness on the part of parents to seek help and medical care for children who were assaulted. Infant rape can be life threatening. The tearing of the perineum and other severe injuries can cause hemorrhaging or infection that, particularly in communities where medical care may not be immediately available, may cause death. Furthermore, because of the assumption that many of these occurrences are due to men's interests in a "cure," many of the infants are at great risk of contracting HIV, not to mention other sexually transmissible infections.

In April 2000, Human Rights Watch reported that male students and teachers sexually assaulted female students on a regular basis in schools in South Africa. There is little or no punishment for the men and boys who perpetrate these crimes because when incidents are reported to school officials, there is usually no outside investigation. These crimes do not get to the appropriate judicial courts. Instead, the schools try to handle the reports internally which maintains secrecy and denies the girls any due process rights. Girls impregnated by teachers must leave school and may never be able to return, jeopardizing their literacy and future employment (Jewkes et al., 2002). This also means the abusers who go unpunished continue to rape and assault, and other victims may attend school with their abusers. When the abuser is a teacher, there is even greater likelihood that the perpetrator will go unpunished (Human Rights Watch, 2001h).

Conditions That Increase Women's Vulnerability to Sexual Violence

Women's vulnerability to sexual violence is universal. The patriarchal social and political institutions within most countries that support male dominance including male sexual rights over women's, make all women potential targets. However, there are conditions that further exacerbate vulnerability and dangerously compromise women's safety. Some examples are war, prison, refugee status, and homophobia.

RAPE DURING WAR

Although war imposes severe crises for families living within a war region, the burden to provide for family members, care for them, keep them safe, and nurture the family structure falls upon women. According to Vivian Stromberg, executive director of MADRE, an international women's rights organization, "When bombs destroy homes, hospitals, schools and food markets, people's basic needs do not disappear—they intensify. Because of their universally assigned role as caretakers, it is left to women to meet the tremendous needs generated by the sharp rise in trauma, disability, disease, and homelessness that are the known outcomes of war" (MADRE, 2003). When atrocities such as rape victimize women further, entire families and communities pay the price.

Sexual crimes against women during war may have several dimensions that could be intertwined: misogyny or hatred of women, destruction of human dignity, ethnic cleansing or destroying a race by "contaminating" the gene pool, damaging the men in a culture by taking the valued virginity of the women, or controlling women perceived to have challenged patriarchal limits (Lykes et al., 1993). On many levels, rape of women during war is a "symbolic rape of the body of the community" (Liebling, 2002, p. 5). The crimes against women take many forms. Ojiambo Ochieng (2002) argues that women's bodies become the battleground upon which the conflict is raged. "They become objects, over which the various warring factions demonstrate their power and control through rape and torture" (p. 2) During documentation on atrocities in Uganda, gruesome stories of torture of women and girls were commonplace.

There was . . . a seventeen-year-old girl who had to face death when two government soldiers disagreed over who would take her as a sex slave. The two saw the best option for them, being to do away with the girl. She was chopped into in front of her mother! (Ojiambo Ochieng, 2002, p. 2)

While reports of individual attacks and incidents of sexual violence directed at women during war have never been uncommon, in recent years, reports have focused on the use of rape as a systematic method of control to instill fear into a population. During the 1995 Fourth World Conference on Women in Beijing, China, established a platform for action to address the systematic violence against women during wartime. The Platform for Action states:

"Reaffirm that rape in the conduct of armed conflict constitutes a war crime and under certain circumstances it constitutes a crime against humanity and an act of genocide as defined in the Convention on the Prevention and punishment of the Crime of Genocide; take all measures required for the protection of women and children from such acts and strengthen mechanisms to investigate and punish all those responsible and bring the perpetrators to justice." (Strategic Objective E.3)

Today, examples of gender-directed war-created violence are integral parts of reports by human rights groups. "Ethnic cleansing" through sexual violence is now documented as testimonies from the civil wars in Bosnia, Rwanda, and Sudan have been recorded. It is estimated that more than twenty thousand women were raped during the height of the war in Bosnia (1992–1996) although the exact numbers will never be known. Many of these women continue to suffer alone and in silence. Their humiliation is kept hidden. In this way, rape becomes an effective weapon used during wartime. A woman who is raped is intended to be "damaged goods," an insult directed to the men in the culture, "a message to the enemy" (Drakulic, 1994). For women who are humiliated and in many cases intentionally impregnated with the "enemy's" baby as a type of "ethnic cleansing," their futures are bleak (Vickers, 1993; Lykes et al., 1993). For Bosnian Muslim women raped by Serbian men, suicide and infanticide was often reported preferable to a lifetime of humiliation and pain (Drakulic, 1994).

Rape has always been a "side effect" of war. Although a distinctly gendered crime, until the 1990s, rape and its associated atrocities had never been prosecuted as war crimes. This neglect was primarily due to little acknowledgment that sexual violence was a war crime, no real efforts on the parts of governments involved to prosecute those responsible for the gendered atrocities, and little or no recourse or compensation for women who had been victimized sexually as a result of the war (Callamard, 1998). However, on June 27, 1996, a United Nations tribunal indicted eight Bosnian Serb military and police officers in connection with the rape of Muslim women during the Bosnian war, the first time sexual assault was treated as a war crime.

In Rwanda it is estimated that two hundred fifty thousand to five hundred thousand women were raped as a result of the 1994 four-month genocide attempt against the Tutsis living there (Human Rights Watch, 1996). It is estimated that over one-third resulted in pregnancy. The children born of these atrocities are known as *enfants mauvais souvenir,* or "children of bad memories" (Green, 1999). Rapes were sometimes followed by other brutalization: knives, sticks, and machetes were used to cut the sexual organs, inside and out. Other women were murdered after being raped. Women who survived were told "that they were being allowed to live so that they would 'die of sadness'" (Human Rights Watch, 1996).

In 1997, the Special Rapporteur on violence against women to the United Nations visited Rwanda at the government's invitation. During her time there, she observed the testimony of witness "JJ" during a trial against a man accused of war crimes, including sexual violence.

They threw us into the building where they were drinking and smoking marihuana. A young man rushed at me. He led me to the corner of the room. He undressed and put his clothes on the ground. I asked him what he was doing; he said I had no right to ask him anything. In fact, he did humiliating things to me even though I was a mother. When he finished the first time, he started a second time. I was so exhausted. I was almost insensitive. He left me and climbed into the area where other persons were being raped. I could hear the cries of young girls but could not stand up to see. While I was recovering, a second person came and made me lie down again. He undressed. When he pulled out his penis, he still had his underwear on. He also raped me. By now I was practically dead. Maybe he realized I was going to die since he left me

*after he had finished. A third person came while I was there. When he saw me
rolling on the ground, he put on a condom. When he finished, I thought I was
going to die for sure. I could not put my thighs together anymore. When they
finished they went away. . . . After the meeting the Interahamwe made us
return to the Cultural Centre. When we arrived inside, they did the same thing
they did before. They raped us again. I was raped twice. . . . The rapes were
public; they raped us in front of the children. The rapists were rascals. Try to
imagine a mother raped by young boys.* (United Nations, 1998)

One rape hotline group, in supporting sexual assault victims of the
Croatia and Bosnian war, came to the following conclusion: "Violence
against women and war against women exists at all times and everywhere;
during war it intensifies and increases. The war has indeed proved that
women calling the hotlines already know most forms of war violence. One
woman recently said to us 'I am not afraid of war, living with my husband,
I am already twenty years in war'" (Mladjenovic and Matijasevic, 1996).

Sudan has been dealing with civil wars for decades. The wars, driven
by religious feuding, rebels of different persuasions, and disputed oil reve-
nues have brought famine, disease, human rights atrocities, and economic
chaos to the country. A preliminary peace accord signed December 31,
2004, is designed to bring peace related to the north-south conflict (Lacey,
2005). Unaffected by the peace accord, however, is Darfur, western Sudan,
which continues to be what has been dubbed "the world's greatest humanitarian crisis" (Amnesty International, 2004b, p. 1). Crimes against humanity
carried out by government-sponsored nomadic units known as "Janjawid"
("armed men on horses") continue. Since February 2003, the Sudanese
government has supported the nomadic groups whose indiscriminate
attacks, bombings, murders, torture, and rapes of the mostly farming civilians has displaced over a million people (Amnesty International, 2004b;
Lacey, 2005). Many are now displaced refugees in bordering Chad. Reports
collected by human rights groups, nongovernmental organizations (NGOs),
and reporters have indisputable evidence that rape and sexual slavery of
women and girls is occurring with frequency and is uncontrolled. In
attempts to humiliate the communities, women have been raped in public,
in front of husbands, children, and parents. In some cases, Amnesty International reports the Janjawid have broken the legs and other limbs of their
sexual assault victims to keep them from escaping. One woman reported:

*When we tried to escape, they shot more children. They raped women; I
saw many cases of Janjawid raping women and girls. They are happy
when they rape. They sing when they rape, and they tell us that we are just*

slaves and they can do with us how they wish. (Amnesty International, 2004b)

As a result, women who have been tortured in this way are ostracized by their families and communities. Women who are raped are "tainted" and no longer welcome at home. Pregnancies that result from rape are considered shameful and the children born to the women are evidence of the shame. Hence, many live with the horrors they experienced in silence. Amnesty International estimates that many rape victims do not seek shelter in displacement camps in Chad for fear of facing their families and others who know about what happened to them. But because of this silence, it is difficult to gauge the numbers of rape victims in Sudan as the conflict continues, despite an April ceasefire that all sides have virtually ignored (Amnesty International, 2004b; Masciarelli and Eveleens, 2004; Human Rights Watch, 2004a).

As countries eventually rebuild after a conflict, women raped during the war are often forgotten victims. They live with the memories, stigma, and shame of what happened regardless of the outcome of the armed conflict. In many cases, they have suffered unmentionable acts and yet they can never return home, are rejected by their families, have no medical or economic resources available to them, and may be living with and forced to support children who are the product of their victimization.

POLITICAL PRISONERS

Women raped during war may also be taken prisoner. Social conditions may expose incarcerated women whose politics, race, or social activism is not consistent with the dominant ideology to abusive or violent practices.

During the years of apartheid in South Africa, women detained by the apartheid government because of their antiapartheid activities were often raped and assaulted as a form of political control and terrorism.

The worst thing about living in hiding is being frightened, especially as a woman. I know women who have been stripped while they were detained. They were threatened with rape, and their children were similarly threatened with rape. . . . The police want to break down strong women (in detention) because they don't give them the information they're seeking. Sexual violence epitomizes that whole dynamic of cutting women down to size, which is why it is such a powerful element in torture. (Fester, 1989, pp. 248–49)

Reports of sexual torture of Latin American women who were being held as political prisoners determined that the torture essentially took away not only human dignity but the woman's identity. Because women are more often the caretakers of a community and strongly identify with their roles as mothers, those who sexually torture play on these identities when devising ways to victimize women.

The aim of violence targeting women per se is to change the woman from "Madonna to whore" and "to teach her that she must retreat into the home and fulfill the traditional roles of wife and mother." Thus, through the process of socialization, violent sexual treatment administered by the state becomes most cruelly doubly disorienting; it exacerbates and magnifies the woman's already subservient, prescribed, passive, secondary position in Latin American society and culture. (Lykes et al., 1993, p. 535)

Regardless of the reason for imprisonment, women are at risk when incarcerated and at the mercy of authorities to whom their rights have been transferred. Sexual assault of women inmates in the United States is not uncommon (Stein, 1996), and the complaints by the inmates go unheard. Robin Lucas, a federal inmate, served time in a federal detention center for men. During that time she claims "Male prisoners routinely had access to the women's cells" (Stein, 1996, p. 1). The men would bring alcohol for her and request sexual favors. Her complaints were ignored and instead she was ostracized and called a "snitch" by the male prisoners in the unit. As a consequence, three male inmates gained access to her cell one night and beat and raped her. When they left, her cell was relocked after them (Stein, 1996).

REFUGEES

According to a United Nations report, 80 percent of the refugees worldwide are women and children. Refugee status increases women's vulnerability to rape, sexual harassment, abduction, and physical violence (Watts and Zimmerman, 2002). They are sometimes obliged to exchange sexual favors for much needed food sources, documentation, or to escape further violence (Green, 1999).

Reports first emerged in 2001 regarding refugee camps in Ghana and Sierra Leone where aid workers were allegedly demanding sexual favors from girls in exchange for food for the family. The reports stated that those distributing aid and assistance were demanding the sex from mostly young girls (between thirteen to eighteen years of age), but some boys, in return for the supplies. The allegations of sexual abuse and violence were all similar in nature. Sometimes the sexual abuse was in exchange for things as simple as a bag of flour or a bottle of oil. But for those who have had nothing for so long, these items become an invaluable commodity. It is a particularly powerful force when children who have been traumatized already through homelessness, war, orphanhood, and so on are involved. The additional consequences from this kind of sexual abuse are obvious: disease, pregnancy, and HIV infection.

Somali women living in refugee camps in Kenya were reportedly attacked when in search of firewood or water. Sometimes the perpetrators were "bandits," but others were involved as well, including allegedly Kenyan police who were charged with protecting the camps. In one seven-month period, 192 rapes were reported, although it is estimated the numbers could be ten times as many (Green, 1999).

Women's vulnerability was most recently highlighted by stories of sexual attacks against women who sought shelter in refugee camps after the December 2004 tsunami in Asia. According to United Press International, women and girls in refugee camps in Sri Lanka reported sexual assault, abuse, and in one case, a gang rape when the women left the camps to find food or water (United Press International, 2005).

HOMOPHOBIA

In countries where there is acknowledgment of women who partner with women (as opposed to those countries where public acknowledgment would be life-threatening), homophobia is a constant threat. Even women suspected of being lesbians are at great threat of sexual violence. A woman in Australia had the following experience:

*J*ason brought three friends with him. One of them came up to me, he asked me out and I turned him down, and he was really quite okay about it. . . . And then about half an hour later, he came back saying to me "Oh, my mate tells me you're gay and I wanna do something about it" and "All you need is a good fuck." And he was drunk but not staggering kind of drunk, but he was pretty drunk . . . and he attempted to rape me. It was pretty clear-cut attemped rape, by which point I managed to get him off and get out of there. . . . [After returning to work] it was public knowledge what had happened at that party . . . and then within a week of that party, I started to get harassing phone calls at home: "I know where you live, I'm gonna get you." This person knew I'm *a lesbian, knew that I worked with __, knew what hours I worked.* (Mason, 1997)

Woman to Woman Sexual Violence

Sexual abuse of women who partner with women is not a well-researched topic. Data from the United States and the United Kingdom that shows evidence of this crime is limited. Just as data on intimate partner violence in gay couples has only recently surfaced in the west, there is a paucity of data on sexual violence in female couples. Some of the reasons are wrapped up in assumptions about women's passive nature and inability to commit these kinds of crimes as well as reluctance by feminist communities to examine the problem. There is even less known about women who attack other women sexually but are not in intimate relationships. Rare crime reports of women sexually abusing other women within the context of other crimes committed have done little to help understanding of this phenomenon. Because of the overwhelming numbers of women sexually assaulted by men worldwide, a consideration of sexual violence of women by women has drawn little attention.

Worldwide, most nations do not acknowledge or accept women in same sex relationships. Simply "coming out" would threaten their lives. Furthermore, studies that have used samples of women in same sex relationships may not ask the kinds of questions that would identify this type of violent experience.

However, a 1986 study found that among self-identified lesbians, 5 percent reported attempted rape by a date and 7 percent had been raped by either a female or male assailant (Girshick, 2002). Girshick reports other studies have found as high as almost one-quarter reporting sexual abuse in a lesbian relationship (2002). The descriptions of incidents reported by women who were assaulted by women are very like those reported by women assaulted by men. One woman recounts:

I am now twelve years sober, but in my drinking days, somewhere between the ages of twenty-four and twenty-six, I was raped by my then girlfriend. We were both drunk and high. She tied me to a bed and used a broom handle. I was seriously hurt. (Girshick, 2002, p. 79)

Other circumstances of women assaulting women may occur with the involvement of men. One woman who was kidnapped by a woman and her boyfriend reported:

*W*hat *I do remember overall is being terrified I would be killed or kept there forever. The woman periodically used the man as a tool to hurt me at her order, to punch me, and so on. I was forced to kiss her on the lips; she fondled my breasts. I was forced to perform oral sex on her while she called me a bitch and a liar and told me I was no good because I couldn't make her get an orgasm. She threatened to burn me with the crack pipe; she threatened to shove wire coat hangers and bottles up in me.* (Girshick, 2002, p. 82)

While the vast majority of sexual crimes are perpetrated by men and boys against women and girls, to acknowledge all types of violence will lend greater acceptance rather than silence to those who've had these experiences. As one woman wrote:

I *want to use my real name. It's like being true to myself. It's keeping good faith with myself. I don't have to hide anymore. Every time that I'm upfront about being a survivor, it strengthens [me]; it deals with a bit more of that fear and shame.* (FitzRoy, 1997)

SUCCESS STORIES AND PROMISING PRACTICES

Attempts to reduce the incidence of sexual violence have varied in effort and success. In the United States, the rape crisis movement that started in the 1960s promoted women's consciousness groups that raised awareness and shattered the silence that victims had lived with after their attacks. Although the contexts of the rapes varied (some in marriage, some stranger, some by acquaintance, etc.), what was discovered was that the common thread in women's experience was the response to their disclosure. Victim blaming was the standard. Although women were blamed for the assault, programs still warned females to walk in groups and lock their doors and windows. In the 1970s, hotlines were created for women to use after an attack. Grassroots rape crisis organizations were formed in many communities. Research during the 1980s reported that women may be threatened more by someone known to them than by a stranger. By the early 1990s, women were warned about romantic dates, to watch how much alcohol they drink, and to be alone with only those they are confident they could trust. Still, prevention efforts did little to slow or reduce the numbers of incidents. It is now understood that any attempt to reduce sexual violence must involve those most likely to commit it—men.

Below are two African examples that, while vastly different, could show some effect in slowing the impact of sexual violence on women.

Men as Partners (MAP) in South Africa

The Men as Partners (MAP) program in South Africa started in 1998 and was a collaboration between EngenderHealth based in the United States and Planned Parenthood Association of South Africa. The MAP program describes its goal to "promote gender equity in order to foster the sexual and reproductive health of both women and men" (Peacock, 2002). In response to the HIV/AIDS concerns and violence against women reported in South Africa, the MAP program was initiated in eight provinces in South Africa with two primary objectives: (1) to challenge men's attitudes and behaviors that jeopardize their own health as well as that of the women and children in their lives and (2) to support men to mobilize and become actively involved in stopping violence against women.

The apparent success of MAP is due to the careful attention paid to culturally relevant factors that exist. First, as a result of the long antiapartheid movement in South Africa, the country has a history of men mobilizing and working together on human rights issues. Second, because men are generally socialized in groups such as in religious activities, sports, schools, and so on, there is a natural opportunity for collective group action. MAP took advantage of these conditions.

Collaboration with large organizations of South African men, including labor unions and community-based groups was the primary recruitment strategy. Trained facilitators helped organize workshops. The interactive activities that participants explore are always built around gender issues and encourage the familiar goal of mobilizing and organizing together on a particular social action. The series of interactive workshops developed examine more than one specific issue; instead the program helps men look critically at the interrelationships of issues such as gender equity, reproductive freedoms, violence against women, and HIV/AIDS while examining alternatives to male socialization.

The MAP program reported that posttraining evaluations were conducted with MAP participants as well as men who did not participate in the workshops. After MAP workshops, over 70 percent of the participants reportedly believed women should have the same rights as men. A quarter of the control group believed so. Eighty-two percent of men in the MAP program believed it was not normal for men to beat wives, but 38 percent of the control group reported such a belief. Eighty-two percent of MAP men acknowledged sex workers could be raped during their work, but only

33 percent of the control group men believed that fact (Peacock, 2002). Although this type of evaluation does not report long-term change or violent behavior reduction, it indicates progress on challenging norms and educating men to think in ways that may support women's safety and rights.

Umoja

A completely different approach to preventing violence against women can be found in Umoja, Kenya. Umoja which means "unity" in Swahili is comprised of mostly women and children. It started when women were reportedly raped by British soldiers, and they were forced to leave their homes because of the dishonor they brought to the community. As a result, the women formed their own village where they have established themselves. They support themselves and their children by making bead necklaces that are popular with tourists. Unlike what they could do in some of their home villages, they send their children to school, buy new clothes with the money from the necklaces, and live in peace. Other women from around Kenya who have been abused or sexually assaulted have joined the village. When angry husbands have come to the village to demand their wives return, together the women insist they leave or if necessary, they engage the help of the local police (Lacey, 2004). The village offers a safe haven away from those who threaten women the most: men both known and unknown.

CONCLUSION

In order to understand the role that sexual violence plays in the maintenance of power, control, and men's dominant rights in gendered societies, individual incidents must be juxtaposed against the historical, cultural, social and political backdrop in which they occur. The sociohistorical context in which rape survivors live is particularly critical to victim survival and recovery. It is the way violence, gender, sexuality, and power intersect within cultures that is the backdrop within which women make sense of their rape experience (Luo, 2000). Furthermore, understanding the context in which individual incidents occur, including the "social opinion and moral force" (Luo, 2000) to which women and men are exposed that fundamentally denies male-female equity and institutionalizes male dominance, is the only option for deconstructing the crimes and effectively preventing future ones

(Gil and Anderson, 1999). The contextual factors outlined in this chapter expose the complexity of sexual violence that is fueled by social, religious and political restrictions on women's freedoms and used to protect the interests of patriarchal structures that dominate the political and social landscape around the world.

6

SEXUAL SLAVERY

It is claimed that after the third menstruation, the priest is entitled
to sexual intercourse with the girls.

(Dovlo and Adzoyi, 1995, p. 11)

Women's sexual enslavement takes many forms. Examples of the practice are bonded labor, forced marriage, child labor, human trafficking, forced prostitution, sexual servitude, and traditional slavery (Herzfeld,
2002). Poverty, greed, marginalization, misogyny, and power create the
foundations for slavery. Women are enslaved anywhere from a few months
to their entire lifetimes. While slavery affects women and men, some forms
are gender-specific, exploiting women and girls disproportionately, particularly sexually. This chapter describes particular circumstances of slavery: sexual servitude and imposed marriagelike circumstances that women are
forced to endure.

THE SCOPE OF THE PROBLEM

It is almost impossible to determine how many girls and women are subject
to sexual slavery in the world today. Sexual slavery is closely related to the
trafficking trade (which is described in more detail in chapter 7). However,
while trafficking is primarily a clandestine operation, some of the types of
sexual slavery described here have been legitimized by religious and social
justifications that protect the practices. This makes it difficult to accurately
assess the numbers of females enslaved because while the practice may be
built on the sexual exploitation of girls and women, its institutionalization
does not define it as such. In armed conflict situations, women live in terror
with no one to tell about their enslavement; reports are hard to come by.
Women enslaved during armed conflicts are often kidnapped and then
released, with only sporadic accounts that surface, further complicating

attempts to quantify this concern. For the examples of sexual slavery listed in this chapter, statistics have been offered when available.

The Trokosi

The Trokosi system is an ancient practice in western Africa. The custom is related to a traditional fetish belief system which proposes that gods or spirits live within ritual objects and shrine priests. Many believe the shrine priests communicate with the war-gods which gives them great power in the spirit realm. The Trokosi system is practiced in parts of Ghana, Togo, Benin, and Nigeria. It is estimated that there may be as many as twenty to thirty thousand Trokosi slaves within the four countries (Rinaudo, 2003; Aird, 2000; Dogar, 1999; Simmons, 1999) and approximately 160 shrines in Ghana alone (Boaten, 2001). The term "Trokosi" is derived from the word "tro" which means gods and "kosi" which means a slave girl.

Under the Trokosi belief system, when a crime is committed, the family of the guilty party must give a young female virgin to the local shrine priest to appease the war-gods (Goltzman, 1998; Aird, 2000; Boaten, 2001). If the family of the offender does not abide by this law, it is believed that bad fortune, such as death or disease, will befall the family. The young girls chosen to serve the local priest at the village shrine are, in general, expected to do so for their entire lives.

In Ghana, two patrilineages most commonly carry out the Trokosi practice: the *Ewes* of Tongu and Anlo and the *Dangmes* of the surrounding region of Accra. It has been a tradition there for hundreds of years. The life of a Trokosi slave is one of powerlessness, shame, and humiliation. Perhaps the greatest injustice is that the girls are serving sentences for crimes committed by distant relatives. Oftentimes the sin was committed so far in the past that the girls cannot identify the crime committed or who in their family was responsible for the offense. The severity of the crime most often determines the length of servitude or number of generations that serve from one given family. For example, if there is a homicide, families are required to send generation after generation of virgin daughters to atone for the incident. Some families believe so strongly in the practice as a safeguard against misfortune, they have sacrificed five generations of virgin daughters to the priests (Aird, 2000). On average, a Trokosi slave will be kept in servitude by the priest for over ten years. If a Trokosi slave dies or escapes and her time in slavery is not completed, the family must replace her with a new virgin daughter. Thus, the practice may continue for generations.

The priests determine the entire sentence of servitude for the slaves and when the crime is repaid. If a priest grows tired of a servant, he can release her from the shrine. However, a new slave provided by the family must replace her, and the former slave may be called back at any time because she is viewed as a "slave to the gods" for her entire life (Aird, 2000). The children produced from slaves are known as "trokosiviwo" and belong to the priest. Should a priest die, the Trokosi are inherited by the "new" priest who is heir to the deceased (Aird, 2000).

The life of a Trokosi is filled with hard labor and sexual service. Each young girl is forced to work at both household and farm-related jobs. Not surprisingly, she is not paid for her work (Wiafe, 2000). Priests may require slaves to work more than twelve hours a day, in harsh conditions, providing no compensation for their labor. The enslaved women are required to present any income from farming or petty trade to the priests and receive meager or no aid from outside sources. The fetish shrine owners, who the priests work under, are generally elder members of the clan. They are also invested in the Trokosi system as they acquire all economic profits from the servants' labor. The Trokosi shrines are managed like businesses where goods and money are highly valued by the priests (Aird, 2000). In fact, the owners and priests will not even allow visitors to the shrine unless they bring some sort of offering with them, such as alcohol, cash, or food.

Although her family essentially abandons the girl when she is turned over to the shrine, a Trokosi slave's family is still expected to provide any food and clothing their daughter needs for survival. However, many families do not comply with this expectation because they are often afraid to visit their daughters at the shrines. Poverty, malnourishment, and starvation of the slaves is not unusual (Aird, 2000; Boaten, 2001).

The Trokosi slaves are expected to provide sexual favors on demand. The traditional belief is that the slaves, by having intercourse with the priests, are actually having intercourse with the gods (Goltzman, 1998). The priests' sexual control and demands are legitimized by their claim that Trokosi are really priestesses whose duty is to engage in intercourse with the gods. Forced sexual intercourse customarily begins at an initiation ceremony (called *tsi de da ta*, meaning baptism). During this ritual, the deity (who is represented by the priest) copulates with enslaved girls who have achieved puberty (Ameh, 1998). The priests are then at liberty to have sexual intercourse with a Trokosi slave whenever they desire. An initiation ceremony could be imposed on a girl as young as nine years old (Dovlo and Adzoyi, 1995). Some Trokosi servants are sent to shrines at even younger ages.

In the regions where Trokosi is practiced, the number of children a man fathers determines his status. Therefore, there is an incentive for priests to procreate with Trokosi in order to raise their status. Once a girl begins menstruation, she must submit to the sexual desires of the priests, even if this includes rape on a regular basis, which is often the case (Aird, 2000). As a result, almost all of the enslaved girls are impregnated, thus creating an entire shrine of children who are seen as illegitimate in the eyes of fellow Ghanaian community members. The Trokosi are completely responsible for raising the children born from intercourse with the priests, and in many instances the priests neglect the children and refuse to have anything to do with them. This brings about a continuous cycle of often unwanted, uncared for children who live in abject circumstances and poverty at the shrines (Goltzman, 1998; Boaten, 2001).

Despite the reported treatment of the girls, many Ghanaians do not challenge this practice (Goltzman, 1998). Because of the deeply rooted religious beliefs, villagers fear that if they do not obey the Trokosi practice, they will anger the war-gods and bring unending bad luck upon their families. Families often relinquish their daughters to local shrines convinced that to not do so would result in bad luck for the entire family and the community. Community members are so faithful to this practice that they may even return escaped Trokosi for fear of the misfortune harboring slaves would bring them.

If slaves are released from the shrine, survival on the outside is difficult. With the exception of nongovernmental organizations (NGOs) that focus on liberating the Trokosi, women left on their own are not educated nor do they have employable skills. This, coupled with a lack of personal resources, leave former Trokosi slaves unmarriageable and facing a future of poverty.

Religious doctrine justifies the Trokosi slave practice for local West Africans. Village priests, who enforce the slave practice, reason that they are merely carrying out the commands of the war-gods. The war-gods are the deities that promote the custom of Ju-Ju based on the African belief in spirits. Ju-ju is contingent on the belief that deities with magical energies can be called upon for help in daily survival (Kwabena-Essem, 1995).

Because the deities are essential in providing protection, giving children to infertile women, blessing the community, and carrying out justice, community members have created a complex structure of rituals to support them (Boaten, 2001). The deities are responsible for punishing those who commit a crime. In the case of the young Trokosi girls, deities punish those unfortunate enough to be born into the wrong family. While the reports from the Trokosi girls demonstrate instances of brutality, poverty, sexual slavery, and hard labor, some local communities consider Trokosi a legitimate religious and cultural practice because justice is served in the name of the gods. Although many Westerners argue that this kind of practice is inhumane, priests firmly hold that this is a practice based on deep religious beliefs and their relationships with the deities.

THE LIVES OF TROKOSI SLAVES

The accounts of women who have been bound to the Trokosi system describe a difficult life:

We were living like slaves. We were made to suffer hunger. We had no soap for our bath. We did farm work under severe pressure. In the nights the priests just ordered any one of us to sleep and have sexual intercourse with him. If you felt sick, it was the responsibility of your people to give you medication. In fact, it was terrible for a human being to live in such a condition. (Boaten, 2001, p. 95)

Dora Galley spent seven years imprisoned as a Trokosi slave:

I had to cut down trees and uproot tree stumps to burn into charcoal to sell and make some money to take care of myself. I did not have the right to take crops from the farm unless the "priest" allowed me to. Occasionally my parents sent me some food, but that was kept in the priest's room and I had to request it any time I needed some. I was forced to have sex with the priest as one of the rituals in the shrine, but luckily I did not get pregnant. (Ben-Ari, 2001, p. 1)

Patience Akope lived at a shrine for twenty-one years. During that time, she became pregnant.

The priest did not allow me to visit the clinic for prenatal care or to go to the hospital. Throughout the pregnancy, I had to fend for myself. (Ben-Ari, 2001, p. 2)

In one extraordinary case, Julie Dogbadzi was able to escape from a life of servitude to the priests. Julie found refuge at the Ghanaian offices of International Needs, a Vancouver-based Christian missionary and aid organization, after fourteen years of physical and sexual abuse by the priest to whom she was enslaved. Julie is seen as a heroine among the thousands of women who serve as Trokosi. Her parents gave her to the shrine priest in Kebenu when she was seven in compensation for a petty theft committed by Julie's grandfather, whom she had never met.

During those fourteen years of physical and sexual abuse in the name of the shrine priest, she bore two children. After her escape, she began a one-woman campaign to try to end the Trokosi custom. Julie worked with government groups, NGOs, and International Needs Ghana and has continued to challenge the practice (Dogar, 1999). She described her life at the shrine in an interview with Rana Dogar:

I was given to one of the oldest women in the shrine, also a slave. She was so tired she couldn't even take care of her own children, so I had to fend for myself. I started to cut firewood to make into charcoal, and I took it to a nearby town to sell. I got to keep only 50 percent of my wages, so I was virtually starving. I had no food, no clothes, no education, and no health care.

My family was afraid that if they came, some misfortune would befall them.

When I was twelve, one of my grandfathers had come to the shrine village. He didn't visit me, so I decided to follow him. To do this, I had to cross the river. He was in a canoe, and I fell into the water trying to swim to him. I told him about the priest and what he was doing. But I was sent back to the shrine.

Once you are in the shrine, you become the property of the priest. Every woman in the shrine is made to sleep with the priest. The first time he tried to rape me, I ran away to a nearby village. But I was brought back.

When they get you back, you are beaten until you collapse. I still have some scars on my body to show from those beatings. Every day I would think of escaping, but I realized there was no place for me.

Once you are sent to the shrine, you usually stay there until you die. And even after you die, your family may have to replace you with another virgin. They can pacify the gods by giving the priests a lot of money. But if your family is poor, then that's the end. They'll be providing virgins until God knows when.

Once, when I was three months pregnant, I decided to go to the farm and get a cob of corn and roast it. The priest caught me and got very angry. He asked three other men to hold me down and tie me to a table. They put ropes on my feet, legs, and hands, and I was beaten mercilessly. I thought I was going to lose the baby. I was weak afterwards and almost dying. I resolved from that pain that there was no way I was going to stay in the shrine. One day later I escaped through the bush.

Although the Trokosi custom has been in existence for hundreds of years, it has only received attention as a form of enslavement in the last few decades. As a result of the media attention and some key testimonials such as that by Dogbadzi's, the government in Ghana has responded to the need for laws addressing issues of human rights. The Trokosi practice is in direct opposition to a multitude of laws under the 1992 constitution of Ghana (Boaten, 2001; Quashigah, 1999; Aird, 2000). The priests' denial of schooling to Trokosi children is also a violation of the Ghanaian Constitution. In 1998, Ghana's legislation outlawed all forms of forced labor, which included Trokosi and in 2001, Ghanaian president John Agyekum Kufuor stated "Girls should go to school, not to a shrine" (Ben-Ari, 2001).

Although political leaders and new laws forbid the practice, many argue there is no enforcement. Furthermore, opposition to dismantling the Trokosi system is so strong, that women who are freed from the shrines are often unable to assimilate back into society. They are stigmatized and ostracized because they left the shrine. A study of two thousand women who were liberated between 1997 and 1999 reported that over three-quarters of the women ultimately returned to the shrines from which they escaped because it was too difficult to survive outside the shrine, they had no means of support, and/or they believed that they were cursed by the fetish priests and were afraid for their safety (Wiafe, 2000). Although there is a strong network for maintaining the Trokosi tradition, some groups have successfully challenged the practice.

The Devadasi System

The Devadasi tradition is an ancient system in India with roots in the performing arts (Kersenboom-Story, 1987). While it is a different practice than that of the Trokosi, today it still sentences a girl to a life of sexual enslavement. The Indian government has banned this practice but the Devadasi practice, like that of the Trokosi, is a religious-based system that makes it difficult to change. Like the Trokosi system, it targets poor, young girls. The dedication of Devadasi girls has been occurring for thousands of years. Although there have been attempts to remove it, it is estimated that fifteen thousand girls become Devadasi annually (Power, 2000).

The Devadasi practice results from India's caste system where the measure of social status is based on the caste strata to which one belongs. Those in the upper castes hold great social prestige, wealth, and superior reputation, while those in the lower castes are poor, working-class, and are regarded with little respect. Status is based on the family one is born into and where one's caste lies. The caste at the top of the hierarchy is Brahmin, while the lowest caste is now known as the Dalit, or "untouchables" (Shankar, 1990). The upper caste is perceived and treated with great privilege while the lowest of classes is severely discriminated against and expected to serve the upper, "cleaner" castes (Shankar, 1990).

Each year, over one hundred thousand cases of rape, murder, arson, and other crimes are committed against Dalits (Human Rights Watch, 1999a; 2001b). While in some cases, Dalits are now more visible than ever (and compose a significant proportion of representation in the Indian Parliament and ministries), there are still circumstances in which they are denied ownership of land, work in slavelike roles when employed, and are abused and killed by police and higher-caste members. In parts of India, they are still segregated from using the same wells, temples, churches, and classrooms as other community members of different castes (Human Rights Watch, 1999a; 2001b). As Dalit rights movements have been created to advocate for them in the early 1990s, violence has escalated against them.

In almost all cases, Devadasi girls come from the Dalit caste. It is the economic deprivation of the caste that motivates poor families to agree to the sexual slavery of their daughters; they are in desperate need of the money paid for the girls (Kirloskar and Cameroon-Moore, 1997; Shankar, 1990). Once parents hand their daughters to the local temples as human offerings, the girls are symbolically married to God. After their first menstrual period, the girls are turned into sexual servants for upper-caste men in their villages (Power, 2000). While some men keep their Devadasi as personal servants, others make them available to other men, cost-free.

The process of dedicating prepubescent girls to marriage with a deity or temple takes place in the southern states of India (Human Rights Watch, 1999a). The term "Devadasi" translates into "female servant of deity." These girls are not permitted to marry an earthly man because commitment to temple service represents a marriage to God (Shankar, 1990). In medieval times, these women servants of the deities were known as expert artists in music and dance. However, throughout the centuries, the Devadasis became exploited by the upper classes. Their servitude transferred from the gods to kings, priests, and lords, and finally to the wealthy men of today's society. Essentially today this dedication to the deity means living a life of cheap prostitution that initially is based on religious duties (Shankar, 1990).

Ashana was seven when she was married to the gods. Now an adult, she looks back on her time as a "jogini" (the title used for girls forced into prostitution as a result of the Devadasi system) with sadness:

> Since the day of the initiation, I have not lived with dignity. I became available for all the men who inhabited Karni. They would ask me for sexual favours and I, as a jogini, was expected to please them. My trauma began even when I had not attained puberty. (Carroll, 2002)

A ceremonial dedication binds the girl to the service of a deity, religious institution, or temple. Once her parents decide to dedicate her, a marriage ceremony occurs between the girl and the god. In some cases the eldest of the Devadasi women ties a marriage necklace called a mangal sutra around the girl's neck; in other cases it is the priest who ties the necklace as he chants (Human Rights Watch, 1999a; Shankar, 1990). These red and white beaded necklaces adorned with silver and gold medallions stand as a visible marker of the girl's status for other citizens to identify (Power, 2000). Devadasi women call these the beads of bondage (Kirloskar and Cameroon-Moore, 1997, p. 28).

According to the laws of the ceremony, girls are dedicated before they are eight years old. During the event, musical instruments are played and there are elaborate dances. Ceremonies are performed in secret places such as small temples and private residences. Most priests demand a generous fee or gifts for conducting the ceremonies. The companion or urban brothel that will reap the benefits of the girl's services pays for her initiation. On the day of the event, family members gather together for the ceremony. They cook sweet dishes to commemorate the dedication.

Once the dedication occurs, the community is informed and the Devadasis receive offers to "deflower," or have their virginity taken from professional men; it is less common, but not unheard of, for the priest be the first to have sexual intercourse with the girl. Parents of the Devadasi generally favor men from the upper caste to deflower their daughters (Shankar, 1990). The man who is the first to have sexual intercourse with the girl has access to special benefits. In exchange for some form of payment, the male can engage in sexual relations with the Devadasi for as long as he wishes. For the men, the maintenance of one's own Devadasi is encouraged as it marks greater prestige in ownership. Yet after this deflowering process, the girl must serve other men sexually as well, with the understanding that they will leave her house when her initial patron returns. The number of Devadasi owned by a man determines his status.

The lives of Devadasis are filled with poverty, shame, and exploitation. Thousands of Dalit girls forced into the Devadasi system face dangerous conditions as they prostitute themselves to the upper-caste community and later to unregulated urban brothels

A thirty-seven-year-old woman living in a district of Bombay says:

My life is finished because of this. I never thought I would become a Devadasi. I never thought I would be a prostitute. (Kirloskar and Cameroon-Moore, 1997, p. 28)

NGOs estimate that at least five thousand girls are secretly auctioned annually; many later die from diseases or AIDS-related illnesses (Human Rights Watch, 1999a).

JUSTIFICATION FOR THE PRACTICE

One reason that the sexual slavery of Dalit girls and other women in the lower caste has continued with such success is that it is a religiously sanctioned practice. The practice of dedicating girls to the temple is held as a religious deed because its main purpose is to appease the god or deity (Shankar, 1990). The Devadasi practice is propelled by an intense connection between religious doctrine and religious practice. Joachim Wach explains the reckoning of such practices by noting, "No act of worship can exist without at least a modicum of cultic expression" (Shankar, 1990, p. 19). In other words, the practice of prostituting these women's bodies is regarded as a religious experience and therefore socially permissible.

A spokeswoman of a women's organization for Karnataka (the state capital of Bangalore) explains that their practice has a very strong religious grounding (Kirloskar and Cameroon-Moore, 1997). In the Karnataka state, the Goddess Yellamma temple is used for a mass initiation of young girls to the Devadasi practice (Shankar, 1990). In the past, thousands of girls have been dedicated at this temple. When the government of Karnataka discovered this mass dedication, they passed legislation to ban the practice. Social service groups thus began antidedication campaigns both to stop the practice and to rehabilitate those already enslaved as Devadasi (Shankar, 1990). However, the custom remains strong because of the legitimacy that religion brings to it. Instead of ending the practice, in many villages, the priests of temples initiate girls secretly to evade encounters with the police and law officials (Shankar, 1990). Therefore, the practice of the Devadasi initiation, while illegal, continues to occur.

POLITICAL RESPONSE TO THE DEVADASI SYSTEM

Although the Indian government has increased its efforts to end the Devadasi tradition in the last fifty years, the result is far from successful. The practice has not ended but has become more discreet. Because of a government ban on the Devadasi practice since 1988 (Carroll, 2002), dedications are no longer performed in temples, but in private, concealed locations. Poverty and the accepted subjugation of women help to perpetuate the system. As of 1997, an estimated one thousand girls were dedicated annually (Kirloskar and Cameroon-Moore, 1997).

The UN Human Rights Committee has urged that action be taken immediately to end this practice. However, legislation regarding Devadasis is inherently intertwined with laws pertaining to Dalits and treatment of citizens from the lower class. The discrimination inflicted upon this group is taken seriously by the international community that has challenged the Indian government to do a better job of addressing the issue of caste "untouchability" (Human Rights Watch, 2001b). Yet despite legislation against this practice, many of the laws remain unenforced (Human Rights Watch, 2001b). Essentially, activism against the Devadasi practice has been unsuccessful.

The activist community has expressed great moral opposition to the Devadasi practice and finds it particularly troubling that it specifically targets poorer, Dalit girls. Many activists believe that the practice is "designed to kill whatever vestiges of self-respect the untouchable castes have in order to subjugate them and keep them underprivileged" (Human Rights Watch, 2001b). They believe that by maintaining Dalit women as prostitutes to upper-caste men, it supports a social and economic superiority of the upper castes over the lower ones.

International activists are attempting to reduce the struggles that Dalits face. In December 1999, the National Campaign for Dalit Human Rights, a grassroots group for Indian human rights submitted over 2.5 million signatures to the Indian prime minister regarding the injustice of the caste system. Sister Bridget Pailey is a nun who has challenged the Devadasi practice for twenty years. "The parents simply don't see any other possibility. Somebody has to be dedicated, or the goddess will be angry" (Power, 2000, 39). She has been able to implement subtle changes to improve the circumstances for the girls, such as clothed dedications at the ceremony, as opposed to the past where young girls were dedicated naked. But until changes are made to reduce the poverty that Dalits endure, the Devadasi system will remain an unfortunate alternative for girls born into abject poverty and discrimination.

Other Forms of Sexual Slavery

In 1994, Rwanda faced genocide and atrocities as a result of a civil war. An attempt by radical Hutus to remove all ethnic Tutsis in the country resulted in the death of almost one million people (Amnesty International, 2004c). Women, in particular, experienced extreme brutality and torture. Tutsi women were raped and murdered with ease. Moreover, many were held in collective and individual sexual slavery. Collective sexual slavery included rape and sexual service to a group of Hutu militiamen during the genocide period (Nowrojee, 1996). Individual sexual slavery was tied to forced marriage in which women were coercively held as "wives" to militia men. Oftentimes these were the same men who murdered the women's husbands and children.

While most women were killed immediately by Hutu militiamen, some survived because they were communally detained to serve the men sexually. For many of these women, this servitude meant constant individual rape and/or gang rape (Nowrojee, 1996). Some women were held in these circumstances for as long as the war lasted. After the war was over, their futures remained insecure at best. Militia forced some to leave the country and live in surrounding countries. Some women escaped back to their homelands, while others remained in neighboring countries.

One enslaved woman, Marie, fled to a commune to hide with a family friend after her entire family was killed. When the Hutu militia found her, they brought her to a government office where she was detained by soldiers who shot escapees. Marie recounted the following events:

> *They took the women to the bush and told us that they were going to kill us. They started to beat us. Some women were beaten to death. Then they took those of us who were still alive and forced us to walk to Nyamabuye (the neighboring commune). There were about two hundred women from the two communes. They chose the young women. They raped many of us. They were saying "we want a Tutsi wife."*
>
> *When we reached there, they took our clothes and made all of us sit down in a big area. At night they came around with torches to look for the beautiful women. They shone the torches in our faces and they kept saying "you come, you come." The first time they chose six women. They were raped by up to five militia. They kept changing the women through the night. When they chose me, I begged them, "please kill me." I was raped by three men.* (Nowrojee, 1996)

Afterward she was chosen by the militia for communal servitude with other women, after a forced march where many women died:

> *By the time the group reached Kabgayi, only approximately thirty women had survived the ordeal. We were held there by the militia for close to one month with other Tutsis until the RPF (Rwandian Patriotic Front) came into the area on June 2, 1994. During that time, they would come and rape*

*the women whenever they wanted. Luckily, I was not raped again, and I was
able to get some medical treatment.* (Nowrojee, 1996)

A Tutsi woman, Constance, recalled her experience after her husband
was killed by militia:

> *They ordered me and some other people I was with out of the bushes. They
> killed all the men and children right away and said that we three women
> would be killed the following day. . . . They took us to an old bar/cabaret . . .
> and locked us in there . . . There were many other women held in there. The
> Interahamwe would come whenever they wanted and take us outside to rape.
> There were women from ages fifteen to fifty in there. The women there had all
> been raped.* (Nowrojee, 1996)

Unlike the collective group, individual sexual slavery isolated one
woman to serve one militiaman from the Hutu group. These "forced marriages" were the only means of survival for some Tutsi women. When the
militia traveled to villages killing community members, they chose some
women as their sexual servants. These women were held captive in the
homes of the militiamen. They were referred to as "women of the ceiling"
because in many instances they were hidden between the roof and the ceiling in order to avoid being found by others (Nowrojee, 1996).

The women who lived in these situations were required to be loyal to
the men who were responsible for murdering their husbands and children.
The loyalty was expected in payment for letting them live.

According to twenty-three-year-old Ancille:

> *One of the Interahamwe started hitting me. He cut me on the leg and told
> me that I was going to be his wife. I had seen him before because he was
> from the Shyanda commune. He took me to his house and other Interahamwe
> came to look at me. He would lock me in the house in the day and in the
> evening he would come home and I would be his wife. . . . Other times, he
> would become angry and shout at me for sitting and spending the day thinking
> about my dead family.* (Nowrojee, 1996)

Ancille described her perception of militiamen as husbands:

> *We call these men our husbands. But they were not a true love. I hated
> this man. Maybe later on you could even be killed by them. Before the
> war I had a fiancé. . . . This happened to a lot of young girls—even school
> girls around eighteen years old were kept like this. In my commune I know of*

three women. One of these women is still with her "husband." (Nowrojee, 1996)

Nadia was eleven years old when a militiaman said he was taking her as his wife:

He only came to rape me, but he never brought any food. He came about five times. He would say, "Lie down or I'll kill you." So I was afraid. I would just go to the bed. He threatened to kill me with his machete. He would keep the machete near the bed while he raped me. (Nowrojee, 1996)

In another case, a militia leader married four girls to men in his militia group. According to one of the girls:

I knew I was condemned to this. . . . I thought this is a death, like other deaths. . . . I thought to be taken as a wife is a form of death. Rape is a crime worse than others. There's no death worse than that. The problem is that women and girls don't say what happened to them. (Nowrojee, 1996)

Without family, skills, or income, forced marriages provided the only means of survival for these women. Twenty-three-year-old Venautie still lives with the member of the militia who initially raped her. She has a child with him:

I still live with him, and I think of him as my husband because he gives me food and lodging. Every day (during the genocide), he told me that he would kill me. . . . When I realized I was pregnant, I thought that I had to accept it because it came from God. Now I am the only Tutsi living here. . . . As long as he does not want to kill me, I will stay with him because I could not find another husband. (Nowrojee, 1996)

Some Tutsi women stay with their new "husbands" because no other men would want them and because these women lack the resources to leave. Despite the end of the genocide, fear of their "husbands" and other hostile conditions leave them no alternative. Venautie lives with fear every day:

His brother tells him that he should not live with a Tutsi—that he should kill me. (Nowrojee, 1996)

In the last decades, thousands of women have been taken into sexual slavery in Afghanistan by enemy forces and physically and sexually assaulted.

Both Taliban forces and forces grouped in the United Front have assaulted, abducted, and forcibly married women during the armed conflict, targeting them on the basis of both gender and ethnicity (Human Rights Watch, 2001a). Taliban forces were reported to have abducted girls from villages they defeated and girls from other ethnic minorities and forced them into marriage (Coomaraswamy, 2001; McGirk and Plain, 2002). These marriages were tantamount to legalized rape. "They sold these girls,'" says Ahmad Jan, the Kabul police chief. "The girls were dishonored and then discarded" (McGirk and Plain, 2002).

The Taliban burst in with their guns and torches. None of the women even had time to put on their veils. With the women stripped of their burkas, the Taliban fighter selected the young attractive women. Nafiza was one of them. She had green eyes and waist-length black hair. With the butt of his AK-47 rifle, a Taliban invader slammed Nafiza into the dust and dragged her, crying and pleading, to the highway. There, Arabs and Pakistanis of al-Qaeda joined the Taliban to sort out the young women from the other villagers. One girl preferred suicide to slavery; she threw herself down a well. Nafiza and women from surrounding villages, numbering in the hundreds, were herded into trucks and buses. They were never seen again. (McGirk and Plain, 2002)

More than six hundred women vanished in the 1999 Taliban offensive (McGirk and Plain, 2002). Such abductions are considered such a great disgrace that the women's families almost never discuss them, or they say that their daughters are dead or married in Pakistan. It is likely that some of the women did end up in Pakistan, where they were sold to brothels or kept as virtual slaves inside (McGirk and Plain, 2002). They never go back home. They believe that their families would not welcome them back.

In 1991, rebels known as the Revolutionary United Front (RUF) began a ten-year war in Sierra Leone that supposedly ended with a peace agreement in May 2001. During the war, RUF perpetrated some of the most heinous human right's violations imaginable. Civilians were thrown from windows, burned alive, massacred in large groups and tortured by severing limbs, burning body parts, and gouging eyes. The rebels targeted civilians because they believed civilians were loyal to the government. In the vast majority of cases, they chose victims randomly. Further horrors were reported when the rebels gathered women and girls by the thousands and tortured, gang-raped, and mutilated them. Some were kept as permanent sex slaves and have yet to be returned to their families.

Human Rights Watch reported the stories of girls who were taken by the rebels. The girls explained that once rounded up, they were taken to a rebel command post where they were raped on a daily basis. Girls who have escaped report that many of the girls taken by the rebels remain behind rebel lines to this day. "Those who remain within the rebel ranks most often become attached to one rebel who then refers to her as his rebel wife" (Human Rights Watch, 1999c, p. 28). Some girls who were taken were as young as eight years old.

I was abducted from my home with several other neighbor women on January 8 and made to carry looted goods all the way to Waterloo. I spent over a month with the rebels and during that time was raped countless times. In our rebel camp there were scores of other abductees from Freetown including a young girl name Mariatu. She was just beginning to get breasts, and I estimated her to be no more than twelve.

One afternoon in later January as we were both being raped in the bush, I saw six men use her, one after the other. She was screaming and crying in pain, and I could see she was bleeding. After the second or third man, she went silent and I thought she had passed out. After they'd finished with both of us, I brought her water and said "Mariatu, you must drink, but she wouldn't wake up, I think she was dying. There was too much blood. After a few hours they came, picked up her little body, and carried it into the bush. I never saw her again. (Human Rights Watch, 1999c, p. 32)

Journalist Naomi Wolf referred to these atrocities as a type of "sexual holocaust on an unprecedented scale" (Oprah, 2003). There are some individuals who are risking their lives to work with the rebels and get the girls returned to their families. When the families are reunited, there is a ritualized welcoming that lets the child know that they are not held responsible for what happened to them. According to Wolf:

They bathe her feet and then an aunt or a cousin or a mother or father, if they're still alive, will drink the water from underneath the child's feet saying to the child "You're completely accepted back. Whatever you had done to you or whatever you were forced to do, whether you were forced to kill or whether you were forced to be a soldier or whether you were raped or turned into a slave, you know, we accept you completely. (Oprah, 2003, p. 5)

Other Incidents of Slavery

In some cases, individual men kidnap women to use as personal sex slaves. This was the case when police uncovered a dungeon in the home of John Jamelske in Dewitt, New York, U.S.A. On April 9, 2003, Jamelske was charged with kidnapping, rape, sodomy, and sexual abuse. The police believe that Jarmelske had enslaved women at different times since the 1980s and kept them as sex slaves. When they searched his home, police uncovered an underground concrete bunker as well as photographs of women chained to a wall and diaries Jamelske forced the women to keep, recording everything from when they ate to when they had been raped (Associated Press, 2003). As of April 29, 2003, five women had come forward and reported having been held. The length of time they were imprisoned varied. A sixteen-year-old was held for six months; a fourteen-year-old was imprisoned for two years (Smalley and Mnookin, 2003; Associated Press, 2003).

Finally, it is easy to imagine how the Internet facilitates instant access to women and girls who are lured into sexual slavery or are abused and exploited as a result of online contact. Women in Russia advertise themselves over the Internet as mail-order brides. As a result, men intent on using them for prostitution or pornography have easy access to women looking to leave their country (Goonesekere, 2001). Internet chat rooms are used by sexual predators to identify young girls who can be coerced into dangerous sexual interactions. A survey of over sixteen countries found that over 70 percent of Internet users under twenty-four years of age use chat rooms; girls who used them were twice as likely as boys to be contacted regarding sexual overtures. Technology has aided communication between predators and victims and established highly effective methods to entrap women into dangerous circumstances.

PROMISING PRACTICES
AND SUCCESS STORIES

Women's enslavement as a result of civil unrest and war flourishes during dangerous conditions that makes it difficult to document or quantify the number of women forced into slavery. But efforts to challenge traditional systems have managed some success. For example, understanding the historical roots and the cultural barriers to eliminating the Trokosi practice has helped liberate many girls and women from the shrines.

Supporters of Trokosi find the laws against it and efforts to liberate the slaves an intrusion on traditional values, particularly pushing a Westernized agenda. Regardless, as of 2000, it is estimated that approximately 60 percent of Trokosi have been freed due to the work of NGOs and local participants who, through education and communication have sensitively engaged individuals and groups to reevaluate the practice and promote ending it (Ameh, 1998).

International Needs Ghana has taken on the challenge of ending the practice, although they recognize how the system is enmeshed in traditional and religious roots. This cultural sensitivity is likely the reason for its success. They understand that ending traditional practices takes time.

With legislation that outlaws Trokosi, an important early part of the initiative to end the practice involved making sure the authorities understood that this practice exists and the laws against it. International Needs Ghana trained police officers, many of whom did not know about Trokosi and therefore did not know about laws against it (Ben-Ari, 2001).

Then International Needs Ghana approached priests keeping girls at shrines. A slow process of communicating with priests and convincing them of the human rights aspect to this practice has been continuous over the years. It is painstaking because other groups counter that this interference challenges religious freedoms and cultural expression. However, International Needs Ghana understands that raising awareness of these practices and advocating for human rights while strengthening legislation and enforcement will make a difference.

International Needs Ghana reports that they have liberated more than three thousand females from shrines. A school has been established where the women and girls can learn a trade that may make them employable or help them support their children. With help from AusAid in Australia, International Needs has received a grant to provide training and education to nine hundred released Trokosi. The goal is to release and train one hundred slaves per year (Rinaudo, 2003).

CONCLUSION

There are many types of sexual slavery. Sexual slavery may result from organized cultural or religious circumstances, war or civil unrest, or from coercive entrapment and exploitation. It may even be the result of a psychopath's sexual fantasies. Technology has facilitated some of the contacts and in some instances, it is a close "cousin" to trafficking in intent and management. Often, the women who are enslaved just "disappear." Regardless of the circumstances that lead to women's entrapment, sexual slavery is a direct result of systems that support the sexual objectification of women's bodies. This objectification may start as early as adolescence and may continue throughout the life span. Women are particularly vulnerable during the reproductive years. Women's sexual objectification is a root cause of many atrocities committed against women and is certainly the foundation of attitudes that condone or promote types of sexual slavery. The dehumanization of so many women demands more rigorous attempts to liberate them.

7

TRAFFICKING IN WOMEN

"I own you," he said. "You are my property, and you will work
for me until I say stop. Don't try to leave. You have no papers, no
passport and you don't speak the language."

(Lederer, 1999a)

The commodification of women is historically rooted in cultural and
social mores. Women have been given to men in marriage, taken in
battle, exchanged for favors, traded, bought, and sold. It comes as no surprise, then, that women are highly sought commodities by those who buy
and sell humans. Today, trafficking in women for sexual exploitation and
forced labor has proven to be one of the most lucrative forms of organized
crime. It is estimated that this market produces profits of $7 billion annually
(Kanics, 1998). This chapter explores the factors that make women vulnerable and profitable to those who buy and sell them. As a global human rights
concern, transnational attempts to contain trafficking show some success
although until the economic and social factors that jeopardize women's
safety are improved, and law enforcement efforts prioritize the identification
and conviction of traffickers, women (and children) will still be at great risk.

SCOPE OF THE PROBLEM

It is extremely difficult to collect data on the number of women directly
victimized by trafficking. The United Nations estimated that four million
people are trafficked each year, most of who are women (Kanics, 1998).
Although there has been no internationally agreed upon definition for the
"trafficking in persons" the United Nations defines the circumstances as follows:

"Trafficking in persons" shall mean the recruitment, transportation, transfer,
harbouring, or receipt of persons, by means of the threat or use of force or

other forms of coercion, of abduction, or fraud, of deception, of the abuse of power or of a position of vulnerability or of the giving or receiving of payments or benefits to achieve the consent of a person having control over another person, for the purpose of exploitation. Exploitation shall include, at a minimum the exploitation of the prostitution of others or other forms of sexual exploitation, forced labour or services, slavery or practices similar to slavery, servitude or the removal of organs. (United Nations Office for Drug Control and Crime Prevention, 2002)

Unstable social conditions for women contribute to trafficking. Arranged marriages and mail-order bride systems rely on vulnerable women with few alternatives; civil unrest and armed conflicts displace women and families with no economic alternatives; organized crime thrives in places where there is economic and political instability where women become vulnerable and valuable commodities; and sex tourism has become an important economic boost to some nation's economies (Mattar, 2004).

Women are most frequently trafficked to work as sex workers, factory workers, agricultural workers, domestic workers, or to be bought as wives. The endlessly flourishing sex industry provides a steady market for women. For example, in Japan the demand for sex workers is far above the local supply. Women are brought into Japan from many other nations including Thailand, South Korea, and Burma. The annual earnings of the sex industry is somewhere between 33.6 and 84 billion dollars (Human Rights Watch, 2000a).

Since the Vietnam War in the 1970s, Thailand has become a prime location of the sex industry where foreign men flock for sexual favors. It has been estimated that 60 percent of Thailand's tourists visit for the sexual "paradise" (Kuo, 2000). Package sex tours to Thailand including airfare and hotel have been provided to employees of transnational corporations as fringe benefits (Global Fund for Women, 1995). Many of the women trafficked from Cambodia, China, and Laos are forced into prostitution in Thailand to support the industry (HumanTrafficking.org, 2004). U.S. military ships will occasionally stop by Thailand for "rest and recreation." One woman described this practice as if the troops are being brought in for a mass rape of her nation (Global Fund for Women, 1995).

It is estimated that approximately forty-five thousand to fifty thousand women and girls are brought to the United States each year by traffickers (Matar, 2004). The women come from around the globe including Africa, Latin America, Mexico, Russia, and Southeast Asia as well as Central and Eastern Europe and China. Many of these women and girls are forced into the sex industry due to poor social and economic conditions in their home countries coupled with the demand for cheap labor in the United States. This practice exposes them to a host of other ills in addition to unsafe labor conditions and slavery. Because many in the sex trade are forced to engage in unprotected sexual activity, the rates of HIV transmission are high. One particular trafficker was purchasing HIV-positive females so that he could force them into slavery believing they had no reason to live and nothing to live for (O'Neill, 1999).

Brides for a Price

The market for brides is a component of the trafficking industry. In one circumstance, the stereotypical submissive nature of women in East Asia makes them targets of men in the West who are looking to dominate and control within the confines of marriage. With the advent of the Internet, the number of mail-order bride companies has increased almost exponentially. Women can be purchased and sent to men with the simple click of a computer "mouse." With financial interactions taking place over the Internet, there is less probability for detection of the crime. There is no guarantee that men ordering these brides are searching only for wives. In many cases the women may be forced to become involved in pornography and/or the sex industry (Hughes, 2000).

The search for a bride is not limited to men in industrialized countries. The sex imbalance in several developing countries such as India and China (see chapter 3, Femicide: Infanticide and Feticide) also increases the demand for trafficking. In these countries the percentage of women in the population has been steadily decreasing; therefore, there has been an influx of women from neighboring countries. In China in 1999, it was estimated that at the turn of the century, ninety million bachelors would be in search for a wife (Ren, 1999). It has been estimated that eight thousand women, mainly from Vietnam, are trafficked to China annually to fill the void left by the decreased female population in the country due to the one-child policy in place (Manthorpe, 1999). The demand for women in some areas coupled with the oversupply of vulnerable and desperate women in other areas is partially what makes trafficking in women so easy (Quy, 2000).

Forced Prostitution

Among other factors, the trend toward the legalization and regulation of prostitution in several nations has increased the demand for sex workers. When the demand surpasses the availability, women in neighboring countries are enticed to help supply the goods. Sex industries require a constant supply of fresh "goods" due to the physical and emotional abuse of the women involved (Hughes, 2000).

In countries where prostitution is not legalized, the trade is looked upon as unavoidable (the Western phrase "women's oldest profession" suggests legitimacy of the industry). Men are thought of as promiscuous in nature, and women are needed to help satisfy this natural characteristic. In stark contrast, women who are prostitutes are thought of negatively; therefore, while some women are needed to satisfy men sexually, other "respected" women are the ones sought for marriage (Seabrook, 1996).

In Greece, prostitution is thought of as a "threat to societal order" (Lazaridis, 2001, p. 76). Prostitutes are stereotyped as dirty and diseased. However, prostitution continues to be legal because sometimes a man's "sexual urges needed to be served by (someone) other than 'honest decent women'"(Lazaridis, 2001, p. 76). This "virgin/whore" dichotomy is a familiar theme in gender politics; in some cultures, like the United States, the same woman is expected to be virtuous and saintly in appearance and demeanor in public while simultaneously willing to be sexually objectified to satisfy men's sexual urges in private.

Women who are forced into prostitution find themselves in a double bind. Not only is forced prostitution a form of sexual slavery, but the increased risk of disease, disability, pregnancy, and injury, not to mention stigma, social isolation, and cultural disgrace may have lifelong impact and permanently prevent them from ever becoming respected citizens. Once forced into prostitution, it is enormously difficult to get out.

My story begins in May of 1997 in Veracruz, Mexico when I was approached by an acquaintance about some jobs in the United States. She told me that there were jobs available in restaurants and that I would earn enough money to support my daughter and my parents in Mexico. I accepted the offer and a "coyote" brought me to Texas.

I was transported to Florida and there, one of the bosses told me I would be working in a brothel as a prostitute. I told him he was mistaken and that I was going to be working in a restaurant, not a brothel. He said I owed him a smuggling debt and the sooner I paid it off, the sooner I could leave. I was eighteen years old and had never been far from home and had no money or way to return.

I was constantly guarded and abused. If any of the girls refused to be with a customer, we were beaten. If we adamantly refused, the bosses would show us a lesson by raping us brutally. We worked six days a week, twelve hours a day. Our bodies were sore and swollen. If anyone became pregnant, we were forced to have abortions. The cost of the abortion was added to the smuggling debt. (Protection Project, 2002)

Women forced to prostitute themselves are at great risk of sexually transmitted diseases and HIV infection. This is exacerbated by the lack of medical care and treatment available to trafficked women. As a result of limited contraception and repeated rapes, many women forced into prostitution become pregnant. In most cases these women are forced to undergo abortions (Bell, 2001) because a pregnancy would take away from their ability to work. Clients are often not required to wear condoms and if the woman requests the use of a condom, she risks being beaten. Refusal to wear condoms and lack of availability most likely contributed to the rapid spread of HIV/AIDS in Southeast Asia (Beyrer, 2001).

When trafficked internationally, women are less likely to speak the language or understand that services are available. In some cases, trafficked women are not eligible for government-subsidized services that might otherwise be available to citizens of that country.

One of the few methods of escape from the brutality in brothels is to become a recruiter. Women sometimes return home to recruit new victims (Hughes, 2000). However, there are consequences to women who take on this responsibility:

> *When I went back home, I found out that my mother had died a year ago. My father loved me, but my village refused to accept me because I was considered a bad woman. Village leaders threatened my father that he had to leave the village if he accepted me* (Poudel and Smyth, 2002, p. 81).

It is very rare that a woman may be able to return home and be accepted. In a few instances, women who are able to bring money, goods, and security back to their family may be able to return home and do so under more honorable conditions (Wennerholm, 2002).

Forced Labor

The subordination of women is reflected in economic, educational, and employment disparities between genders. The exploitation of female labor has become an important source of foreign exchange to some countries. In the Philippines for instance, the women in the sex industry, known as "overseas contract workers," are paying off the national debt by stimulating the economy. All of the money they send home to their families improves the economy of the Philippines (Global Fund for Women, 1995).

These high profits are not limited to Asia. A Russian woman can earn up to $100,000 annually for the pimp who controls her (Hughes, 2000).

The expanding middle class in countries like the Philippines and Indonesia has allowed for more men to afford to purchase sexual services. Therefore the demand for workers increases (Wennerholm, 2002). In Thailand, the expanding rice export industry has caused more men to move into the cities, and this has increased the demand for sex services in these cities (Seabrook, 1996). Not surprisingly, the continuous increase in demand for sex is causing traffickers to seek women from all over the world to fill the shortage of sex workers.

The trend of women being brought into countries for labor is not exclusive to the sex industry. Many industrialized countries are faced with the challenge of having to cut costs in order to maximize their profits. In these cases, the use of a cheap and undeclared labor force is very attractive. Because women are less likely to be educated and have fewer opportunities to work in skilled professions, women are more vulnerable to traffickers who can promise substantial work elsewhere. Offers to work in factories abroad entice women unable to secure economic options in their home countries (Wijers and Lap-Chew, 1997). Although factory-type jobs can be filled by both men and women, one African employer indicated that girls were preferred because they were more "cooperative" than boys (Dottridge, 2002).

Factories often seek female employees, not only because they are more obedient, but because the factory may serve other purposes. The biggest industry in Nepal is the carpet industry. The carpet factories employ thousands of women and are managed predominantly by men. The girls and women who work in these factories are sexually abused and raped by their adult coworkers, managers, and brokers for the factories. In some cases these factories run underground brothels which doubles the demand for women (Human Rights Watch, 1995).

Extreme poverty plays a crucial role in supporting trafficking of women. Due to the economic and social oppression of women in some countries, women look for employment abroad (Demleitner, 2001). Some of the women who agree to enter the sex industry are not aware of the horrors that await them. One woman indicated that she thought prostitution would be a lot like the Hollywood film "Pretty Woman" (Hughes, 2000). These women are also driven by the myth of female liberty in the West, thinking that moving will automatically guarantee them freedoms (Wijers and Lap-Chew, 1997).

In countries where a son is valued more than a daughter, poverty, debt, and hunger may leave families with only one choice—to sell their daughters—because having a daughter is an economic burden (Diamantopoulou, 2001). The selling of daughters in India is not unusual because selling a daughter is a way to avoid having to pay her dowry later in life. In most cases, the parents do not understand what they are selling their daughters for but are blinded by the possibility of large profits. In Nepal, a family may not understand and even complain about why the Nepalese police may imprison them for selling their daughters (Poudel, 1994).

Some girls may elect to enter the sex industry as they feel a duty to repay their parents for protection and care (Wennerholm, 2002). Debates rage about the rights of sex workers and the "choices" they make. When women enter the industry as a result of poverty or familial obligation, the market forces that support the sex industry are called into question. Women are thus seen as an expendable commodity. It is ironic that these "expendable commodities" are in essence putting food on the table back home.

Recruitment of Women

Globalization and modern technologies facilitate trafficking today. The Internet has made the market in women very efficient, providing easy access to women and wives through computers (Diamantopoulou, 2001). Large international networks that are well organized, well run, and well funded create sophisticated organizational structures by providing countries of origin, countries of transit, and countries of destination to traffickers. The opening of borders, as with the collapse of the Soviet Union, have allowed for greater travel, migration, and trade. Since this collapse, Russia and Ukraine have become valuable places for the easy movement of women out and through (Hughes, 2000). In addition, the increased migration acts as a perfect cover for traffickers who rely on the ability to transport women between nations (Hughes, 2000).

Globalization has also caused many industrialized countries to open their borders to financial assets and tighten their migration policies. The increase in women searching for employment abroad coupled with harsher migration policies are putting women at even greater risk of falling prey to traffickers. Traffickers look for women who are desperate to cross the borders. Unfortunately, with the desire to move abroad, women become vulnerable, thinking traffickers will let them go free once in their country of destination (Wijers and Lap-Chew, 1997). Criminal business profits from poverty, despair, war, crisis, and ignorance. Traffickers are able to use the vulnerability of women in situations of desperation to their advantage.

There are several different types of recruiters. Individual recruiters may find women in bars, cafes, or clubs.

*O*la had met a man in a disco in Warsaw; he offered her work as a stripper in a club in Holland. She was excited about the opportunity and left with him. When she made it to Amsterdam, she was forced to prostitute herself in a window and give all her earnings to her pimp who beat and drugged her. (La Strada-Ukraine, 2001 p. 2)

Some traffickers recruit through contacts with families or community members. These recruiters then sell women (much like wholesale products) to bigger networks, which act as the retailers in the business. Others are a part of a greater organized crime network that has specific offices such as a recruitment agency office, document procurement office, transport office, and prostitute management office. The recruiters belong to many different networks, and sometimes they are just individuals looking for some extra money.

Recruiters understand the urgent needs of the women and then use this to their advantage. They note the circumstances from which the women come; some may come from areas of extreme poverty, abusive households, or dysfunctional families. They listen to how these women want to change their lives. When the opportunity arises, the recruiters offer to make the dreams of these women come true. They make promises of marriage and introduction to potential husbands in areas with a higher standard of living. Sometimes they even pretend to be in love with the women and ask for their hand in marriage. In several instances, the traffickers sit through a marriage ceremony and then take the women to be sold out of the country. Men called "Ghataks" in Bangladesh make rounds of the rural areas in search of women to marry Indian men. These marriages, however, are a sham. The women are then sold by the men they believe to be their husbands (Wijers and Lap-Chew, 1997). In a village near Cairo, girls are married to much older men from other Arab countries. These men may stay for a few months with their new wives and then head back to their country where it becomes impossible for the wives to trace them. The wives are often left to fend for themselves and end up in prostitution. In some cases, a man will take the young girls back with him and make the girls responsible for caring for his other wives (Mikhail, 2002).

Women are also duped with promises of paid jobs with which they could send some money home to improve the living conditions of their parents. The promised jobs include but are not limited to waitresses, domestic nannies, and dishwashers. One fourteen-year-old girl in Thailand was taken to a tea shop, where she was told to rest before starting to work. When she awoke, she asked where the food was that she should begin serving. Her employer informed her that she would not be serving food but that she would be selling her body (Global Fund for Women, 1995).

It is also possible that women get in touch with these recruitment agencies through advertisements for help needed abroad placed in newspapers and magazines. They are not warned of the possible dangers:

> *Terri, a university-educated woman but unemployed, responded to an advertisement in a popular employment magazine in Budapest. The ad said a Canadian family was looking for a Hungarian-speaking nanny. The agency advertising the job escorted her to Canada. Upon Terri's arrival in Canada, her employers stripped her of her work permit and passport, and she was forced to perform "risqué dances onstage and illegal acts in the 'VIP private rooms.'"* (McClelland, 2001, p. 22)

If the effort to make women agree to leave with the recruiters fails, recruiters sometimes resort to force, kidnapping, and rape.

> *Kasia, a twenty-five-year-old woman from Warsaw, had no interest in working abroad, but her marital difficulties created a situation for easy recruitment. Kasia turned down an offer for a high-paying job in Germany. After her refusal to comply, she was kidnapped and taken to a cottage where the recruiters tried to gang rape her into submission. She was raped by three men for three days repeatedly.* (Johnson, 1999)

Rape is often used to leave women with no choice but to join the traffickers. In some areas that value virginity highly, rape soils these women and leaves them with no family support or economic resources. The only reason why rape may be discouraged in the trafficking of women is because the virginity of a woman has a high price tag. Virgin girls are sought after because they bring a lower disease threat. The fear of disease and more specifically, HIV/AIDS, has caused traffickers to recruit younger women and girls. There have been cases reported of girls as young as seven years old recruited for the sex industry (Miko and Park, 2000). Virginal girls are at great risk of contracting many sexually transmitted diseases, including HIV. Because of their virginal status, their "customers" have no reason to use protection of any kind. Young girls may not be fully developed and their genital area is easily torn and infected. These girls do not remain disease-free for long.

In addition to being disease-free, young women are thought of as being more compliant and less likely to rebel against the conditions associated with forced labor (Jordan, 2002). Therefore, the recruitment of younger women makes clients happy and makes the job of traffickers easier.

Conditions That Support Trafficking

Women may attempt to move abroad because of poverty, the lack of employment or marriage opportunity, or because of civil unrest or armed conflict in their home country. For example, the collapse of Communism in the former Soviet Union and the wars in Eastern Europe have left many people destitute. It is not unusual to find women there with the desire to move abroad and start a new life. In order to escape from the chronic poverty in Burma, many Burmese flee to Thailand or may enter Thailand as contracted workers. Trafficking networks have flourished due to these circumstances; they take advantage of the circumstances and facilitate the movement of people, such as from Burma to Thailand (Beyrer, 2001).

In some countries, women who are raped, divorced, or widowed are ostracized by the culture. As a result, they may be killed to restore "honor" to a family shamed by a rape or pushed into flames with the corpse of her husband as a result of widowhood. Or, once labeled as used goods, women in these situations have little choice and are forced to fend for themselves. Extremely vulnerable, they are prime targets for traffickers. Some women even enter prostitution willingly, claiming that it is what they deserve (Wennerholm, 2002).

Once these women are procured, travel documents, either legitimate or fraudulent, are used to cross borders. Generally the woman pays a fee to the traffickers because she believes the traffickers are doing a favor to her in facilitating the crossing of borders. Upon their arrival in the destination country, the women are stripped of their passports and other documents as a means to prevent their escape. Traffickers use illegal immigration to their advantage, instilling the fear of arrest and deportation into the women. The women find themselves abroad with no means of return, and it is not until this moment that they begin to understand that they may be forced into prostitution and work in deplorable conditions. There is no way for anyone to identify which agencies or recruiters offer legitimate work and which do not before they decide to work with the agency. One woman, Swe Swe, was recruited into sex slavery when she traveled from Burma to Thailand in hopes of finding a good job. A man she met insisted on helping her find a job. She was unaware of what was happening until her first client undressed and raped her. While he forced himself on top of her, she repeatedly banged her head against the wall, until she was bleeding. She wanted so badly to run away. However, her inability to speak or read Thai kept her in the brothel and caused her to lose all hope (Human Rights Watch, 1993).

An increasingly popular method of obtaining women is through abduction. This is particularly true in China, where women are kidnapped and sold as wives to men. It was established that between 1974 and 1991, approximately 176,000 women and children were kidnapped from one province in China (Biddulph and Cook, 1999). In Algeria, Sudan, and Chad, young girls are often kidnapped by gangsters who rape and sexually abuse them. These kidnappers refer to their abductions as temporary marriages (Mikhail, 2002).

Women are forced to work from dawn to dusk, with little or no pay. They may average between ten clients a day to as many as three dozen in one night (Wijers and Lap-Chew, 1997). They are raped and beaten by employers or customers daily. Prolonged abuse leaves trafficked women infertile and diseased. Sick women are often denied medical care or forced to work to pay off medical bills they incur as a result of the abuse. Many women live every moment of their lives in extreme fear and shame because of cultural gender expectations that have them believing they are criminals instead of victims. In order to prevent their escape and ensure their obedience, women are threatened daily with violence. In one report, a woman who had tried to run away had the tendons in her feet cut to prevent further attempts at escape (China Rights Forum, 1995).

In order to instill fear, women receive clear messages about what can happen if they do not comply with the traffickers' wishes. One escaped woman remembers seeing a video about a Bulgarian woman who had her knees bashed in for not obeying her pimp (La Strada, 2001). Police reports in Italy indicated that a prostitute is murdered every month, sometimes as a warning as to what may happen if a woman refuses to work (Hughes, 2000). Jaem, a woman in Japan, was reportedly beaten and kicked while her employers asked if she knew anything about the escape of two other women from the brothel (Human Rights Watch, 2000a). It is no wonder that once enmeshed in the world of traffickers, a women's terror is used as a weapon against her.

Transnational Attempts to Contain Trafficking

Can people really buy and sell women and get away with it? Sometimes I sit here and ask myself if that really happened to me, if it can really happen at all. (Hughes, 2000, p. 1)

As of 1999 there were 154 countries that had laws against trafficking although the penalties range from mild (the more antiquated laws) to severe (the more recent laws are more stringent) (Mattar, 2004). Although there is now more international cooperation than ever before to address worldwide trafficking, legislation will do little by itself to diminish the incidence rates of abused women and girls. Trafficking is highly profitable because it involves a great number of corrupt people, from police to border guards, organized crime syndicates, and state officials (Human Rights Watch, 1993; 2000a). While laws may exist in principle, they are often ineffective or unenforceable.

Attempts to thwart trafficking have varied around the world. The United States has passed a law that includes monitoring governments' efforts to stop trafficking. In 2000, the U.S. government passed the Victims of Trafficking and Violence Protection Act of 2000 amended with the Trafficking Victims Protection Reauthorization Act of 2003 to strengthen criminalization and prosecution of traffickers worldwide. The law addresses both forced prostitution and forced labor, focusing on prevention, protection, and prosecution (Protection Project, 2002). It is broad in scope, encouraging international cooperation and preventive measures to diminish the numbers of women and children trafficked each year. "It also requires the Department of State to scrutinize more closely the efforts of governments to prosecute traffickers as well as evaluate whether our international partners have achieved appreciable progress over the past year in eliminating trafficking in persons" (Powell, 2004; Protection Project, 2002).

Other countries have taken a different legislative approach. For example, the legalization of prostitution is a strategy to allow a government to better control the thriving sex industry that supports trafficking. In Greece, the legalization of prostitution has allowed for Greek women (age twenty-one and above) to register themselves as prostitutes. However, this legalization has caused the number of female foreign workers to increase. Between 1991 and 1995 it is estimated that 13,677 foreign women were trafficked into Greece. Since none of these women are Greek, they cannot register as prostitutes and thus are not awarded the same protection as the registered prostitutes (Lazaridis, 2001).

Because the legalization of prostitution may increase the trafficking of women into countries, these efforts have yet to define success. Furthermore, "as the number of prostitutes increases, organized crime groups cash in on women's bodies" (Ren, 1999, p. 8). The trafficking of women is actually less risky to profiteers than the criminal movement of other items such as drugs or arms. The consequences for moving drugs may be more severe in some places. Using women's fear to keep women silent assures a sense of security to the traffickers. Because women can be reused and resold, unlike drugs, which are consumed, it is more profitable in the long run. The high profit and low risk combination makes it a very attractive business (Edwards and Harder, 2000).

The increased cooperation between nations in efforts to combat trafficking has led to international communication and networking, stringent and prosecutable laws that criminalize trafficking, tailored prevention efforts that address the root causes, and protecting and repatriating victims. Many organizations are collaborating across borders to develop policies, network, and work with international human rights organizations in order to abolish trafficking (Global Fund for Women, 1995). Nongovernmental organizations (NGOs) have taken a lead in the prevention efforts and are reporting some measurable successes. Since many women are often illiterate, some organizations use creative educational techniques, such as books on tape or short street plays to warn women about the potential dangers from traffickers. Because traffickers often seek women from high poverty communities, attempts to improve or change the economic conditions for women are underway. Often, they will teach women simple skills that result in products that can be sold for profit (fish nets, rug, clothes), keeping women from having to seek employment abroad or from being lured to nonexistent paid jobs in cities. Direct service organizations provide support to women who are being prostituted or to women that have returned home from prostitution. They provide health and mental services and work on rebuilding self-esteem. They provide education for trafficked victims and educate communities about the threat of trafficking. Most important to many regions, these organizations provide an economic alternative to forced prostitution and labor by improving schooling opportunities, developing small business opportunities, and improving the economic conditions for women and girls. The best examples of attempts to thwart trafficking incorporate all of these efforts (education about trafficking, education to improve skills, economic opportunity, restitution, and reintegration into communities for those women who return from having been trafficked). Two of these organizations are highlighted below.

SUCCESS STORIES AND PROMISING PRACTICES

Winrock and La Strada-Ukraine

In 1997, two NGOs, Winrock International and La Strada-Ukraine (International La Strada, founded in the Netherlands, does work throughout Central and Eastern Europe) collaborated to address trafficking of women from the Ukraine. In order to be effective, they identified what they considered the root causes of the large numbers of Ukrainian women targeted by traffickers: (1) a lack of economic opportunity (75 percent of the unemployed in Ukraine are women and 71 percent of young people report feeling as though they have no social opportunities), (2) restrictive Ukrainian gender roles that demean women and leave them vulnerable, and (3) inefficient legal and enforcement systems. An effective program would have to be multifaceted and focus on these three main issues (La Strada-Ukraine, 2004; Winrock International, 2004; Maksymovych, 2004).

Seven "Women for Women" Centers were organized in cities with twenty-four-hour hotlines operated by trained women. The counselors answer calls related to domestic violence, sexual assault, and abuse as well as inquiries about opportunities abroad and marriage agencies. They assist family members of women who have disappeared after traveling to work abroad. A team of lawyers provides pro bono consultations for women who are either victims of trafficking or who are thinking of traveling abroad with an agency promising them work. The centers also provide job and skills training and help women start their own businesses. There are educational programs about the scope and depth of the problem of trafficking in the Ukraine, and through personal accounts of trafficking victims, women hear how traffickers trick women. Other educational efforts provide information to women about their rights, about violence against women, and exploitation (Maksymovych, 2004).

Although the Ukraine passed legislation outlawing trafficking in 1998, it was inadequate. For two years, La Strada lobbied the Ukrainian government until the legislation was revised to be more effective (La Strada-Ukraine, 2004).

Since July 2000, Winrock/La Strada reports over 17,500 women are no longer seeking employment abroad and over 37,000 women have received training on basic job skills and business enterprise to make them more economically viable. Of 18,000 women enrolled in vocational skills courses, over 5,000 have been employed after completion of the training and more than 4,700 have stayed in school. Over 30,000 women have learned about trafficking through the various educational initiatives by the NGOs and since December 1998, it is calculated that 70,200 have called the Women for Women Center hotlines (Winrock, 2004).

Prior to 1998, virtually no legal cases of trafficking were prosecuted. Between March 1998 and December 2001, 145 cases were initiated. In the year 2003, trafficking victims who returned to testify were picked up from the airport and transported to a safe haven. As a result of this safety net, 278 women testified against their traffickers (Office to Monitor and Combat Trafficking in Persons, 2004). That same year, forty-one trafficking cases were tried, and there were convictions in twenty-nine of them. Winrock/ La Strada-Ukraine is an excellent example of a comprehensive program directed at the root causes of trafficking that is making a difference.

Maiti Nepal

Nepal is a small country surrounded by two powerful giants: India and China. Due to poor economic conditions, the trafficking of women and girls from Nepal has been increasing since it began in the nineteenth century. The women and girls trafficked out of Nepal today usually end up in India and are reportedly sold for as little as four American dollars (Protection Project, 2004). Maiti Nepal, founded in 1993, has as its primary focus the rescue of girls who have been forced to prostitute themselves and the provision of economic alternatives to women and girls from the poor regions of Nepal. Maiti Nepal provides transition and safe housing to trafficked women, where educational programs teach the young women and girls about health, their rights, basic reading and writing, and some job-related or income-producing skills. There is a hospice run by the organization for women living with AIDS who have been rescued. The organization is also engaged in working to prosecute traffickers and help women testify against those who recruited and kidnapped them.

Maiti Nepal works closely with NGOs in India to rescue girls brought there and return them to Nepal. Between February 1997 and July 1999, Maiti Nepal reports having provided education and training to 120 girls (IPEC, 2001). While the numbers reported may be small, there is no measurement for the qualitative difference this organization makes in the lives of women who have been abused, exploited, and raped.

CONCLUSION

The problem of transnational women trafficking is a moral problem, a public order and labor problem, a human rights problem, a migration issue, and an organized crime concern. The complexity of this issue "without borders" requires focused effort to understand and eradicate. Legislation will support some of what is needed to address worldwide trafficking, but efforts must be comprehensive to prevent the exploitation of women and girls victimized by a sex industry that objectifies and dehumanizes them as much as it desires them. The solutions must be as complex as the problem and focus on the roots and underlying causes that put women's lives in jeopardy. There is no easy solution. Consistent efforts like those of La Strada and Maiti Nepal within regions highly vulnerable to trafficking, as well as cooperative arrangements with NGOS across borders, appear to provide some promise in intercepting and rescuing highly sought commodities—women and girls.

8

INTIMATE PARTNER VIOLENCE

How to Beat Your Wife without Leaving Prints

—The title of an article in a Romanian edition of *Playboy*

Intimate partner violence around the world is extensive (Davies, 1994; Chatzifotiou and Dobash, 2001). As is the case with other violent practices outlined in this book, an overriding theme of intimate partner violence is that violence within relationships is accepted as part of dominant patriarchal cultures, with few resources available to women who are victimized. Sometimes referred to as domestic violence, the incidents, more often than not, are considered a private matter within a household or within personal relationships and in most countries, law enforcement does not provide any security for women. In many countries, intimate partner violence is viewed as both a social problem and an individual problem on one hand, while denial and minimization regarding its existence is simultaneously present. This constellation of factors results in the practice and acceptance of women being beaten, scarred, burned, and/or murdered by those they live with and often love.

This chapter outlines cross-cultural examples of violence perpetrated against intimates with specific examples from North America, Asia, and Europe. It is mostly concerned with interpersonal violence between men and women but reviews interpersonal violence with women who partner with women. It also includes cultural contexts from which emerge distinct violent practices such as dowry-related and sati deaths, as well as acid attacks.

THE SCOPE OF THE PROBLEM

It is estimated that between 10 to 50 percent of women worldwide have been beaten by their intimate partners (Heise, Ellsberg, and Gottemoeller, 1999). In the United States, it is estimated that at least 1.5 million women are victims of domestic abuse each year (Centers for Disease Control, 2002; Loue, 2001; Straus and Gelles, 1990). U.S. women are six times more likely than men to experience violence committed by an intimate. According to the data collected by the National Crime Victim Survey, women are more likely to be injured during violence committed by someone close to them than by strangers (Bachman and Saltzman, 1995), and this has been confirmed repeatedly by studies examining this phenomenon in the United States. Women who are murdered by husbands or other male intimates account for 50 percent of female murder victims (Browne, 1992).

Data from around the world confirms the pervasive nature of the problem. Wife battering is common and found in such different countries as Bangladesh, Barbados, China, Columbia, Costa Rica, Guatemala, Kenya, Israel, Spain, and Norway (Mehotra, 2001b; Piispa, 2004; El Mundo, 2004; Herzog, 2004; Xu et al., 2005). Although overall, homicide rates have decreased in North America during the last ten years, the numbers of women killed by male partners in Canada have risen (Sev'er, Dawson, and Johnson, 2004). Almost 30 percent of Canadian women have been beaten by their husband, and four out of five people murdered by their spouses in Canada are women murdered by men (Morris, 2002).

Regional data highlights the problem in South America. In Chile, it is estimated that 60 percent of women are physically abused by their partners. A study conducted in Quito, Ecuador, found more than 80 percent of the women interviewed reported being beaten by their intimate partners (Dobash and Dobash, 1992). In Peru, 70 percent of all crimes reported to the police are by women beaten by their husbands. One study in Lima found over one-third of women reported physical abuse, and almost half were sexually coerced (Flake, 2005). Husbands who murder their partners in Brazil are often exonerated. Accusations of infidelity on the part of the wife provide the necessary justification for the husband's behavior; he had to do what he did to maintain his honor. Acting in one's self-defense is then a legitimate way to avoid prosecution for the killing (Fineman and Mykitunk, 1994).

In Latin America and the Caribbean, family and intimate partner violence is the most common violence reported (Arscott-Mills, 2001). One study found that 30 to 50 percent of women with partners in Latin America and the Caribbean are victimized by psychological abuse. In a study with abused Nicaraguan women, who had been beaten, only five out of 188 had *not* been sexually assaulted as well. Some women report that the ongoing psychological abuse is more difficult to bear than the physical beatings (United Nations Population Fund, 2000a). A study of Jamaican women showed that not only were many Jamaican women abused, there was a high level of injury, including broken bones (Arscott-Mills, 2001).

An Australian study conducted in health-care provider offices found almost one-quarter reported being assaulted by their intimate partner in the last year and of those women, approximately half admitted that they had never told anyone about the assaults (Loue, 2001).

In Africa, it is assumed that wife-beating occurs in most regions and is often socially acceptable. One report suggests that in Zambia, "a man could kill his wife and incur less of a jail sentence than if he stole a goat" (Green, 1999, p. 41). In Ghana, where polygyny is accepted by many of the disparate cultural groups that inhabit the country, males dominate within the family. Estimates there are as high as one in three women may be victims of interpersonal partner violence (Adinkrah, 2004).

Societies deemed to be more equitable economically and socially are not immune. Although Finland prides itself on being a gender equitable society and did not conduct its first study of intimate partner violence until 1997, the results showed that 40 percent of adult women reported being the victims of physical or sexual violence (Piispa, 2004).

Southeast Asian women are at great risk of interpersonal violence. In Sri Lanka, 60 percent of women are beaten, and 51 percent of the partners used weapons. In Pakistan, 70 to 90 percent of women experience domestic violence. It comes as no surprise that few women in Pakistan seek medical care after beatings. "When asked about the domestic violence victims who have been examined at his office, the head medical doctor for Karachi explained that '25 percent of such women come with self-inflicted wounds'" (Human Rights Watch, 1999b). One study of Indian women found the majority of women who were interviewed disclosed daily abuse and almost three-quarters reported that they feared for their lives (Panchanadeswaran and Koverola, 2005).

Research conducted in Papua New Guinea found that the majority of wives there have been hit by their husbands as it is seen as a normal part of married life (Davies, 1994). A study of Korean women found that over one-third of the wives reported being battered by their spouses during the last year (Heise, 1994b). Combined, the data from many regions around the world paints a universal picture of high numbers of women experiencing intimate partner abuse.

It is generally agreed that intimate partner violence is a leading cause of injury among women of reproductive years, making it a global public health issue (Doyal, 1995). Aside from the obvious health risks associated with the direct violence perpetrated against women in the home, women who suffer from intimate partner violence have a significantly higher level of anxiety and depression than women who have not been victimized. This may lead to higher rates of suicide in victims than nonvictims (Davies, 1994). Sleep and eating disorders, suppressed anger, self-blame, fear of sex or intimacy, risk of sexually transmitted diseases, and risk of pregnancy have all been associated with victimization. Other medical problems such as hypertension, chronic pelvic pain, irritable bowel syndrome, asthma, and a host of gynecological and psychiatric disorders have been associated with victimization (Heise, 1994a).

The challenge to making cross-cultural estimates of the numbers of women beaten in their homes demonstrates the cultural complexities of the problem; in many cultures, the extent of the violence is difficult to determine. Some cultures would deem any public disclosure of battering offensive so it remains a hidden problem. Many countries do not engage in any research to determine the extent of the problem. Due to social or religious beliefs, many cultures do not define battering as a problem. Some countries support wife-beating as an attempt to control women. The women themselves sometimes expect battering as an inevitable part of an intimate relationship.

In some cases, countries are faced with catastrophic health concerns that require all of the health-care resources available to them (e.g., HIV/ AIDS). Health threats that are predominantly female-based, like battering, do not get the attention they deserve and are minimized compared to the other public health issues. Some of this may be due to the fact that reports from medical facilities regarding injuries due to battering do not fully account for the extent of the problem. Many women do not have access to medical treatment or choose not to seek medical interventions for fear of reprisal, ostracism, or shame. Some women seeking shelter from violence are abused by those they seek help from, such as police or military officials (Heise, 1996).

Although it may be difficult to estimate cross-cultural numbers, there are striking similarities in the experiences reported by women worldwide. Qualitative data reveal the hidden nature of the problem as a "private family matter" (a well-known Brazilian saying is "you don't stick your spoon into someone else's pot") is common. Victim blaming that perpetuates abuse and exonerates abusers can be found worldwide, and there is a chronic lack of support services and resources for women whose lives are endangered. The individual experiences of women are then exacerbated by cultural specifics, such as religious doctrines that support wife-beating, different types of abuses suffered by women in different cultures, cultural expectations of women in the marital home, the sanctity of marriage, and misogynist power structures that ignore women's presence and dismiss female contributions, aside from childbearing. Other common experiences reported by women relate to the "reasons" given for a beating which may include disobeying the husband, initiating some control over sexual relations such as refusing to have sexual intercourse with the husband or asking the man to wear a condom, failing to have meals prepared on time, questioning the husband on matters considered inappropriate for women such as finances, going somewhere without the husband's knowledge or permission, challenging a husband about an extramarital affair, or not caring properly for the children. Use of family planning methods without a husband's consent may also be reason for a beating (United Nations Population Fund, 2000).

Women who are beaten by partners often suffer years of victimization and may never find relief or an end to the violence. Because traditional values in many cultures teach that marriage is the most important social condition, women are often afraid to or are unable to leave the confines of the marital home. Patriarchal conditions encourage women to live their lives according to what they were taught and what is culturally sanctioned: man is the master in relationships and in the home.

Most of what was initially known about intimate partner violence was a result of research conducted since the 1970s. North America, Europe, Australia, and New Zealand were the first sites to research domestic violence as a social condition. More recent investigations provide a glimpse into this problem in many more cultures worldwide, thereby expanding our understanding of the similarities and differences of this type of violence. Most of the research has focused on dominant cultures, although there are now some studies that describe violence against women in native, refugee, and immigrant populations (Davies, 1994; Bui and Morash, 1999; Human Rights Watch, 2000b; Raj and Silverman, 2003). While once considered the domain of the lower socioeconomic masses, we now know that it is not race-based, ethnicity-based, religion-based, or even gender-based (although the overwhelming majority of victims are women).

Violence directed at a partner may not be the only violence in a family. A complicated example of family and intimate partner violence hidden by secrecy and psychological torture got the attention of the American public in 1987 when six-year-old Lisa Steinberg was admitted to a hospital emergency room in New York City in 1987. The adults raising her, Hedda Nussbaum and Joel Steinberg, were responsible for her abuse, beating, and death.

*H*edda Nussbaum was a writer of children's books and an editor at Random House Publisher in New York City. Enthralled by attorney Joel Steinberg after meeting, the two moved in together. According to Nussbaum, after Joel Steinberg hit her the first time in the late 1970s, she chose to ignore *the violence, hoping it would never happen again. The violence continued and escalated. Ultimately, Steinberg brought home an illegally adopted girl whom Nussbaum and Steinberg began to raise. Finally, the abuse by Steinberg perpetrated against the girl, Lisa, became so severe that she was admitted to the hospital. As a result of the injuries from Steinberg's beatings, Lisa died on November 6. On the same day that Lisa was admitted, Hedda Nussbaum was examined by a physician.*

Dr. Neil Spiegel was the examining physician. "She was a forty-five-year-old woman that appeared much older than her stated age," he said later. She suffered from anemia and was a "hunchback" due to calcium deficiency. Spiegel testified that her injuries consisted of cuts on her lip, broken cheekbones, a broken nose, a large bruise on her right buttock, multiple broken ribs, and ulcers on her legs so widespread that they were life threatening. She was physically as badly injured as any battered woman I have ever seen—short of those who were killed," a social worker later told reporters (Gado, 1987).

For most women, once it starts, the violence persists while they are in the relationship and will likely increase in severity and frequency. Many women try to flee the violence if they live in communities where resources are available, but many more may not. The risk of violence may even increase for women who leave an abuser (Romito, 2000).

While intimate partner violence may not be a new phenomenon, it is likely to be on the rise due to changing political or social conditions. It is difficult to maintain an effective research base on the changing environments within cultures that spawn violence against women. Some theories suggest that when men are economically threatened or believe their control is being eroded, they may resort to violence in response to social and political turmoil (Arscott-Mills, 2001). However, without longitudinal data that is relevant to the period of change within a country, it is difficult to support this argument; these theories assume that there would be evidence of increased violence against women as well as against men because the social conditions would increase violence overall, and men would also be victimized (by other men). Because this does not appear to be the case, and overwhelmingly women are victimized by partners when there is social mayhem, cultural patriarchy and misogyny provide a better explanation as a root cause of intimate partner violence. Furthermore, because some governments argue that woman battering is a result of displacement or social/acculturative stress due to the environmental changes occurring in some countries, the government is exempt from having to examine the cultural roots that condone woman battering and the patriarchal conditions that exacerbate it.

While this perspective "justifies" battering as a result of changing political and social environments, it conflicts with the descriptions of violence that come from members of the community. Instead, what emerges as an explanation for battering from individuals within cultures experiencing upheaval, is victim blaming (e.g., she didn't listen to her husband, she should have been more attentive, she didn't properly care for the children). Comments on the specifics of the case (e.g., he was drunk) are also noted when asked about circumstances that contribute to intimate partner violence. The external political climate including gender inequity is generally not considered to be one of these circumstances.

Cultural Contexts of Violence

While much of the violence and murder associated with intimate partners is universal due to male domination within the family, many women are exposed to situations that are culturally specific. Acid attacks, bride burning, dowry death, sati, and honor killings are not frequently committed in the United States but are found to occur in greater frequency in other parts of the world. (See chapter 9 for a more thorough discussion of honor killing.) These issues are discussed in greater detail below as examples of the role that cultural norms and expectations play in violence targeting women.

ACID ATTACKS

Acid attacks have been reported in Southeast Asia (most particularly India, Bangladesh, Burma, Cambodia, and Pakistan) as an increasingly "effective" way to perpetrate violence and control women and girls. As a result of men feeling rejected by potential brides or lovers or because of loss of dowry, acid is used to make the woman or girl a less appealing "commodity" to other suitors (Khan, 1999; Lawson, 2002).

Most victims are attractive, young females (over three-quarters of victims of acid attacks in Bangladesh were females, the average age was twenty-one years) (Bari and Choudhury, 2001; Lawson, 2002). Illicit relationships or love affairs are often the impetus for these violent attacks. Acid is typically thrown over the face, neck, and upper part of the body through a window after dark when the victims are asleep or reading, or over the lower part of the body and genitalia after refusal of a sexual proposal or marriage (Bari and Choudhury, 2001).

In Cambodia, sixteen-year-old Tat Marina was an actress and model in 1999. She was one of nine children, and she supported her family with her modeling and acting career. She became the mistress of the Undersecretary of State in Cambodia, Svay Sitha. At first, she was not interested in his proposed relationship, believing him to be married. They became involved once he convinced her that he was not. When she discovered the truth that he was married, she tried to end the relationship. When Sitha's wife discovered her husband was having an affair with Tat, she and her bodyguards reportedly kicked and beat Tat until she passed out. Then they doused Tat with acid. Tat had third degree burns over almost half of her body. Tat said "I should have died that day. I probably would have died if I didn't think about my parents and my younger brother and sister. . . . I coughed up blood sometimes, or sometimes blood came through my nose." (Smith and Kimsong, 2000)

In Cambodia, society generally scorns people disfigured by acid as well as people who have affairs with married men. Furthermore, once Tat's attack became publicized, the incidence of acid attacks in Cambodia increased (Smith and Kimsong, 2000).

BRIDE-BURNING AND DOWRY DEATH

Traditionally, Indian females' lives are divided into three distinct stages: premarital, marital, and postmarital or widowhood (Puri, 1999); all three stages are defined in relationship to the men in their lives (Johnson and Johnson, 2001). Because to be never married or divorced in India is a disgrace for a woman and her family (Rao, 1997), many women are forced into unsatisfactory and even dangerous marriages. Brides report being denied food, harassed, abused both mentally and physically, and tortured by their husbands and in-laws, without any resources available to escape the marriage. Marital abuse is usually a precursor to bride-burning and dowry death (Jain, 1992; Gautam and Trivedi, 1986).

The original intent of a dowry was not to pay a groom's family to take the bride but to safeguard the bride in the event that some harm would come to the groom. It was to be an inheritance that belonged exclusively to the bride to use as a safety net (Caleekal, 2001). It was also intended as a way to provide for daughters in a culture where only sons inherit upon the death of their parents (Natarajan, 1995). D'Souza and Natarajan (1986) propose that the real reason for a dowry is to compensate for a woman's low economic value. However, this custom has been corrupted and is now used primarily as payment to the groom (Caleekal, 2001). The better educated the groom, the larger the dowry demanded by his family. Dowries were originally intended to serve three functions: a gift which provides the donor with spiritual wealth, economic compensation for the groom's family for taking on the additional burden of one more mouth to feed, and as a form of inheritance for the bride to support herself should her husband die before her (Johnson and Johnson, 2001; Anandhi, 2001). Dowries have come to include large sums of cash, appliances, cars, televisions, clothes, and jewels (Puri, 1999; Van Willigen and Channa, 1991; Anandhi, 2001). A larger dowry will assure a groom with good credentials. If the groom has female siblings, part of the dowry he receives will be incorporated into his sister's dowries (Van Willigen and Channa, 1991). Even though more women are becoming educated and employed, the practice remains commercialized because of the market value of grooms with desirable qualifications (Vindhya, 2000; Rao, 1997).

The dowry system in India has been blamed for perpetrating violence against women (Panchanadeswaran and Koverola, 2005) and identified as "an instrument of torture and oppression of the bride and her parents" (Gangrade and Chandler, 1991, p. 263). Reasons cited for a violent response to insufficient dowry (abuse and bride-burning) are alcohol consumption by the husband, the wife not producing a male heir, disobedience on the part of the wife, female infidelity, infertility, and sterilization (Rao, 1997; Johnson and Johnson, 2001). Wives may be threatened with divorce so that they can be replaced by women who can bring more income into a family (McWilliams, 1998).

Dowry deaths are cultural rather than religious in origin; they have been reported among Hindus, Muslims, and Christians (Stein, 1988). These murders most likely take place when the wedding has been arranged quickly (Scheneck, 1986; Kelkar, 1992; Miller, 1992; Van Willigen and Channa, 1991) or in order to arrange a second marriage that is perceived to be more satisfactory. In some cases, the bride might be driven to suicide (Natarajan, 1995, p. 299). Most Indian women who commit suicide have been abused for many years before they take their lives (Kishwar and Vanita, 1984).

Dowry-related deaths are usually labeled as accidental kitchen fires (Amnesty International, 2001; Oldenburg, 2002). The women will be found burned to death in the kitchen in a kerosene-soaked sari, or they die several days later in the burn wards of hospitals. Some women have also been found drowned in the wells where they gather water or poisoned with insecticides or poisonous plants (Natarajan, 1995).

For nineteen-year-old Rinki, dreams of a happily married life were never to be. Barely a month after her marriage, she was allegedly tortured and then set ablaze by her in-laws for insufficient dowry. Rinki was married to Anil. Soon after the marriage, Anil's father demanded a color television instead of a black-and-white one and a motorcycle. When Rinki's mother failed to meet their demands, Rinki was subjected to severe physical torture, allegedly by her mother-in-law and husband. Her mother was informed that Rinki had been burned to death when a kerosene lamp accidentally fell on her and her clothes caught fire. However, it appeared that the victim was first attacked, as her teeth were broken. Injuries were also apparent on her chest and wrist. (Hitchcock, 2001)

Female children bring economic and social burdens to a family in India (Sewell, 2000), and families must be able to produce considerable wealth for each daughter's dowry. However, dowries do not need to be as large if the bride can contribute economically to her husband's family. For example, lower class women in southern India are considered economically more valuable because they contribute to agricultural production (Johnson and Johnson, 2001). In addition, if a dowry is required for marriage of a daughter, a poorer family may be unable to afford one. In this case, it may be perceived as preferable that poor families kill an infant girl or abort a female fetus than contend with the social dishonor associated with having an unmarried daughter (Sarvate, 2000). The major root cause of female feticide and infanticide is a strong cultural and economic preference for sons. (Female infanticide and feticide are discussed in greater detail in chapter 3.)

The 1961 Dowry Prohibition Act became part of India's Penal Code as a result of a sizable increase in the number of Indian brides who died early in their marriages due to mysterious or suspicious circumstances (Caleekal, 2001). It was not until 1983 that domestic violence became punishable by law in India (Hitchcock, 2001). Amendments to rape and dowry laws were brought about as a direct result of the pressure brought to bear by the active women's movement in India, but these laws have been ineffective in stopping the violence because of loopholes or entrenched cultural values (Agnes 1998; Vindhya, 2000; Oldenburg, 2002; Panchanadeswaran and Koverola, 2005). Any attempt to seek police involvement in disputes over dowry transactions could result in members of the woman's family being subject to criminal proceedings and potentially imprisoned for having provided a dowry initially, since dowries are illegal in India (Hitchcock, 2001).

In 1986, harsher legal amendments (Section 174, CrCP) required investigations of suspicious bridal deaths with penalties for these deaths ranging from seven years to life imprisonment or even death. If the woman dies, there is rarely a conviction, and the groom and his family are then free to seek another bride and another dowry.

In the late 1990s, Vimochana, a women's group, studied dowry deaths in Bangalore, in southern India. They reported that many murder accusations were dismissed as accidents by the police. The information obtained during a police interview with a dying woman, usually taken with her husband and relatives present, is often the determining factor regarding whether a criminal investigation will proceed. Victims frequently make statements while they are in a state of shock and/or under threat from their husbands' relatives. The statements often change in later interviews (Hitchcock, 2001). During the investigation into the cause of death, the police are sometimes bribed, resulting in very few arrests (Anandhi, 2001). Sometimes the assailants avoid arrests and convictions by fleeing.

Of the 1,133 cases of "unnatural deaths" of women in Bangalore in 1997, only 157 were treated as murder while 546 were categorized as "suicides" and 430 as "accidents." Furthermore, of the 550 cases reported between January and September 1997, Vimochana reported that 71 percent were closed as "kitchen/cooking accidents" and "stove-bursts." (Hitchcock, 2001; Miller, 1992). The fact that most of the victims were young wives was either ignored or treated as a coincidence by police.

Since India has experienced increased prosperity, the number of dowries has also increased (Sarvate, 2000). There has been a significant increase in dowry disputes, dowry related murders, and suicides since the Dowry Prohibition Act became law. In the 1990s, there was a steady increase in the reported number of burned brides (Caleekal, 2001; Oldenburg, 2002). In the region of Rajasthan, police reported an almost 25 percent increase in dowry deaths between 1997 and 1999 (Amnesty International, 2001). Deaths in India related to dowry demands have increased fifteenfold since the mid-1980s from 400 a year to around 5,800 a year by the middle of the 1990s (Hitchcock, 2001). It is likely that more cases are being reported as a result of increased activity of women's organizations. Or perhaps the incidence of dowry-related deaths has increased. The degree of underreporting is unclear.

B. K. Rojavathi, an elementary school teacher narrowly escaped an attempt on her life by her husband. She was married in May 1999; her husband was given a large dowry in cash, jewelry, and household goods. Soon after the marriage, Rojavathi's husband and father-in-law demanded more dowry from her. On July 16, her husband tricked her into accompanying him to an isolated forest where he tried to strangle her with a chain that she was wearing. When that was not successful, he returned with a can of kerosene from his scooter and poured it over her. A forest guard saw him just as he tried to light a flame. Her husband fled the scene, the police were informed, and she was taken to the hospital. The husband and the rest of his family fled. Rojavathi, injured from the attempted strangulation, and her body bruised from the blows her husband inflicted, managed to recover from her injuries and shock. (Menon, 1999)

In comparison to the older women in the household, the status of the daughter-in-law is quite low (Johnson and Johnson, 2001). Abuse of daughters-in-law begins when the husband or his family harass the woman for greater dowry (Kelkar, 1992; Van Willigen and Channa, 1991). The harassment is not committed exclusively by the males in the family. Women (i.e., mothers-in-laws, sisters) may also abuse a new bride. The women involved in the harassment may believe that they do not have a choice because they are expected to follow the orders of the men in the household or suffer retribution themselves. Oldenburg argues that mothers may commit abuse and murders on behalf of their sons so their sons remain "innocent" and therefore still of marriageable status while searching out a new bride (2002).

There is cause for concern that dowry related deaths are spreading into more Indian states, including the southern part of India (where it had been much less of a problem until recently), and among the Dalits and lower middle-class families (Oldenburg, 2002). Kapadia (2002) suggests the modern changes taking place in India, while helpful to economic development, have influenced gender identity and role to the extent that male identity has become central to modern Indian society. This "translocal modernity" perpetuates women's subjugation by strengthening the male position of power in the culture. A direct result of this is the spread of dowry related crimes, not only in India but in countries like the United States where immigration has drawn NRIs (nonresidential Indians) but for whom the traditional cultural identities and expectations remain strong.

However, Oldenburg (2002) has an alternate view. She suggests that increased dowry deaths may represent a greater threat to the cultural male dominance. With Indian women's increased sense of economic and social independence may come more confrontation and resistance to control. The outgrowth of violence used against women may represent an attempt to rein in women's challenge to gender relations rather than a declining status for women as proposed by Kapadia. It is because women are stronger and more vocal that there is a greater need for violence used in a feeble attempt to deter women's growing independence in India.

SATI

Sati, or self-immolation, although also illegal, still occurs in India. It is not a common practice, but it is still reported to occur in rural parts of the country

(Birodkar, 2002; Narasimhan, 1994). "If a woman's main reason for living is to serve her husband, she no longer has a purpose once he is dead. Therefore, she must show her eternal devotion by throwing herself on his funeral pyre" (Johnson and Johnson, 2001, p. 1060). The widow herself may believe that she has been remiss in her duties as a wife by not prolonging her husband's life. Therefore, Sati restores her honor in death (Oldenburg, 2002). Many believe that if a woman chooses Sati, she will be granted magical powers to return to her people as a spirit and spread good. She is seen as a heroine within her community (Narasimhan, 1994).

In 1999, Charan Shah, a widow in Uttar Pradesh, north of Delhi, threw herself onto her husband's funeral pyre and burned to death. (Sen, 2001)

In 1987 there was a much more widely publicized case of an eighteen-year-old widow, Roop Kanwar, who burned to death on her husband's funeral pyre. However, in that case many people were arrested for contributing to her death. There were allegations that some of her relatives drugged her and forced her to burn alive with her dead husband. (Sen, 2001)

There have been debates about whether Sati represents "free choice." The majority of women in India traditionally and historically have not been permitted to voluntarily make any major decisions in their lives. Traditional Indian women in the twenty-first century may be allowed input into their choice of a husband, but the family selects the group of men from which she is permitted to choose. She historically has moved from her father's home to her husband's home and is expected to obey her husband and her mother-in-law. She may not decide if she will go to school, if her daughters will go to school, or if she will work outside the home. Furthermore, once widowed, a woman's status in India is very low. She is generally considered an unwanted burden, and taboos may prevent her from participating in housework because she is liable to be considered unholy and impure. Some believe it was because of the widow's "karma" that her husband died. She is likely to be shunned and abhorred. Therefore, a woman who believes that she has no choice may commit Sati. The reality is that a choice can be made only between viable alternatives; for many women there are none (Sen, 2001, p. 30).

Historically, Sati was sometimes performed by women even before their husbands were actually dead, if their city was besieged by the enemy and defeat was imminent. It was considered preferable for a woman to kill herself than to risk being dishonored at the hands of the enemy (Birodkar, 2002). Many in India argue that Sati is a sacred tradition, and those women who commit Sati by burning alive voluntarily with their husbands should be worshipped. However, others perceive the practice as the logical progression of social aberrations like dowry, widow denigration, women's inequality, obsession with male progeny, and marginalization of women from the mainstream of life. Narasimhan argues that people's social perceptions need to be changed radically and the collective conscious needs to be roused against such ritualistic practices (Narasimhan, 1994).

OTHER INTIMATE PARTNER MURDER

In its most extreme form, violence against women in the home becomes murder. It is estimated that overall, one-half of women who are killed are murdered by an intimate partner or husband. The major distinguishing characteristic of intimate partner murder is acceptance of this fate by the women in the abusive relationships. As with intimate partner violence, worldwide women are generally blamed for their behavior that led to the murder or their poor judgment in choosing their violent partners or their inability to understand the threat in the home and flee.

The U.S. stabbing murder of Nicole Brown Simpson whose ex-husband, O. J. Simpson (former pro-football player and movie star), was accused of the crime, received international attention. On July 12, 1994, Nicole Brown Simpson and a friend, Ronald Goldman were stabbed to death outside Nicole's Brentwood, California condominium. On July 17, O. J. Simpson was charged with the crimes. During the trial, Denise Brown, Nicole's sister, testified that Nicole had confided that O. J. had abused her during their marriage and that she feared for her life. Evidence that supported this testimony was allowed into admittance during the trial. After seven months of a highly publicized trial, on October 3, 1995, Simpson was acquitted of the two murder charges. (CNN, 1995; *USA Today*, 1996)

Easy availability of firearms in the United States contributes to the number of women killed each year. The U.S. military has investigated the role that military training and war experience plays in violence perpetrated against spouses. During one six-week period in 2002, four military wives were murdered at Fort Bragg, North Carolina. Two of the soldiers who killed their wives committed suicide following the murders (Krasula, 2002).

Homocide rates tend to increase during severe social or political upheaval. For example, the spousal homicide rate in Russia is dramatically higher than in the United States. "The likelihood of murder of a woman as opposed to a man by an intimate partner is nearly three times greater in Russia than in the United States" (Gondolf and Shestakov, 1997). This makes Russian women the most vulnerable of all women in industrialized nations. Gondolf and Shestakov attribute this extreme risk to women to the social and economic upheavals that Russia is regularly prone to, the high level of normative violence in the culture (reflected by the strong militarism and high level of crime in the country), and the conflicted status of women who work both in the public workplace but still are responsible for daily household demands and primary child-care responsibility. The high level of alcohol abuse in Russia is also a contributing factor to the violence. Women in Russia have few opportunities to escape violence in the home; there are severe housing shortages and very few resources or agencies for battered women (1997). Police in Russia are known to dismiss women's complaints of abuse, and there have been reports of officers' refusals to take a report from women victims. In other circumstances, police are accused of refusing to respond to emergency calls from women being beaten in their homes (Human Rights Watch, 2001h).

During the peak of the troubles in Northern Ireland, police resources were taken up almost entirely with the violence associated with the political struggle (McWilliams, 1998), even though between 1991 and 1994 (when the first peace agreement between England and Northern Ireland was enacted) twenty women in Northern Ireland were killed by a common-law partner or husband (McWilliams and Spence, 1996). This is more than one half of the number of women who were killed as a result of the political violence during that period, but the victims of domestic murders received comparatively little attention (McWilliams, 1998). The police and the culture view domestic violence and murders quite differently from murders involving a political element. This is illustrated by the fact that murders not related to the political situation are referred to as "ordinary decent murders" (McWilliams, 1998).

The reality is that women who are killed by their intimate partners have usually suffered violence for some time. The murder is often the end result of a long history of abuse, assault, and battery. However, when a man is killed by his intimate partner, it is often a form of self-defense; the women who kill do so while defending themselves during a violent episode or resort to killing their mates because it is the only way they can see to stop the violence that has been repeatedly perpetrated against them. According to Dobash and Dobash, "no matter who dies, the antecedent is often a history of repeated male violence, not of repeated female violence" (1992, p. 6).

LACK OF SERVICE PROVISION FOR VICTIMS

Shortage or lack of housing puts women at greater risk of violence within the home by forcing them to stay in an abusive relationship, sometimes in order to provide shelter for their children. Some women may be unable to take their children with them but will not leave without them. In some cultures, family members may be reluctant to take in a fleeing woman. It may dishonor the family to know that the wife has fled to her family of origin. If they take a woman in, the family may be ostracized for what would be perceived as "interfering" in a marital squabble. In some cases the family may even side with the abuser. Women forced to stay with abusers may choose to become prisoners within their own homes rather than make their children homeless or leave their children with the abuser without the mother's protection.

In many countries there are no supports, legal or social, available to women who might otherwise flee violence in the home. Attempts at strengthening laws that address violence in the home are not deterrents to the violent behavior, primarily because the social roles between men and women do not change with the laws. Nor are there serious consequences for individuals who break the laws.

When Japan became one of the last major industrialized nations to criminalize domestic violence in 2001, complaints to law enforcement rose 50 percent once the law was enacted. Although a law criminalizing domestic abuse may encourage victims to step forward, Japan maintains a dominant patriarchal culture that subordinates women. Marital rape remains legal in Japan. The silence and secrecy of domestic abuse in Japan still holds (as in many other countries), and many still believe that what men and women do behind closed doors is private and no one else's business (Yoshihama and Sorenson, 1994).

*K*imiko was married in 1965. Shortly after the arranged marriage, her husband began breaking things: objects and appliances in the home. Then he began throwing things at Kimiko. Eventually he began attacking Kimiko directly. "Sometimes he beat me once a year, sometimes several times. If he'd been violent all the time, I would have left him much earlier." But the psychological abuse was unending. He was possessive and watched her every move. He complained about the way she spoke, what she wore, how she comforted herself, and the way she served meals. Virtually, every night after work, he cross-examined her about whether she had left the house that day, when she had returned, whom she had seen. (Magnier, 2002)

Men need not physically attack or abuse but simply intimidate women into submission. The fear that abusive men instill in their partners is often enough to maintain control over the women. For many women, the social stigma attached to this kind of abuse keeps them silent and reluctant to seek help. Because there are (only) emotional and psychological scars rather than physical ones, many women trivialize the abuse in an attempt to justify what their husband or partners do to them.

Women Who Partner with Women and Interpersonal Violence

Until the 1980s, little was documented about abuse in same-sex relationships. The majority of research about domestic violence had focused on heterosexual couples in the Western world. Because same-sex relationships are outlawed in many countries, there remains a paucity of research worldwide about the problem.

The percentages of women in same-sex relationships who experience abuse appear to match those of women in heterosexual couples (Ristock, 2003). In one U.S. study, more than one-half of the respondents had experienced abuse during their first same-sex relationship (Ristock, 2002). There are obvious cultural and social taboos associated with same-sex relationships in many countries that forbid women from seeking the support and services they need. In some countries, simply "coming out" threatens their lives. Many women are unable to leave or put an end to an abusive relationship. For lesbians, economic dependency, a paucity of resources or places to go, and fear of being identified as a lesbian in a homophobic culture pose additional obstacles.

In an abusive lesbian relationship, the abuser may use the lesbian identity as a source of power and control (Loue, 2001; Ristock, 2003). She may threaten to "out" her partner if she tries to leave or tell someone about the relationship. "Outing" is a serious issue in Western cultures that continues to deny gay citizens full rights. In other cultures, being exposed as lesbian, "outed," or even perceived as being a lesbian, could result in alienation, discrimination, persecution, and/or death.

For some battered lesbians, confiding to a health-care provider that injuries are the result of physical abuse by an intimate simply may not be an option. This may result in untreated injuries and emotional and psychological scars. In *Naming the Violence* (Lobel, 1986) Donna Cecere described the abuse she suffered:

> *The physical abuse I endured ranged from pushing and being restrained against my will to slaps and a tackle, which produced a back injury that*

left me in pain for several months. I never sought medical help, mostly out of fear of having to explain or lie about what had happened. My injuries were not visible, except perhaps in my mood. There was the time that she made a move to strangle me and was shocked that I bothered to defend myself. (p. 25)

In some countries such as Australia, United Kingdom, and the United States, there are a growing number of services available to battered lesbians, but there may still be obstacles to seeking help. Fear of identifying an abuser may be the same for lesbians as it is for straight women. Threats and intimidation by the abuser may be doubly hard on lesbians, for whom a small, tight-knit community of lesbians may be the only source of support and "family." Lesbians who leave their abusers may find themselves completely isolated, having already been estranged from their family of origin because of their sexual orientation. There is a crucial need for more research and attention worldwide to women who abuse and are abused by female partners.

PROMISING PRACTICES AND SUCCESS STORIES

Countries around the world have implemented national policies and legislation to address intimate partner violence. However, large-scale policies appear to do little to affect change on the personal level. Laws and legislation may criminalize behavior or allocate funds for services and prevention efforts, but they rarely implement social or cultural change. For example, the U.S. Violence against Women Act provides grants for community police training, safe homes for women and children, and improved enforcement of laws but does little to challenge social inequities that give rise to these problems in the first place. Patriarchal structures that support gender-based violence continue unchallenged by most policy initiatives. However, policy on a community level can help by putting violent behaviors under scrutiny and requesting accountability. Policies that address the fundamental issues that help create and support gender-based violence may do more to prevent it than sweeping, generalized national legislation. Human rights work, poverty and illiteracy reduction, economic opportunity, changes in the gendered division of labor, and male involvement in the prevention of violence can create a network of environmental change that will support the amelioration of gender-based violence.

In a document outlining men's role in ending gender-based violence, the United Nations (Lang, 2003) highlights many programs on community and individual levels that involve men in preventing violence against women and girls. For example, an increase in paternity leave, child-care availability, and flexible work hours in parts of Scandinavia and Europe are policy attempts to create an environment where men are more involved in child rearing and family activities. By establishing a more equitable household environment, the thought is that men more involved in family life where inherent patriarchal and power dynamics are reduced, may be less likely to commit intimate partner violence. In Pakistan, images of victims of acid attacks are sent to policymakers to raise awareness of violence against women, in line with the English expression "a picture is worth a thousand words." Training for police officers in Pakistan helps the men understand the responsibility in enforcing the laws against violence against women and the gender disparities and stereotypes that create inequitable power dynamics in their own families. In Brazil, there is an outreach program for men and boys called the Guy-to-Guy Project where trained youth from poverty areas work with other young men in examining behaviors that lead to violence against women and girls.

Efforts to involve men and change the gendered power structure must be consistent and long term in order to show any measurable change in reducing violence against women. But other initiatives that support women who have been victimized have had more immediate success in providing necessary shelter and protection when escaping violent relationships.

In the mid-1980s, as a result of strong feminist activism, Brazil was the first country to organize all-women police stations where victims of partner and sexual violence could find supportive and willing law enforcement officers to handle the crimes. Staffed by trained female officers, there are now over three hundred in the country (Santos, 2004). These stations have increased the investigation and arrests associated with intimate partner violence and helped raise awareness of the laws against family violence. In the cities, these stations have had over ten thousand complaints annually, which is a much higher number than those registered in the traditional male-dominated police stations (Hautzinger, 2002). While these stations are not without their problems, a compelling argument can be made that women may be more apt to criminalize violent behaviors perpetrated in the home when there is a law enforcement system that facilitates investigation and prosecution of the crimes on a local level.

Concerns about the role that dowry plays in family life and its association with violence against women inspired a creative approach to violence prevention in India. Population Communications International (PCI) is a nonprofit organization dedicated to healthy and sustainable development around the world. One of the efforts developed by PCI was to collaborate with the local Indian media to create sensitively constructed radio soap operas that challenge the collective attitudes in the culture. Developing appealing entertainment that addresses social issues has increasingly become a way to initiate prosocial behavior (Sood, 2002). Using entertainment-education (sometimes called "edu-tainment"), PCI developed storylines that addressed challenging social, health, and economic development issues.

The radio soap called Tinka Tinka Sukh (Little Steps to a Better Life) was broadcast in 1996–1997. In India, it is estimated that the radio show's regular listeners numbered as many as forty million people. The topics in the storyline addressed individual and community issues: equality between the sexes, dowry, family planning, poverty, community responsibility, and HIV/AIDS. Many of the issues addressed by the soap opera are those that are considered fundamental causes of violence against women (Sood, 2002).

Communication theories hypothesize that the more relevant an issue is to an individual, the more likely that an individual will attach importance to that issue. In some cases, greater motivation for critical thinking will follow. Listeners who identify to some degree with the characters and the storyline will be more prone to discussion and consideration of those issues (Sood, 2002).

The yearlong broadcast of Tinka Tinka Sukh elicited thousands of responses from listeners for inspiring many local discussions on social matters, including the role that dowry plays in women's lives.

My brother got married recently, and we did not even bring up dowry. Our entire village has collectively decided to renounce dowry. In fact, there have been three weddings in our village in recent months where the issue of dowry never came up. There were some people who previously wanted to take dowry but based on the education we received from the radio, the discussion on dowry has now ceased. (Chandra Bhan Yadav, a listener of Tinka Tinka Sukh, Sood, 2002)

Although the impact of the radio show on preventing violence against women has not been measured, it is a noteworthy effort at creating community involvement in cultural issues that require community attention. Most entertainment-education efforts have been used to promote prosocial behaviors in cultures where collective concerns take precedence over individual ones (Sood, 2002). According to PCI, "the purpose of the serial drama, while entertaining and educating its audience, was ultimately to motivate the listeners to take charge of their health, seek out health services, and improve their own lives" (PCI, 2003).

CONCLUSION

The reality is that for most women in abusive relationships, escape is nearly impossible due to social restrictions imposed on them. When the violence is committed by male family members, many social and political institutions desert the women because the violence is seen as male prerogative or a method to maintain the social and economic power over women in the household. For women who do escape, they may be stigmatized without a marital connection, may experience poverty due to loss of support by the husband, and may live in fear that the abuser will come after them and find them.

Many women live in a constant, daily state of terror, isolation, and fear. Some argue it is a form of worldwide terrorism. Most governments respond to violence against women with legal solutions. As noted, this solution may have both benefits and limits. In most countries, violence against women receives no special treatment. That is, the laws that regulate other violent behaviors are used as templates to address violence against women. This approach proves inadequate due to the gender and cultural root causes of the violence directed at women (Connors, 1994). Without an adequate understanding of the cause of violence against women, prevention initiatives will be ineffective. The efforts listed above show creative attempts to change social norms and challenge the beliefs that may lead to interpersonal partner violence.

Although vulnerable and without proper resources outside the home to assure safety, some women who do flee find any alternative better than living in terror at home. To women, like Kimiko in Japan who ultimately left her husband, the vulnerability and fear is worth it.

> I feel so happy that I've escaped a life of terror. I'm free. I'm free.
>
> (Magnier, 2002)

9

HONOR KILLING

I would not have want [sic] to harm my own child, but I had no
choice. Nobody would buy my produce. I had to make a living for
my other children. (a farmer who felt forced to kill his daughter
cited in Turgut, 1998)

Unlike the other chapters, there are no women's voices in this chapter,
only women's stories told by others who knew them. The victim's
voices were silenced by the very act that is the focus of the chapter. They
were killed in the name of honor.

This chapter will focus on crimes of honor primarily in Turkey, Jordan,
Iran, and Egypt; however, honor killings occur, often with some regularity,
in Afghanistan, Bangladesh, China, Great Britain, Ecuador, India, Iraq,
Israel, Italy, Korea, Lebanon, Pakistan, Palestine, Morocco, Sweden, Syria,
Uganda, and Yemen as well (Muslim Women's League, 1999; Sarhaddi Nelson, 2003; Flattum, 1999; Amrani, 2002; Ortner, 1978; Baker, Gregware,
and Cassidy, 1999; Jehl, 1999). In Latin America these murders are called
crimes of passion (Mayell, 2002).

This chapter will address the customary, cultural, and religious justifications for honor killings. In addition, the relationships between honor
crimes, patriarchy, and illiteracy will be explored. There have been reports
of women murdered in the name of honor in parts of the world where this
practice has heretofore been uncommon, and the reasons for this spread will
be discussed. Many countries have tried unsuccessfully to eliminate these
murders by passing what is apparently ineffective legislation; however, there
have been several promising approaches to reducing this problem, which
will be reviewed at the conclusion of the chapter.

SCOPE OF THE PROBLEM

The United Nations estimates that more than five thousand women worldwide are killed each year in the name of honor (Rice-Oxley, 2004). Family

173

honor is achieved through different expectations for men and women: man-
liness in a man and sexual purity of a woman (Youssef, 1973). There are
many motivations for these killings, depending on the culture in which they
occur. In the countries where "honor" is valued, a man's self-worth and
social status are tied to women in his life as extensions of his honor (Baker,
Gregware, and Cassidy, 1999). What happens to women is a direct reflection on men's respectability in a community. Female adultery and premarital
sex are the most severe violations of patriarchal community norms in certain
societies and the ones that elicit the harshest punishment (Baker, Gregware,
and Cassidy, 1999).

In a Greek mountain community, family dishonor has been linked to
a wife's disobedience, with adultery viewed as the ultimate betrayal. The
husband becomes a neighborhood laughingstock and there is speculation
about sexual potency or lack thereof (Campbell, 1964). Furthermore, adultery betrays the entire family because the family expects to have control over
the sexual behavior of all of the females in the family. This betrayal provides
ample "justification" to murder the responsible party (Campbell, 1964).

Elizabeth Kim was just a small child when she watched her grandfather
and her uncle kill her mother for bringing dishonor to the family by having
her out of wedlock in a small Korean village in the middle of the twentieth
century. Elizabeth does not know how old she was at the time, but it was
several years after the end of the U.S. involvement in the Korean War. Elizabeth's father was an American GI. Her grandfather demanded that her
mother sell Elizabeth into slavery to restore the family honor. When Elizabeth's mother refused, her father then told her that the only way to restore
the family's honor was to kill Elizabeth's mother. She was hanged to death
in front of Elizabeth; then her relatives burned Elizabeth's genitals and they
sent her to an orphanage (Kim, 2000).

Women bring shame upon a family for having been raped, for wanting
to be educated, for selecting their own spouses, for marrying outside their
caste or class, for marrying outside their ethnicity, for marrying outside their
nationality, for not obeying their husbands, for having premarital sex, for
having extramarital sex, for being pregnant outside of wedlock, for simply
being suspected of having lost their virginity, for being seen with or talking
to a male other than a relative, because a man wants another wife, or
because their whereabouts were unaccounted for during which time they
could have been with a man (Amrani, 2002; Ruggi, 1998; Associated Press,
1999a). According to Jehl (1999), in the Arab world, female chastity determines respect in a family; lack of it causes shame. An unchaste woman is
sometimes considered worse than a murderer. A woman's chastity reflects
not just on the woman, but also her entire family and even her tribe (Jehl,

1999). Women in many countries where honor killings occur are encouraged to observe purdah (Purdah is the physical covering of women within an enclosed space) and remain sequestered in their designated private, safe space to assure their honor by eliminating their vulnerability to rape or illicit sex (Mandelbaum, 1988). Not surprisingly, this limits women's options and their ability to earn their own money, become educated, socialize, or contribute in meaningful ways to the community.

Honor crimes are treated leniently in many parts of the world where women are considered the property of their husbands or fathers, regardless of class, race, or ethnicity. Since the man owns the property, he can decide what to do with it. Treated as property, women are considered a commodity to be bought and sold (Khan, 1999).

Kifaya, a Jordanian girl of twelve, was intelligent and full of curiosity. But when she returned home one evening from a walk in the neighborhood with some friends, she was confronted by her enraged father. Shouting that she had dishonored the entire family, her father proceeded to beat Kifaya with sticks and iron chains until she was dead. He told police he killed his only daughter because she went for walks without his permission (Halaby, 2000).

Honor killing occurs most often in areas where illiteracy rates are high, poverty is severe, and there is a strong community belief in the notion of family honor (Kahn, 2004). A review of Jordanian cases of homicide in 1995 found that thirty-eight of eighty-nine murder victims were women, but most striking was the fact that the vast majority of the women were murdered by a male relative, usually their brother. The women are accused of dishonoring the family in some way, usually due to sexual conduct outside of marriage, but not always. One of the women killed was sixty years old. Her brother murdered her because "forty years ago, she married against the will of the family" (Kulwicki, 2002, p. 80). In Aamiry's (1992) research on honor killings in Jordan, a pattern of abuse was present in families where honor killings took place: "the father abused everyone, the mother abused the children, and the male children abused the female children" (p. 589). A woman's virginity is considered the property and responsibility of the men in her life; first her father, then it becomes a gift for her husband. It is her dowry (Ruggi, 1998). This may be the reason why honor killings are most common in poor, rural areas. Even the poorest of women have the potential of the dowry of her virginity, while only wealthier women can offer a dowry of monetary value (Sev'er and Yurdakul, 2001). In feudal-like circumstances in rural areas, females are sold as commodities for a "pride-price" (Turgut, 1998). Many families prefer to marry their daughters off at a very young age so that they will not have the responsibility of keeping their daughters chaste (Kahn, 2004). The younger the daughters are at marriage, the less likely they are to protest, elope, or commit suicide (Kahn, 2004).

According to Bellamy (2000), in 1997 an estimated three hundred women died in the name of "honor" in one province of Pakistan alone. In Pakistan, as well as in other countries where family honor is paramount, the merest "suspicion that [a] wom[an] has had sexual contact with a man she is not married to" (Khalid, 1997, p. 51) puts her at very real risk for death. Nazir Ahmed killed his twenty-five-year-old stepdaughter in 2005 to restore his family's "honor." He then killed his three young daughters to make sure that they did not shame the family in the same way when they grew up. Pakistan has been trying to reduce honor killings, which are not uncommon there. In 2005, more than 260 honor killings were documented in Pakistan by the rights commission. The independent Human Rights Commission of Pakistan reported that more than half of these crimes are resolved by a cash settlement paid to the victim's families. A new law now requires that the minimum penalty is ten years, and the maximum penalty is death (Tanveer, 2005).

In Great Britain, where family honor does not play as central a role in the culture, 43 percent of female murder victims were killed by a spouse or lover (Mezey and Stanko, 1996), primarily due to immigration of families from countries where honor killing is common. There were an estimated four hundred deaths due to honor killings in Yemen that same year. Egypt reported fifty-two "honor" crimes in 1997. Nora Marzouk Ahmed was killed by her father that same year in Egypt. He cut off her head seven days after she eloped (Flattum, 1999). In 1999, more than two-thirds of all murders in the Gaza Strip and West Bank were believed to be "honor" killings. In Jordan and Aman there are an average of twenty-five to thirty honor killings each year (Goodenough, 1999; Sati, 1997). Thirty-six "honor" crimes were reported in Lebanon between 1996 and 1998, mainly in small cities and villages (Bellamy, 2000). Since these numbers are those cases that come to the attention of the authorities, the actual numbers probably are grossly underrepresented (Sev'er and Yurdakul, 2001).

In addition to the danger of homicide in these cultures, the threat of death creates a culture of fear among women. A man can accuse a woman of anything that would tarnish the family's honor and reputation, and in many cases the woman is given no opportunity to defend herself. In Pakistan, if a woman develops a relationship with a man, but she is forced to marry another man, the disgruntled man may try to harm her through rape, acid attack, or even murder because if he can't have her, no one else will (Kahn, 2004). Women who have tried to escape their family's wrath because they want to marry suitors who are not approved by the family are often hunted down by male members of their families and killed. Women have been known to seek protection from their families by asking authorities to jail them, but even that is no guarantee the women will be given asylum. More than 25 percent of the women incarcerated in Amman's women's prison are there to seek protection from being killed for honor (Hosken, 1999); even so, some women have been raped or killed at the hands of their families while in protective custody (Amrani, 2002).

Authorities are sometimes complicit in these crimes, either directly or indirectly. Women have been returned to their families by the authorities after they have run away with the false assurance that the women will remain unharmed. Even after an honor killing, the police may fail to carry out a thorough investigation and may even assist in the crime or its cover-up (Sev'er and Yurdakul, 2001). Lawmakers create insufficient laws, and judges are responsible for dismissing charges or dispensing lenient sentences for these crimes (Sev'er and Yurdakul, 2001). The legal system and law enforcement agencies, including police officers and prison guards, are complicit in honor crimes by selectively enforcing laws and being lenient toward men who have committed crimes in the name of "honor" and by their abuse and denigration of women who stand accused (Muslim Women's League, 1999). A Pakistani man killed his daughter because he discovered her in a compromising position (having sex). He was convicted to a life sentence but was subsequently acquitted because a high court judge said that "A father can't see his daughter in such a situation" (Javeria, 2002).

Ms. Musarrat fell in love with her maternal cousin, Hassan. Her family did not approve, so an arranged marriage forced her to marry her paternal cousin. She told her husband that she wanted a divorce and returned to her parent's home. She ran away with her lover, Hassan. Her family tracked her down. Two days later she was dead, and the family said that she had died of natural causes (Masood, 2003).

In 1996, Sevda Gok was sixteen years old when she was knifed to death by her fourteen-year-old cousin, Mehmet. He stabbed her with a knife in the stomach and hip and then slit her throat in a public place (the town square in a village in Turkey) so the killing would serve as a warning to others. Mehmet said "She made us suffer, shamed us, disgraced us. We were insulted by people in our community. I restored our honor" (Duzkan and Kocali, 2000).

Yirmibesoglu (2000) recounted the killing of Sevda Gok. Sevda was taken out of school after the third grade. Her father beat her. She used to wander away from her mother at the market. She did not have any close friends. She ran away from home but decided to return after staying in an orphan home for girls. She was worried that she would be killed by her family for running away. She returned only after her father signed a paper promising not to harm her. Her mother said "She liked to go out; she was sixteen, but no one wanted to marry her" (p. 389). There would be no bride price; she was a source of embarrassment to the family. After her death, the forensic report stated that Sevda was a virgin.

Mehmet was sentenced to only two years and eight months because this was a matter of honor, and he was a minor (Yirmibesoglu, 2000).

Men who kill in the name of honor often continue to live as usual after the murder without any threat of social ostracism, or even pangs of conscience (Ismail, 2004). In fact, offenders are often viewed as heroes in their communities (Bellamy, 2000).

In Turkey in 2002, Recve Aslan was killed by her brother to restore the family's honor because she had been raped at the age of eleven and therefore was no longer a virgin (Smith, 2004). Two sisters in Jordan, who were burned to death, were later revealed to have been virgins at the time of their death. No one was arrested for their deaths (Flattum, 1999). "In Pakistan, a young mother of two sons was shot to death by a family acquaintance because she had sought divorce from an abusive husband. Another woman was shot dead in front of a tribal gathering after she had been repeatedly raped by a local government official" (Feminist.com, 2002).

Rape is a particularly effective political tool, because it not only victimizes the individual women, but can demoralize an entire family or community. (This concept is discussed more thoroughly in the chapter on sexual violence.) In the most extreme cases, after a rape, the family and community's honor is marred and the victimization brings shame. While honor killing may occur at the hands of men in the family, the woman herself will be expected and encouraged to commit suicide since her death is a way for honor to be restored (Haeri, 1995).

Laws Pertaining to Honor Killing

There are three approaches to laws within countries where leniency is applied to honor crimes: (1) some countries use statutes to eliminate or reduce penalties for men who kill their wives (Saudi Arabia, Jordan, Lebanon, Morocco, and Syria), (2) others have laws to protect women from their husbands, but these laws are not enforced (India), and (3) still others excuse this behavior through judicial action in which judges have created defenses for men who kill their wives (Brazil and the United States) (Spatz, 1991). In India, intercaste marriages have resulted in honor killings if a woman "defiles" her caste by marrying a man of a lower caste or if she engages in certain intracaste liaisons that are considered incestuous (Chowdhry, 1996). The penalties for these types of transgressions range from social boycotts to death. Article 548 of the Penal Code of Syria provides an exemption from penalty if a man kills or injures his wife or any female accused of committing adultery or other "illegitimate sexual acts with another" (Feminist.com, 2002). Some U.S. courts have formally recognized a "cultural defense" based on cultural, racial, and religious factors that is employed disproportionately to men accused of murdering their wives (Spatz, 1991).

In 1996 Pakistan ratified the Convention on the Elimination of All Forms of Discrimination Against Women but refused to change any aspects of the Pakistani constitution that conflicted with the convention (Amnesty International, 1997). In 1999 the Upper House of the Pakistani Parliament rejected a resolution that would have condemned the practice of honor killing (Resolution condemning honor killings rejected by Pakistani Parliament, 1999).

There are approximately two hundred honor killings per year in Turkey (Smith, 2004). The Turkish penalty for premeditated murder is twenty-four years, but if the crime occurs within a family the sentence is life imprisonment. Particular clauses in the law allow a judge to reduce the sentence by one-sixth. Clause 19 allows the sentence to be cut in half for good behavior. There are also reductions for age, so that if a minor commits the crime, he will get a very light sentence, and he may even be considered a hero (Duzkan and Kocali, 2000). Zaid murdered his divorced sister by stabbing her thirty times because she had been away from home for one week, and people were talking about her. He was sentenced to six months for committing an honor crime and due to mitigating factors under Article 98, he was freed after being sentenced because he had already served six months (Human Rights Watch, 2004b). Under European Union pressure, the Turkish government recently repealed a law that allowed for sentences to be reduced on the basis of "Provocation" such as in the case of honor crimes (Smith, 2004). However, the provision to reduce sentences for "extenuating circumstances" remains, based on demands by the Islamic led ruling party (Smith, 2004). Between 1998 and 1999 there were more than two thousand suicides reported in Batman, Turkey; almost all were girls (Smith, 2004). It has been suspected that these inordinately high numbers may not have been suicides but the result of attempts to protect family members from punishment after having killed in the name of honor.

An alternative explanation is that women are driven to suicide. Women in southeast Turkey are twice as likely as their male counterparts to kill themselves due to social pressures imposed by their families (Sev'er and

Yurdakul, 2001). These young women . . . "cannot control their lives, only their deaths" (Frantz, 2000).

In Jordan, premarital sex is regarded as adultery unless the girl is under eighteen, in which case it is considered rape. An unmarried woman who becomes pregnant is considered a criminal, and her child is taken away and raised as an orphan (Jehl, 1999). In 1999 there were approximately twenty-five reported honor killings in Jordan, which accounted for 25 percent of that country's homicide rate that year (Flattum, 1999). Queen Noor and her husband, the late King Hussein of Jordan, both publicly stated that honor crimes are neither consistent with Islam nor with Jordan's constitution (Queen Noor, 1999).

Jordanian Law considers murder a legitimate act of defense when the act of killing another or harming another was committed as an act of defense of his life, his honor, or somebody else's life or honor. Twice recently the Jordanian Lower House failed to abolish article 340 of the penal code to end the impunity of men who murder female members of their families in the name of "honor" (Ralph, 2000). In 2001, a second clause was added to make the law gender neutral and to punish women who commit honor crimes, even though women almost never do this in Jordan (Human Rights Watch, 2004b). In Jordan . . . "a sixteen-year-old female was raped by her brother, who also threatened to kill her if she told the family. When the young woman found she was pregnant, she confided in an older brother. When the brother who perpetrated the rape learned of this, he tried to kill his sister by cutting her wrists but failed. Another brother revealed to the police that his family and relatives then urged him to kill his sister to cleanse the family's honor. With a kitchen knife, he stabbed his sister to death. Neighbors reported that relatives who had gathered to witness the event cheered and praised the young murderer because he had cleansed the family's honor" (Araji and Carlson, 2001, p. 591).

Islam and Honor Killing

The legal safeguards to protect women and men from indiscriminate and unlawful enforcement of presumed Islamic injunctions vary from country to country in which Islam is predominant. Islam is often cited as justification for honor killing. However, there are varying opinions held by Muslims regarding the acceptability of honor killing. The Muslim Women's League disagrees with those who believe that honor killing is justified by the Qur'an or allowed by Islam.

Many Islamic leaders and scholars condemn honor killing, insisting that it is not based in religious doctrine (Feminist.com, 2002), or the teachings of the Qur'an (Goodenough, 1999; Queen Noor, 1999; Muslim Women's League, 1999; Sati, 1997; Turgut, 1998). "Islam recognizes and celebrates the inherent dignity bestowed by God upon all human beings regardless of race, ethnicity, gender or religion" (Muslim Women's League, 1999). The Qur'an is explicit in its emphasis on the equality of women and men before God:

> *And their Lord has accepted of them and answered them, "Never will I suffer to be lost the work of any of you, whether male or female, you are members, one of another. . . ."* (3:195; see also 33:35)

The problem of honor killings is not a problem of morality or of ensuring that women maintain their own personal virtue; rather, it is a problem of domination and power over and hatred of women who, in these instances, are viewed as nothing more than servants to the family, both physically and symbolically (Muslim Women's League, 1999).

According to the Muslim Women's League (1999) Islam's prohibition on sexual relationships outside of marriage does not differentiate between men and women. As a practical matter, however, women are singled out for punishment of sexual crimes in some countries while the men, even rapists, may be treated with impunity.

In some cultures death to a woman is easily justified, and male witnesses' testimonies are granted more weight in court than female witnesses'. In fact, according to Sharia (Islamic law) four male witnesses, or eight female witnesses are required to convict a man of rape (Ruggi, 1998). Premarital sex and adultery are both punished by Sharia, but the penalty for premarital sex is less. Pregnancy outside of marriage is an obvious indication of sex (or rape), which puts women at a disproportionately increased risk of being punished for premarital sex compared to men. There is no comparable obvious indicator of sexual indiscretion for men. The penalty for extramarital sex according to Sharia law in some countries is death by stoning, where those convicted are buried to their chests and struck by stones not too small so as to unduly prolong the suffering, but not large enough to end their suffering too quickly (Brooks, 1995).

On August 15, 1986, Soraya Manutchehri was buried in a hole up to her shoulders and stoned to death after being convicted of making illicit advances to a widower in a small village in Iran. Her father, sons, and husband were the first to cast stones at her head. The man with whom she was alleged to have had illicit sex was not punished, but he was given the honor of being the first to throw a stone after the male members of her family. Then all the male members of the village were given an opportunity to defend the honor of the village by casting stones at Soraya to kill her. She maintained her innocence but was accused of infidelity by her husband who wanted to be rid of her so he could marry a young, beautiful woman. Her husband rarely spent any time at home, but when he was there he frequently berated her and beat her. After Soraya's death, her body was left out in a field for the animals to ravage. This event occurred after the Ayatollah Khomeni took power, and many men espoused fundamentalist ideals, which included death for extramarital affairs (Sahebjam, 1994). Sharia law is designed to maintain strict social order and is intended to discipline both men and women. In this case Sharia law was inappropriately applied to murder an innocent woman.

Sharia law accounts for only some of these honor killings. In many instances, there is no formal charge, hearing, or guilty verdict. Rather the woman is determined to have broken a customary rule and is murdered by her family, sometimes publicly, but often secretly with the evidence disposed of, to look like an accident or suicide. There is a deep rooted cultural acceptance of honor killing in many communities resulting in inaction to stop it; the consequence is a remedy for husbands and families who are concerned about daughters or wives who become a problem for the family (Ismail, 2004).

Migration and Honor Killing

Due to increasing migration, honor killings occur in many parts of the world where this practice is not part of the majority culture. "On January 22, 2002, Rahmi Sahindal, a Kurdish immigrant from Turkey, killed his daughter Fadime, in Uppsala, Sweden. (For further discussion of this case, see Mojab and Hassanpour [2002a; 2002b].) Fadime, a student in a Swedish university, was visiting her sister when her father shot her dead. The murderer confessed to the crime, telling police that his daughter had shamed the family. Fadime had 'shamed' her father and brother by rejecting an arranged marriage and choosing her own partner. She had also dishonored the family in 1998 in a highly publicized court case against her father and brother who had threatened to kill her. The father received a suspended sentence, while the then-seventeen-year-old brother was sentenced for his part in her death to a year's probation" (Mojab, 2002).

British authorities have taken the problem of honor killing seriously after a number of women were killed in Europe. Heshu Yones was sixteen when her father slit her throat because he didn't approve of her boyfriend. Sahjda Bibi was stabbed to death in her wedding dress by her cousin after she married against her family's wishes at the age of twenty-one. Rukhasna

Naz was killed by her mother and brother for becoming pregnant outside of marriage (Rice-Oxley, 2004). With increasing migration, traditions and practices that were formerly limited to particular parts of the world are being seen in other areas where there are no attempts or laws to understand or deal with such crimes.

Medical Intervention

The extreme importance placed on a woman's virginity has created the development of two related practices: virginity testing and hymen reconstruction. These practices are increasingly common in some traditional cultures where honor killing occurs. While virginity testing is often embraced and encouraged by the culture, hymen reconstruction, or hymenoplasty, is not. Virginity exams are instrumental in controlling women's sexuality (Frank et al., 1999). Hymenoplasty is often illegal and is performed in secret to save the life of the woman.

As noted, in some countries the social norm of female premarital virginity is of critical importance to avoid accusations of extramarital or premarital sexual intercourse (Frank et al., 1999). Virginity tests are requested for legal reasons in the case of suspected rape or to verify an accusation of extramarital sex, adultery, and prostitution (Frank et al., 1999). There are no comparable tests for men to verify extramarital or premarital sex (Sahinoglu Pelin, 1999). Virginity tests are conducted in countries such as Turkey for "social reasons" at the request of the parents of the perspective groom to assure the virginity of their son's bride-to-be. These tests are conducted by forensic gynecologists to determine the presence of an intact hymen. The absence of a hymen may not be indicative of behavior deemed immoral (Frank et al., 1999), but women without intact hymens are assumed to have had premarital sex. Hymens can be torn by physical activity (i.e., doing splits, climbing a tree, gymnastics, bike riding, etc.), rape, or a medical gynecological exam. It is also possible for hymens to stretch but not tear during intercourse (Azam, 2000), so the presence or absence of an intact hymen is not necessarily indicative of voluntary premarital sexual behavior. Virginity exams are often performed against the woman's will and can cause trauma themselves (Frank et al., 1999). Because some traditional cultures demand "bloody sheets" to be displayed after the wedding to avoid dishonor and shame (Choi, 1998), surgical and laser remedies are being employed to increase the likelihood that a woman has an intact hymen on her wedding night (Logmans et al., 1998).

While hymen reconstruction is used by women to appear as if they still have intact hymens, other methods to signify virginity can be tried, such as secretly dripping chicken blood on the sheets after sexual intercourse. Hymen reconstruction is a more drastic approach. The cost of this surgery varies depending on the type of surgery and locale. Egyptian women pay between US$100 to $600, while in Turkey, the cost for a hymenoplasty can be as much as $1,500 (Choi, 1998). Because of the cost, it is not available to everyone. However, these procedures have been successful in reducing honor killing on the individual level. In Egypt, over a ten-year period, this surgery has been credited with reducing honor killing of new brides by 80 percent (Choi, 1998). With migration of families from countries where honor killing is common to countries where it is not, doctors worldwide are having to struggle with the ethics of performing this medically unnecessary procedure. Many physicians have come to view this procedure as "ritualistic surgery," analogous to male circumcision where the justification is the fulfillment of a personal need, rather than a response to a medical condition (Logmans et al., 1998). However, even though this surgery is not being performed to treat a life-threatening condition, the result will be the same; it may be lifesaving. But it is a solution only effective on the microlevel and only available to women of means.

SUCCESS STORIES AND PROMISING PRACTICES

Diana Nammi, director of the International Campaign against Honour Killing, believes that culture can be changed, and that honor killing is not inevitable (Rice-Oxley, 2004). Success in changing a culture that promotes violence against women sometimes comes from the government in the form of laws, sometimes from nongovernmental organizations, and sometimes from a grassroots groundswell of public opinion, but there are also isolated cases in which one very brave and forward-thinking individual performs an act of heroism that improves the lives of many others. Ms. Mukhtaran from Pakistan is one such person.

A Mastoi tribal council in Meerwala, Pakistan, ordered eighteen-year-old Ms. Mukhtaran to be gang-raped to punish her family for the insult of her eleven-year-old brother walking with an unchaperoned girl from the higher class Mastoi tribe. The Mukhtarans were from the lower class Gujar tribe. The Mastoi tribe demanded retribution. Ms. Mukhtaran was gang-raped by six men while hundreds of Mastois cheered. The Human Rights Commission for Pakistan investigated, and the victim's father pressed criminal charges against four of the men who raped his daughter (Tanveer, 2002).

Ms. Mukhtaran was expected to commit suicide. "Just like other women, I initially thought of killing myself," said Ms. Mukhtaran. Her older brother explained, "A girl who has been raped has no honorable place in the village. Nobody respects the girl or her parents. There's a stigma, and the only way out is suicide." But instead of killing herself, Ms. Mukhtaran testified against her attackers and presented the shocking idea that the shame lies in raping, rather than in being raped. The rapists were sent to death row, and President Pervez Musharraf presented Ms. Mukhtaran with the equivalent of $8,300 and ordered round-the-clock police protection for her. Ms. Mukhtaran, who had never gone to school herself, used the money to build one school in the village for girls and another for boys because she believes that education is the best way to achieve social change. The girls' school is named for her, and she is now studying in its fourth-grade class (Kristof, 2005a).

Both boys and girls may benefit from her bravery and selflessness. She has presented an alternative way of viewing the world, has improved literacy, and she and her family have become role models for those who want to break with the tradition of honor killing and victim blaming. However, the deep-rooted beliefs, economic determinants, ignorance, and domination of women by men cannot be eliminated through individual heroic acts (Sev'er, 2005).

A U.S. aid organization has helped administer more than US$100,000 in donations for Ms. Mukhtaran's efforts. She has expanded the schools, has started a shelter for abused women, has bought a van that is used as an ambulance for the area, and has become a ferocious spokeswoman against honor killings, rapes, and acid attacks on women. In June 2005, a group of Pakistani-Americans invited Ms. Mukhtaran to visit the United States. However, the Pakastani authorities then put Ms. Mukhtaran under house arrest and the police cut off her land line. After she had been detained, a court ordered her attackers released, putting her life in jeopardy. Ms. Mukhtaran continued her protests by cell phone. She was taken into police custody, and her cell phone was not answered (Kristof, 2005a).

The Pakastani government finally relented under international pressure and permitted her to travel to the United States in November 2005 to receive her Woman of the Year award presented by *Glamour* magazine. She is now considered an advocate for women's rights, not just a gang rape survivor. While in the U.S. speaking to Congress, she advocated for a mobile team of human rights lawyers to be available to victims of violence to enable them to file a complaint with the police (Tanzeem, 2005). After her case became public and donations for her schools poured in from around the world, she improved the schools and "endowed" them with cows to generate income. She has also purchased an ambulance, built a police station, and has plans to build both a women's shelter and the area's first high school (Kristof, 2005a).

Unfortunately, there have not been any interventions that have resulted in substantial widespread reductions in honor killings. Perhaps education, feminist organizing, and intervention may stop or at least reduce the practice of honor killing in the future (Mojab, 2002). However, much of the world does not embrace feminist ideology. Many people are attempting to eliminate honor killing by bringing this issue to international attention. Nazand Begikhani, one of the founders of Kurdish Women's Action against Honor Killings, is campaigning in exile about honor killings in her community. According to a Kurdish man in London, "Kurdish men are more afraid of Nazand Begikhani than Saddam Hussein" (Arin, 2001, p. 824).

CONCLUSION

Honor killings are gender-based; although both men and women are involved in illicit sexual relations, women are almost always the ones killed for it while the plans and execution of the murders are carried out almost exclusively by males (Sev'er and Yurdakul, 2001). Some believe that honor killing is an attempt to control reproduction, where women are considered a factory for making male babies and men strive to control women's sexual drives and fertility (Sharif Kanaana cited in Ruggi, 1998).

Honor killing is a widely accepted practice in some cultures as evidenced by the fact that there is little public moral or social outrage or community action to stop it (Ismail, 2004). Education is one way to expose people of one culture to alternative worldviews. To change attitudes, increased access to education must include exposure to various moral and social codes that differ from the norm. Education is critical to prevent illiteracy, thereby reducing poverty, and information about human reproduction and access to contraceptives can reduce unchecked reproduction. Unchecked reproduction results in more children, causing socioeconomic deprivation, where the most disenfranchised within the culture become dispensable. Until this ends, men will retain the superiority that allows them to treat women as disposable property (Sev'er and Yurdakul, 2001; Muslim Women's League, 1999).

Queen Rania of Jordan believes that most of the honor crimes in Jordan are committed by extreme conservatives who believe that female acts associated with "honor" violations should be handled by families and/or tribes, rather than the judicial system (Amanpour and Tkach, 2000). Marriage contracts have been reversed due to lack of proof of virginity (Sev'er and Yurdakul, 2001) in remote regions where women are expected to bleed on their wedding night (Turgut, 1998). Sanctions for failure of proof of virginity are likely to be the most severe among rural, strongly patriarchal, traditional, illiterate people who are married at an early age in religious ceremonies (Sev'er and Yurdakul, 2001).

Honor killings cannot be stopped by legislation where judges and police fail to enforce those laws. Lenient sentences for murderers of women are much more common compared to cases of murderers of men, due to perceptions of the worth of women and their role in society (Spatz, 1991). If a community continues to accept honor killing as appropriate, it will continue with impunity. Relations must change within the community and the family to value girls and women for something other than reproduction (Ruggi, 1998).

The questions then become: Why does a family's honor lie between a woman's legs? Is there a better way to establish family honor and still respect cultural values? These are very complex and difficult questions requiring a great deal of discourse between stakeholders: religious leaders, feminists, human rights activists, lawyers, and women who live in these cultures. Honor killing will not stop until members of each of these groups value women as people, not commodities.

> We do not consider this murder, it was like cutting off a finger.
>
> (Wakif Abu Abesh, cited in Jehl, 1999)

III

CONSEQUENCES AND POSSIBILITIES

—

10

THE IMPACT OF VIOLENCE
AGAINST WOMEN

The lunar eclipse occurs at night, the solar in the day. Eclipse
brought about by the birth of a daughter lasts forever.

(Bihari folk song) (Krishna, 2002)

Violence against women evokes fear in women worldwide. Many
women have observed or experienced the physical consequences of
violence firsthand. Scars from female genital mutilation are visible on the
skin. Coworkers notice when a woman arrives for work with a swollen lip
and black eye from a beating by an intimate partner. Acid attacks disfigure a
woman's face in noticeable ways. In some countries, public violence against
women is witnessed, yet ignored.

While altered physical conditions may be more obvious to the eye,
there are other consequences that impact women. Mental and emotional
health are seriously jeopardized by violence but may be less noticeable.
They are no less traumatic and may very well be more so. At the very least,
they undermine a woman's physical health even further. This chapter examines the impact of violence on women's lives. It explores not only the physical and emotional aspect of victimization but considers the economic and
social consequences of violence directed against women.

SOCIAL IMPACT

The more women and girls are brutalized, the poorer their physical health,
self-worth and self-esteem. Women who live in fear spend enormous time
and energy to keep oppressors from harming them. As a result, they may

develop poor interpersonal relationships, low productivity, and pass on the notion that females deserve and should expect very little out of life. A woman may experience the stress and trauma of fear related to violence even if she herself has not experienced the violence directly when she lives in a family, home, community, or culture where violence against women is minimized, or the norm.

Victimization is "an instrument of social control of women" (Khalid, 1997, p. 43). In Pakistan, women, more than men, believe themselves to be in danger of violence, and in order to cope with potential victimization, Pakistani women tend to use precautionary and avoidance strategies more often than men and problem-focused strategies of social support and active coping less often (Khalid, 1997). This results in reduced opportunities for women to advance socially and professionally. The continuous awareness of danger creates a constant state of alertness and a hypervigilance about personal safety (Mezey and Stanko, 1996). These women feel forced to impose limits upon themselves because of their anxiety, thereby reducing their freedom and mobility (Khalid, 1997).

Children in the home add to a woman's dependence and limit the options available to her. Children make it difficult for women to escape dangerous situations. Reproductive freedoms unavailable to women further reduce their choices and many women fear reprisal if found using birth control methods (Dixon-Mueller, 1993). In some cultures men refuse to let their wives practice contraception because they believe that fathering many children signals masculinity and fertility. Some men also believe that a woman will use birth control when she is being unfaithful to keep from having a baby who does not look like her husband (Heise, Pitanguy, and Germain, 1994). Males sometimes prevent women from using effective contraceptives including condoms, which puts women at increased risk for contracting HIV and other sexually transmissible infections from men who themselves are not monogamous. Heterosexual intercourse is currently the primary transmission method of HIV worldwide. Forced sex without condoms causes vaginal abrasions, increasing the risk of the HIV entering the woman's bloodstream. If she suggests condom use, her partner may believe that she is promiscuous or that she believes that he is unfaithful. It is not uncommon under these circumstances for men to respond with violence (Worth, 1989). Victimized women who are employed often have problems at work, such as difficulty concentrating and excessive absenteeism resulting from injuries. Relationships, social functioning, and self-esteem also suffer as a result of violence which can produce feelings of helplessness, vulnerability, betrayal, isolation, and loss (Mezey and Stanko, 1996; Heise, Pitanguy, and Germain, 1994).

PHYSICAL IMPACT

Victims of violence against women experience bodily injury, scarring, broken bones, sexually transmissible infections, pelvic inflammatory disease often resulting in infertility, unwanted pregnancies, miscarriages, chronic pelvic pain, headaches, gynecological problems, asthma, sleep disorders, gastrointestinal disorders, irritable bowel syndrome, injurious health behaviors (such as smoking and unprotected sex), and partial or permanent disability (Heise, Pitanguy, and Germain, 1994). The list is extensive.

The physical impact will vary with different types of violence. Women who suffer from intimate partner violence often suffer from chronic headaches, abdominal pains, sleep and eating disorders, muscle pain, and periodic vaginal infections (Heise, Pitanguy, and Germain, 1994). Women whose feet were bound suffer pain and have difficulty walking. There will be painful scarring after bride burning attempts or acid attacks. Women suffer physically from HIV infection and internal tearing resulting from rape and "ethnic cleansing." Female genital mutilation can lead to excruciating short-term pain and suffering or death. Long-term consequences include extremely painful and prolonged childbirth and/or fetal or maternal death during childbirth. There may be bruised or cut flesh after public whippings or broken bones which don't heal normally after domestic violence. Pain, trauma, fear, and posttraumatic stress disorder (PTSD) are common experiences for victims of all forms of brutalization and violence against females. The physical consequences are both acute short-term physical pain, and long-term chronic health problems for the survivors.

There is also physical impact on unborn fetuses of women who experience violence while pregnant, possibly causing miscarriage or disability of the offspring. Those living in areas of political and social violence are much more likely to have complications during pregnancy, such as preeclampsia (potentially life-threatening disorder often characterized by a variety of symptoms including high blood pressure during pregnancy), premature labor, threat of miscarriage or gestational hypertension (Heise, Pitanguy and Germain, 1994).

Because of fear of discovery, shame, or further violence, it is not unusual for women to leave many injuries untreated without seeking medical care. Fear of disclosing to a medical provider, lack of medical services, or inability to seek services may exacerbate the physical consequences of violence.

MENTAL HEALTH IMPACT

While physical pain may recede in days, weeks, or months, there may be psychological repercussions that can last a lifetime. Profound personality change, depression and suicidality, generalized and phobic anxiety, and PTSD are not uncommon outcomes. Not only do individual stresses result, but often violence against women that is widespread in a culture can cause a generalized complacency about the acts and a common belief that the victimization is inevitable, normal, or deserved.

Women's mental health is more negatively impacted by cultural and situational violence than men's. But what separates one woman from another in terms of the mental aftereffects experienced? What risk or protective factors make certain women or women in certain countries or women victims of certain types of violence more or less likely to undergo psychological distress? There are a variety of conditions that lessen or magnify the effects of violence.

Women who are assaulted have significant levels of psychological distress (Feehan et al., 2001). Women are more likely to experience varying degrees of distress following their victimization based on several factors: the characteristics of the assault, assailant characteristics, victim characteristics, and postassault factors. The social conditions in which women live and the traumas to which women are exposed in different countries, can and do affect women's mental health. Unemployed women are much more likely to experience distress than employed women. However, when women are employed in countries where it is still socially unacceptable for them to be in the workplace, they may perceive a "higher level of threat of violence than nonworking women" (Khalid, 1997, p. 49). Because of their outsider status and challenge to societal norms, these women may be targeted more often or more harshly. When an attack takes place in a woman's home, she is more likely to have a negative emotional outcome, and those women who resist attackers are much less likely to experience distress than victims who do not resist (Feehan et al., 2001). This may be due to the fact that for many, such an experience calls into question the safety and security of their homes. Those who resist feel some pride in having fought the attacker and experience less guilt and self-blame due to their attempts to resist (Bart and O'Brien, 1985).

Depending on the type of violence and the cultural tolerance for the crime, women in different countries are not equally likely to oppose their aggressors. For instance, women or young girls undergoing "circumcision" or female genital cutting (FGC) may be unlikely to resist their victimization or may even request the "initiation rite" for a variety of reasons. Often the girls' mothers are involved in organizing and carrying out the practice, all the while trying to ease their daughters' pain and instill in them the cultural importance of chaste femininity valued by the community. When a relative or partner of the victim is involved in the crime, the victim is more likely to experience psychological trauma (Feehan et al., 2001). A girl may be less likely to defend against her victimization when her mother is involved, thereby additionally increasing the likelihood of distress. A key factor in preventing a girl from resisting is the sanctioning of FGC by the cultures in which it is customary. FGC is still desirable despite widespread acknowledgment of the risks to a women's physical and mental health. As a result of the physical and emotional trauma of FGC, some girls develop PTSD and later in life, women who have been circumcised often face difficulties such as painful intercourse and complications in pregnancy and delivery (Almroth et al., 2001).

In contrast, women living in developed nations are thought to have more autonomy. Comments such as "she could leave him if she really wanted to" ignore the reality of intimate partner violence where gendered power dynamics, a shared history, the violation of a safe space (i.e., one's own home), intense feelings, and often children are involved. And leaving carries with it its own burdens. Furthermore, women are in greater jeopardy when a partner learns she is planning to leave. This action is perceived as a threat to the perpetrator's control over the relationship. Upon leaving, women often encounter difficulties in finding accommodation, a decrease in the standard of living, unemployment, difficulties in obtaining child care, lack of social and family support, and/or loneliness and isolation (Scott-Gliba, Minne, and Mezey, 1995). The obstacles women face can sometimes compound and magnify the emotional effect of the abusive relationship, and the knowledge of these very real possibilities prevents some women from considering a move.

"The development of psychological disorder following domestic assault appears to correlate with the frequency and intensity of the violence experienced" (Scott-Gliba et al., 1995, p. 344). The longer a woman endures a progressively abusive relationship, not only is it more likely that she will suffer a negative physical or mental health impact, but she is also less likely to resist. Learned helplessness is a psychological phenomenon whereby people come to see themselves as having no control over what happens to them (Seligman, 1991). A woman unable to resist has learned that not only is resistance futile but she has become convinced that her worth and independence are no longer viable. "Batterers typically justify their abuse of control and violent behavior on the battered woman's inadequacies and failures" (Krane, 1996, p. 439). This becomes further entrenched when social stigma blames a woman for the personal attacks she experiences. Social support acts as a moderator of violence's effects, but when the perpetrator of the violence is the person who had previously been the greatest source of support, the victim is often left feeling abandoned in addition to brutalized.

Defending against an attacker appears to offer some psychological protective factor for women in violent situations. "Resistance . . . gives the woman a sense of having been in control during the attack, whereas the woman who submits is tormented by a sense of profound helplessness which can persist for years as well as self-doubt as to whether her failure to resist had unknowingly transmitted a wish for sexual relations. A key part of this may be that 'resisters' are rarely accused of collaboration and generally encounter a more positive and supportive response from friends, family, and the criminal justice system" (Mezey and Stanko, 1996, p. 164). In many countries, however, resisting a violent husband—or worse, lashing out against him either physically or by tarnishing his sense of honor—is a criminally punishable offense.

Women fear personal violence much more than men (Mezey and Stanko, 1996). Violence that women experience at the hands of intimate partners probably contributes most greatly to women's generalized fear of crime (Mezey and Stanko, 1996). Women's insecurities about personal safety are by no means unreasonable; on the contrary, they are an accurate appraisal of pandemic abuse. Because domestic and sexual violence are most often perpetrated against women, fear of these two crimes compose the foundation of generalized hypervigilance (Mezey and Stanko, 1996). Different cultures respond to this type of violence in varied ways. For example, wife abuse and battering of Palestinian women results in negative self-esteem, increased levels of depression, and levels of anxiety (Haj-Yahia, 2000). In China emotional abuse by spouses cause women more somatic discomforts, anxious mood, and insomnia than physical abuse (Tang, 1997). In collectivist Asian/Pacific cultures, verbal and psychological abuse are likely to have a more lasting and damaging impact due to internalized feelings of shame and self-blame (Krane, 1996).

Women may experience profound personality change as a result of victimization. Over time, constant violence causes changes in personality, including changes in emotional regulation, consciousness, self-perception, perception of perpetrators, relations with others, and in understanding meaning and intent of messages (Farley et al., 1998). Depression is quite common among women in general and even more common among women who have experienced violence. Sometimes depression leaves a woman feeling so helpless that suicide becomes a viable option. In industrialized countries, men commit suicide at higher rates than women; however, in some countries such as India, female suicides are much more prevalent (Brockington, 2001).

Phobic anxieties often manifest themselves in avoidance of situations reminiscent of the traumatic violence. In the case of stranger rape, many women have "rape-associated fears such as fear of the dark, fear of strange men, fear of the sexual act . . . fear of the consequences of rape, and . . . fear related to the woman's sense of her own vulnerability" (Mezey and Stanko, 1997, p. 168). These fears may appear to generalize to unrelated circumstances (Stewart and Robinson, 1995) and virtually paralyze a woman by keeping her confined to spaces deemed "safe," such as her home.

Characterized by "re-experiencing of . . . trauma, efforts to avoid stimuli which are similar to the trauma, a general numbing of responsiveness, and symptoms of physiologic hyperarousal" (Farley and Barkan, 1998, p. 38), PTSD is a common problem for battered women. Prostitutes tend to have experienced a great deal of violence over the course of their lives. Most have been victims of childhood abuse as well as victims of various types of assault while working (Farley et al., 1998; Farley and Barkan, 1998). Between one-half and three-quarters of prostitutes in the United States, Thailand, Zambia, Turkey, and South Africa, experienced PTSD (Farley et al., 1998). PTSD is only one consequence of prostitution, a job that includes violence against women regularly.

ECONOMIC IMPACT

Economic factors can lead to violence against women, as in prostitution, while violence against women can be the cause of severe economic problems. Legal and medical expenses related to the violence are calculable. "According to the World Bank, in established market economies, gender-based violence is responsible for one out of every five healthy days of life lost to women of reproductive age. Recent studies reveal that gender-based violence is a significant cause of death and illness in women, the result of beatings during pregnancy, marital rape, sexual abuse of girls, forced sterilization, abortions performed in unsanitary conditions, malnutrition, restricted access to health services, and a number of other abuses" (UN

Campaign on Women's Human Rights, 2002). Abused women seek employment but are often not able to keep a job so they become welfare cyclers (going on and off public assistance, spending more time on than off) (Raphael and Tolman, 1997).

Rape and assault victims are generally less healthy and experience more symptoms of illness in almost every physiological system than other women (Koss and Woodruff, 1991). Women who have been victimized are often unable to work because of their injuries or because they are embarrassed by their bruises, and they don't want others to know that they have been brutalized. If they are fleeing the violence, they may never return to their jobs.

Wars and armed conflict cause severe economic insecurity in addition to serious health problems, such as hunger, malnutrition, and the spread of HIV/AIDS. As a result of political instability and economic insecurity, trafficking of girls and women becomes a serious threat (Heyzer, 2004). Education is interrupted by wars, domestic violence, and other types of violence against women. When education is interrupted, the economic impact is grave. Refugee women often have access to school in refugee camps, but they rarely attend these schools (Women's Rights International, 1999). When economic self-sufficiency is interrupted during war, it remains compromised for a long period after the end of the conflict (Swiss et al., 1998). "Prior to the outbreak of war in Liberia, most women farmed their own land or engaged in small market activities to support themselves and their families. As refugees in Cote d'Ivoire they could no longer own land to farm and had to work for wages on Ivorian farms instead" (Women's Rights International, 1999, p. 2). Economic problems cause social conditions that have a mental health impact often resulting in physical difficulties. Violence against women sets a vicious cycle into motion that is very difficult for women to overcome.

CONCLUSION

Underreporting is a major problem in fully grasping the incidence and prevalence of violence against women. Women don't report violence because they believe that others will view it as a private matter, they think others won't believe them, they view the offense as minor, or they fear that there will be reprisals from the offender or his friends (Stewart and Robinson, 1996).

It is no surprise that women who live in physically violent cultures fare far worse than women in less violent cultures, and women who endure abusive relationships fare far worse than those living without daily abuse. It is very difficult to identify only one type of impact caused by an individual violent event. Most violence causes physical trauma, described at length in the previous chapters on specific types of violence. Social and economic problems also result when women are brutalized. However, there are often serious psychological ramifications that result from all types of violence women experience, and this trauma is frequently secondary to the physical or economic impact; it is unrecognized, immeasurable, and disabling.

As violence in its many forms continues to be a part of women's everyday experiences, we become more and more desensitized to its effects. We need to understand the risk and protective factors that affect women's ability to cope as well as understand the motivations and mechanisms of violence. Only when we identify how acts of violence against women are interrelated and fully grasp the scope of this pandemic problem can we adequately address the impact of violence in a meaningful way.

11

WORKING TOWARD A WORLD
WITHOUT VIOLENCE
AGAINST WOMEN

They insult us, and we elect them. Toujan al-Faisal (the first woman to be elected to Jordan's Parliament)

At the end of each chapter in this book, we provided success stories and promising practices to end the specific type of violence presented in that chapter. The programs all had some elements in common. First, they acknowledged the realities of the culture, and to whatever degree possible, respected the sociocultural underpinnings of that community. Second, they were creative. To be effective in implementing social change, it often requires looking at the world from a different vantage point. To keep trying to change a situation using the same strategies that have always been used will end with the same results. This has been the case where the change strategy is to make a practice illegal. In several examples presented here, many different laws have been implemented to reduce the violence, without success. Sometimes there is an institutional culture that is so strongly entrenched that it will require a great deal more than a creative idea and a few years to change the balance of power. Patriarchy is one such universal.

Evidence suggests that patriarchy holds the most prominent position in supporting and promoting violence against women cross-culturally. While other conditions that discourage violence against women may be present, patriarchy neutralizes women's potential within a culture and is the consistent thread throughout cultures where violence against women is accepted, condoned, or institutionalized. There are a variety of correlates of gender violence in cross-cultural studies. Factors that are highly predictive of violence against women include violent interpersonal conflict resolution strategies; economic inequality between genders; masculine ideal of male dominance, toughness, and honor; and male economic and decision-making authority in the family. Conversely, cultures that have very low incidence of violence against women share several characteristics: matriarchal and matrilineal systems, active community intervention in violence, presence of all-female work or solidarity groups, and shelters for women to escape violence (Sanday, 1981; Levinson, 1989; Counts, Brown, and Campbell, 1992; Heise, Pitanguy, and Germain, 1994). In patriarchal cultures where only men have power and the ability to earn money or earn more than women for the same task, a dynamic is set up where women have fewer resources; this extreme imbalance of power establishes the exploitation and oppression of women.

"Saying that the woman's right to work and consequently to financial earnings should be confined to a certain category of mankind, and that the other category has to depend on the generosity of the first for its living—in return, of course, for household and personal services that enable the first category to make the earnings—is a call for economic monopoly, entrenchment of capitol influence, exploitation of cheap labor, and rejection of honorable competition in learning and work. . . . Saying that the woman's right to her husband's money in return for the services she provides—which in the scale of labor are considered menial jobs—is only to have food, clothes, and accommodation is nothing but acknowledgment of a principle much worse than merely the exploitation of cheap labor; it is the principal of slavery. Only slaves work in return for food and clothes, deprived of the right to use their time and effort in what may secure them a better future" (al-Faisal, 1989).

Each culture needs to recognize violence against women as a social problem. Only then, will government and the legal community begin to take action and provide necessary services for victims. However, in the past, when governments have tried to address the problem, the root causes of the violence (e.g., patriarchy and gender inequality) were lost in the discourse. During the early years of the battered women's movement in the United States, domestic violence was viewed as a result of the patriarchal power structures within the home. As the United States grappled with the problem and began to address it, woman-battering became subsumed under the term "domestic violence" and grouped with other private problems that took precedence, such as child abuse, child sexual abuse, and elder abuse. Woman-battering results from an unequal and dangerous power distribution between men and women in society. How one defines the problem determines the success of the solutions. In this case, successful solutions to stop woman-battering in the United States have fallen short for thirty years. While intimate partner violence has been reduced because of the attention and services afforded it, it is far from being eradicated.

Using a term like "domestic violence" influences our ability to examine the problem as it exists. By removing the gendered aspect of the violence perpetrated against women, we don't need to address the harder questions of why patriarchy exists, what are the alternatives, and how do we correct the gender inequality that exists to put all women at risk of violence (Katz and Jhally, 2000).

Most countries that are grappling with the social problem of violence against women in its many forms have a difficult decision to make regarding the definition of the problem and the ultimate successful and broad-based solutions that are necessary to eradicate it. Because this is such a multifaceted problem, the solution is similarly complex. It will take Herculean efforts in the areas of social change, educational programs, personal and governmental commitments, cultural understanding, reproductive freedom and control, legislative reform, enforcement of laws, buy-in of the people in power, and finances. Making these changes will be extremely difficult without destroying the social fiber of the culture in which these practices have been entrenched (Sev'er and Yurdakul, 2001).

Many successful movements against particular forms of violence against women start with grassroots women's movements, such as Maiti Nepal, fighting trafficking of girls and women in Nepal; and the women only village in Kenya called Umoja, established in response to violence against women by British soldiers.

Accurate quantifiable and qualitative documentation is needed to confirm the extent of the violence against women worldwide. Qualitative information on women's experiences is as important as quantitative. Of particular importance is information on the way the violence hinders women's full participation in society and its effect on women's health. International attention and political pressure may help facilitate data gathering by forcing cooperation of governments heretofore unwilling to examine the extent of the problem or those who deny or minimize its existence. Economic sanctions tied to human rights abuses are sometimes effective in this endeavor.

Formal education for girls and job training are key. In Uganda, less than two-thirds of the girls with secondary education have undergone female genital mutilation (FGM), while almost all of those with no education have undergone the procedure (Mbugua, 1997). Change strategies coupled with education have helped to create social change (Johnson and Johnson, 2001).

Alternatives to culturally sanctioned practices have shown some success in decreasing certain violence perpetrated against girls and women. Cows have been successfully offered as payment to shrine priests to buy back the freedom of Trokosi slaves in West Africa (Simmons, 1999). In Nepal, a non-profit group has offered fathers living in poor, subsistence-farming regions a piglet (once fattened, worth $100 to a family) in exchange for a promise to keep their young daughters home instead of sending them to cities as bonded laborers or indentured servants where the risks of physical and sexual abuse are great (Kasdon, 2006).

Alternatives to other practices are worth consideration. For example, the women who perform FGM for a living could be retrained in a different profession (such as health education) to provide an alternative source of income; otherwise performing FGM is their only means of financial support. Additionally, because FGM has played a strong role in marking the rite of passage into adulthood, another practice can be substituted for FGM, such as secondary graduation or a meaningful community rite that does not involve cutting.

Children must be taught the equal value of girls and boys. Women and mothers must believe in the value of women and teach this to their children. Males must embrace the idea that gender discrimination exists, and that all people suffer as a result of it. They must teach that lesson to their sons. For example, if women are educated about the harms and alternatives to FGM, but men are not willing to marry women who have not had the procedure, the practice will not stop. Respected members of the community must endorse the change in cultural practices, and alternatives must be offered. Positive peer pressure needs to be exerted within communities. The best way to alter men's behavior is for other men to shame the behavior that is undesirable (Sev'er and Yurdakul, 2001). Negative peer pressure is currently very effective in reinforcing crimes against women. By changing the social norms, cultures may change behavior. This approach is beginning to garner success in the case of FGM in Kenya where slang terms have been introduced into the lexicon to discourage FGM and where young men refer to a noncircumcised girl as *manyanga,* which is Swahili for young and new (Mbugua, 1997).

Medical professionals must be trained to identify female victims of violence and to secure adequate medical evidence (Amnesty International, 2001). Shelters must be staffed and financed with well-trained professionals to assist victims of violence who are unable to remain in their homes or with relatives (Amnesty International, 2001). Women's organizations within the community require support to be able to effectively deal with the issues and needs of the women within their communities (Amnesty International, 2001).

Gender and class/caste-based discrimination must be addressed within the community and criminal justice system (Amnesty International, 2001). Criminal laws must be strengthened to hold perpetrators accountable; the enforcement of laws must be rigorous and cannot be circumvented by individual preference. In 1983 a high court in India overturned the historic decision of a judge who ruled in favor of a dead bride by sentencing her husband and her parents-in-law to death for her murder (Kumar, 1993). The attitudes and training of judges and police officers must change for laws to be effectively enforced (Singh, 1994). Effective mechanisms for ensuring justice to women must be regularly monitored, evaluated, and amended if necessary (Amnesty International, 2001). State responsibility is clearly underlined in Article 4 of the Declaration on the Elimination of Violence against Women, which stipulates that "States should exercise due diligence to prevent, investigate and, in accordance with national legislation, punish acts of violence against women, whether those acts are perpetrated by the State or by private persons" (WomenAid International, 2003).

After China introduced marriage and divorce reform in 1949 and 1950 legally granting women the right to file for divorce, there was an increasing number of violent acts committed against women resulting in deaths (Chang, 1988). Legislative change without social education for communities, as well as community leaders, to encourage acceptance of the new laws often results in the laws being ignored or creates a backlash, which makes matters worse for the previously oppressed (Hom, 1992; Mbugua, 1997). Civil laws must allow women the same rights as men, including rights to own property, vote, and to be permitted custody of children as well as equitable distribution of assets in the case of divorce (Sev'er and Yurdakul, 2001). Women need to be allowed to initiate divorce when preferred or necessary.

Since cultures differ, so will effective approaches to facilitate change most quickly. In Uganda, using the term "genital cutting" rather than "female genital mutilation" was much more effective in allowing people to hear the message about the dangers of the procedure. The former term is descriptive, while the latter was seen as critical and judgmental (Mbugua, 1997).

Policies that focus on improving the human potential of women could make a difference but would be more effective if job opportunities for women are also provided (Rao, 1997). The requirement of women to be married must be relaxed so women can make life choices based on personal choice, rather than cultural mandate. Increasing taxes on alcohol and rationing alcohol in areas where alcohol consumption contributes to violence against women may also have a beneficial effect (Rao, 1997).

Women need to be permitted equal employment in police and military forces as lawyers, judges, and policymakers. All people in policymaking and enforcement positions must be educated about the special problems, dangers, and concerns women face (Krau, 1998; Bell, 2001). Once laws are written and passed, a higher court system must be in place to assure that the lower courts are handling gender-based crimes without bias (Sev'er and Yurdakul, 2001). Just a handful of women in a predominately male profession will not change the prevailing attitudes in that profession. A critical mass of women is necessary, and women must be in positions of authority, such as judges, deans of law and medical schools, lawmakers, and governmental leaders.

The global community must take a strong leadership role in bringing about these changes. International and national organizations must work together to end brutalization, torture, and violence against women (Amnesty International, 2001). Social changes (including women's rights) have not received the same attention as political and civil rights (McWilliams, 1998; Butegwa, 1999). This may be because political rights are cost free, whereas social rights require governmental financial commitment which many countries are unable to afford (Butegwa, 1999).

Until all of these changes are in place, Sev'er and Yurdakul suggest that women need more immediate help on the local level, such as safe houses, government-sponsored safe passage to other cities and towns under assumed names, witness protection programs, and intensive counseling and skills programs for women to regain psychological health and economic self-sufficiency (2001). These practices seem to help reduce the impact of violence against women in the West, but it is not clear that these approaches would be effective in all cultures.

According to *Women Waging Peace,* an NGO based in Washington, D.C. and Cambridge, Massachusetts, ending violence requires full participation of women at all stages of the process. Since women are key stakeholders in their communities, they can bridge ethnic, religious, cultural, and political differences. Women tend to be more collaborative and less confrontational than their male counterparts. They support and sustain local economies. Women are extremely motivated to prevent, stop, and recover from armed conflicts—motivated by instincts to protect their children and themselves (Garner, 2003).

But because males are usually responsible for violence against women, and the laws created to address it are still inadequate, there needs to be considerable attention on the resocialization of men. Education of small boys and their parents regarding the comparable rights of women should be a priority. If men observe violence against women, they must take action to stop it. Male perpetrators require effective intervention, arrest, punishment, counseling, rehabilitation, and so on. Research needs to be conducted to determine the best way to reach men to stop violence against women, and funding must be allocated to support effective programs aimed at male responsibility to improve this situation. Men need to see this as not just a women's problem but one that affects them in fundamental ways.

The first step toward eliminating violence against women is for a critical mass of people to learn about the atrocities that women experience daily worldwide. The next step is to commit to educate others about these issues. Finally, do something personally to work toward eliminating the violence. Women's lives depend on it.

> *Violence against women is, perhaps the most shameful human rights violation. And it is perhaps the most pervasive. It knows no boundaries of geography, culture, or wealth. As long as it continues, we cannot claim to be making real progress toward equality, development, and peace.*

Kofi Annan, United Nations Secretary General
("A World Free of Violence against Women,"
United Nations Inter-Agency Global
Video Conference, March 8, 1999)

REFERENCE LIST

Aamiry, A. (1992). Domestic violence against women in Jordan. *Al-Raida* 11 (65/66): 33–35.

Abrahms, D., G. Viky, B. Masser, and B. Gerd. (2003). Perceptions of stranger and acquaintance rape: The role of benevolent and hostile sexism in victim blame and rape proclivity. *Journal of Personality and Social Psychology* 84(1): 111–25.

Adebajo, C. O. (1992). Female circumcision and other dangerous practices to women's health. In *Women's Health Issues in Nigeria*, ed. M. Kisekka, 1–12. Jos: Tamaza Publishing Company.

Adhikar, M. J. (2001). India: The battle against fear and discrimination and the impact of violence against women in Uttar Pradesh and Rajasthan. *Amnesty International.* Retrieved July 28, 2002, from http://web.amnesty.org/ai.nsf/Index/ASA200162001.

Adinkrah, M. (2004). Witchcraft accusations and female homicide victimization in contemporary Ghana. *Violence against Women*, 10(4): 325–56.

Adithi. (1995). Female Infanticide in Bihar. Report prepared by Viji Srinivasan, Vijay Parinita, Alice Shankar, Medha Mukul, and Anita Kumari. ADITHI, Patna.

Adongo, P., P. Akeongo, F. Binka, and C. Mbacke. (1998). Female genital mutilation: Socio-cultural factors that influence the practice in Kassena-Nankana District, Ghana. *African Journal of Reproductive Health* 2: 25–36.

Afrol News. (2004). Nigeria adopts anti-female genital mutilation day. February 10. Retrieved January 27, 2005 from http://www.afrol.com/articles/11236.

Agnes, F. (1998). Violence against women: Review of recent enactments. In *In The Name of Justice*, Institute of Social Studies Trust, ed. S. Mukhopadhyay, New Delhi.

Agonito, R. (1997). *History of ideas on woman: A sourcebook.* New York: Pedigree.

Ahuja, R. (1987). *Crimes against women.* Jaipur, India: Rawat Publications.

Aird, S. C. (2000). Ghana's slaves to the gods. *Human Rights Brief.* http://www.wcl.american.edu/hrbrief/v7i1/ghana.htm.

al-Faisal, T. (1989). "They insult us and we elect them . . ." *al-Ray.* September 21.

Allison, R., and J. McCurry. (2004). One child policy leaves China with huge shortage of women. *Guardian,* London. March 23, p. 9.

Almroth, L., V. Almroth-Berggren, O. M. Hassanein, S. S. E. Al-Said, S. S. A. Hasan,

U. B. Lithell, and S. Bergström. (2001). Male complications of female genital mutilation. *Social Science and Medicine,* 53(11): 1455–60.

Amanpour, C., and A. Tkach. (2000). Queen of the dessert: Rainas rule. *60 Minutes* [television series]. New York: CBS. April 2.

Ameh, R. K. (1998). Trokosi child slavery in Ghana: A policy approach. *Ghana Studies* 1: 35–62.

Amnesty International. (1997). The campaign to eradicate female genital mutilation: A role for Amnesty International. http://www.hrea.org/lists/hr-headlines/markup/msg01485.html retrieved 4/3/06.

———. (1999). Campaigning for gay and lesbian human rights. *Focus* 29 (5), September.

———. (2001). India: The battle against fear and discrimination and the impact of violence against women in Uttar Pradesh and Rajasthan. Retrieved July 28, 2002 from http://web.amnesty.org/ai.nsf/Index/ASA200162001.

———. (2004a). International zero tolerance to FGM day: Effective measures needed to protect girls from female genital mutilation. Retrieved April 3, 2006, from http://www.hrea.org/lists/hr-headlines/markup/msg01485.html.

———. (2004b). Sudan, Darfur: Rape as a weapon of war: sexual violence and its consequences. July 19. Retrieved January 2, 2005 from http://web.amnesty.org/library/index/engafr540762004.

———. (2004c). Rwanda: The enduring legacy of the genocide and war. Retrieved May 8, 2006. http://www.amnestyusa.org/countries/rwanda/document.do?id=D2 55BF899579F34A80256E67005A4F1C

Amrani, N. (2002). Honor killings and women's rights. http://www.vibrani.com/honorkillings.htm.

Anahdhi. (2001). Personal interview. Chennai, India.

Araji, S. K., and J. Carlson. (2001). Family violence including crimes of honor in Jordan. *Violence against Women* 7(5): 586–621.

Aravamudan, G. (2001). The Rediff special. Retrieved October 24, 2001 from http://www.rediff.com/news/2001/oct/24spec.html.

Arensberg, C. M., and S. T. Kimball. (1968). *Family and Community in Ireland.* Cambridge, MA: Harvard University Press.

Arin, C. (2001). Femicide in the name of Honor in Turkey. *Violence against Women,* 7(7): 821–25.

Armughal. (2004, April 12). Cradles on sidewalks save illegitimate babies. *Pakistan Daily Times.* Retrieved March 2, 2006 from http://www.dailytimes.com.pk/default.asp?page=story_12-4-2004_pg9.

Arrowsmith, S. (1996). Obstructed labor injury complex: Obstetric fistula formation and the multifaceted morbidity of maternal birth trauma in the developing world. *Obstetrical and Gynecological Survey* 51: 568–74.

Arscott-Mills, S. (2001). Intimate partner violence in Jamaica. In *Violence against women* 7(11): 1284–1302. Thousand Oaks, CA: Sage.

Associated Press. (1999a). Honor killings in Pakistan. http://www.ishipress.com/pak honor.htm.

———. (1999b). Taliban beat a mother and her daughter publicly. April 16. http://rawa.org/lashes.htm.

———. (2002). Chinese man sentenced to death for kidnapping, selling 104 women. AP World Stream. Retrieved March 15, 2006 from http://www.highbeam.com/doc/1P1:53337676/Report%7EC%7E + Chinese + man + sentenced + to + death + for + kidnapping%2C + selling + 104 + women.html?refid = SEO.

———. (2003). Suspect in captive women case 'created own world' in hidden dungeon. CNN.com/Law Center. Retrieved April 21, 2003 from http://www.cnn.com/2003/LAW/4/20/captive.women.ap/.

———. (2005). China to outlaw gender selective abortion. *Fox News Channel*, January 7. Retrieved January 24, 2005 from http://www.foxnews.com/story/0,2933,143640,00.html.

Athreya, Venkatesh. (2001). The Tamil Nadu picture. *Frontline*, 18(09). http://www.frontlineonnet.com/fl1809/18090930.htm.

Azam, S. (2000). What's behind retro virginity? *Toronto Star,* August 15. Retrieved October 11, 2005 from http://www.psurg.com/star2000.html.

Bachman, R., and L. Saltzman. (1995). Violence against women: Estimates from the redesigned survey, BJS. Crime in the United States, 1995. U.S. Department of Justice.

Baker, N. V., P. R. Gregware, and M. A. Cassidy. (1999). Family killing fields: honor rationales in the murder of women. *Violence against women*, 5(2): 164–84.

Baker-Brown, B. (1975). Sexual surgery in later nineteenth America. *International Journal of Health Services,* 279.

Ballara, M. (1993). Women and literacy. *WIN News*, 19(1): 12.

Bandura, Albert. (1978). Social learning theory of aggression. *The Journal of Communication* 28 (3): 12–29.

Bari, S., and I. Choudhury. (2001). Acid burns in Bangladesh. *Annals of Burns and Fire Disasters* 14 (3). September.

Barker-Benfield, B. (1975). Sexual surgery in the later nineteenth century America. *International Journal of Health Services* 51: 568–74.

Barnes, V. L., and J. Boddy. (1994). *Aman, the story of a Somali girl*. New York: Pantheon Books.

Bart, P. B., and P. H. O'Brien. (1985). *Stopping rape: Successful survival strategies*. New York: Pergamon Press, Inc.

Behind the Veil of Oppression. (2001). *Hindu Sunday Magazine*. http://www.yorku.ca/iwrp/afghan/Behindtheveil.htm.

Bell, R. E. (2001). "Sex trafficking: A financial crime perspective" *Journal of Financial Crime,* November.

Bellamy, C. (2000). Statement on violence against women for International Women's Day, UNICEF. Retrieved July 20, 2004 from http://www.prnewswire.co.uk/cgi/news/release?id = 41260.

Ben-Ari, N. (2001). Liberating girls from 'trokosi': Campaign against ritual servitude in Ghana. *Africa Recovery* vol. 15(4): December.

———. (2003). Changing tradition to safeguard girls. *Africa Recovery* 17 (1): 4.

Bennice J., and P. Resnick. (2003). Marital rape: History, research and practice. *Trauma, Violence and Abuse* 4 (3): July, 228–46.

Bertell, R. (2000). Victims of the nuclear age. *Ambassador Online Magazine,* 3(2), July. Retrieved July 24, 2003 from http://nucnews.net/nucnews/2000nn/0007nn/000702nn.htm.

Beverley, J. (2000). Testimonio, subalternity and narrative authority. In *Handbook of qualitative research*, ed. N. Denzin and Y. Lincoln, 215–55. Thousand Oaks: Sage.

Beyrer, Chris. (2001). Shan women and girls and the sex industry in Southeast Asia: political causes and human rights implications. *Social Science and Medicine* 53: 543–50.

Bhatia, B., M. Kawar, and M. Shahin. (1992). *Unheard voices: Kagi women on war and sanctions*. London: Change.

Biddulph, S., and S. Cook. (1999) Kidnapping and selling women and children: The States construction and response. *Violence against women* 5(12): 1437–68.

Birodkar, S. (2002). Dowry, sati, and child marriage. *Hindu Social Customs*. http://sudh eerb.tripod.com/practices1.html.

Bishkek International School of Management and Business and the United Nations Development Programme. (1995). Kymyz, computers, customs, and other writings: A collection of accessible texts for learners of English in Kyrgyzstan. *Being Stolen*. Bishkek, Dyrgyzstan.

Blake, C. F. (1994). Foot-binding in neo-Confucian China and the appropriation of female labor. *Journal of Women in Culture and Society*, 19(3).

Blewett, K., and B. Woods. (1995). The dying rooms. Documentary [videotape].

Boaten, A. B. (2001). The trokosi system in Ghana: Discrimination against women and children. In *African women and children: Crisis and response*, ed. A. Rwomire. Westport, CT: Praeger.

Bolles, L. (2002). Why women kill their children. American Anthropological Association. Retrieved February 4, 2005, from http://www.aaanet.org/press/motherskilling children.htm.

Borst, M. (1992). Women and domestic violence: An annotated bibliography. Linden, Netherlands: VENA.

Bosch, X. (2001). Female genital mutilation in developed countries. *Lancet*, 358: 1177–1179.

Boutros-Ghali, B. (1995). Speech made at the Fourth World Conference on Women in Beijng, China. September 9.

Boyle, E. H. (2002). *Female genital cutting*. Baltimore and London: Johns Hopkins University Press.

Brayton, J. (1997). What makes feminist research feminist? The structure of feminist research with the social sciences. Retrieved July 2, 2003 from www.unb.ca/web/ PAR-L/win/feminmethod.htm.

Brenner, C., and H. Ashley. (1995). *Eight bullets: One woman's story of surviving anti-gay violence*. Ann Arbor, MI: Firebrand Books.

Brenner, S. (1996). Restructuring self and society: Javanese Muslim women and "the veil." *American Ethnologist*, 23 (4): 673–97.

British Medical Journal. (1867). The debate of the obstetrical society, April 6, 407–8.

Brockington, I. (2001). Suicide in women. *International Clinical Psychopharmacology*, 6(2): 7–19.

Brodsky, A. (2003). *With all our strength: The revolutionary association of the women of Afghanistan*. New York: Routledge.

Brooks, G. (1995). *Nine parts of desire: The hidden world of the Islamic woman*. New York: Random House.

Browne, A. (1992). Violence against women: Relevance for medical practitioners

Council on Scientific Affairs Report. *Journal of the American Medical Association* 267 (23): 3184–89.

Brownmiller, S. (1975). *Against our will: Men, women and rape.* New York: Simon & Schuster.

Bui, H., and M. Morash. (1999). Domestic violence in the Vietnamese immigrant community. *Violence against Women* 5(7): 769–95.

Bunch, C. (1990). Women' rights as human rights: Towards a re-vision of human rights. *Human Rights Quarterly* 12: 486–98.

Burns, A., R. Lovich, J. Maxwell, and K. Shapiro. (1997). *Where women have no doctor.* Berkeley: The Hesperian Foundation.

Burt, M. R. (1991). Rape myths and acquaintance rape. In *Acquaintance rape: The hidden crime*, ed. A. Parrot and L. Bechhofer, 26–40. New York: Wiley.

Butegwa, F. (1999). International human rights law and practice: Implications for women. http://www.cwgl.rutgers.edu/butegwa.html.

Caleekal, A. (2001). Dowry death: Its gruesome reality and future interface in a digital cultural revolution. Retrieved January 15, 2002 from http://www.digitalism.org/art doc/ddeath.html.

Callamard, A. (1998). Breaking the collusion of silence. In *Common Grounds: Violence against women in war and armed conflict situations*, ed. I. Lourdes Sajor. Asian Center for Women's Human Rights: Philippines.

Came, B., D. Burke, G. Ferzoco, B. O'Farreli, and B. Wallace. (1989). Montreal massacre: Railing against feminists a gunman kills 14 women on a Montreal campus, then shoots himself. *Maclean's Magazine.* Retrieved December 18, 1989 from http://www .rapereliefshelter.bc.ca/dec6/macleans.html.

Campbell, J. K. (1964). Honour, family and patronage: A study of institutions and moral values in a Greek mountain community. Oxford: Clarendon Press.

Carroll, R. (2002). *Devadasi.* Skeptics Dictionary. http://skepdic.com/devadasi.html.

Catalano, S. (2004). National crime victimization survey: Criminal victimization, 2003. U.S. Department of Justice, Bureau of Justice Statistics.

Census. (2001). Female child population. Retrieved April 10, 2003 from http://www .femalechildpopulation/India.html.

Center for Reproductive Law and Policy (CRLP). (1999). Retrieved March 15, 1999 from http://www.crlp.org/fgm_wwsub.html.

Centers for Disease Control. (2002). Intimate partner violence fact sheet. Retrieved January 1, 2003 from http://www.cdc.gov/ncipc/factsheets/ipvfacts.htm.

Central Intelligence Agency (CIA). (2002). World fact book, sex ratio. Retrieved December 15, 2004 from http://www.umsl.edu/services/govdocs/wofact2002/fields/2018.html.

Chandrasekhar, S. (1994). *India's abortion experience.* Denton, TX: University of North Texas Press.

Chang, M. H. (1988). Women. In *Human Rights in the People's Republic of China*, ed. Y. Wu et al. Boulder, CO: Westview Press.

Chatzifotiou, S., and R. Dobash. (2001). Seeking informal support: Martial violence against women in Greece. *Violence against women* 7 (9): 1024–50. Thousand Oaks: Sage.

Chaudhry, L. (2000). World of pain. *Village Voice.* Retrieved October 12, 2000 from www.villagevoice.com/issues.

Chege, J. N., I. Askew, and J. Liku. (2001). An assessment of the alternative rites approach for encouraging abandonment of female genital mutilation in Kenya. USAID: Frontiers in Reproductive Health. September.

Chen, R. (1999). Violence against women in Taiwan: A review. In *Breaking the Silence: Violence against women in Asia,* ed. F. Cheung, 174–84. Hong Kong: Equal Opportunities Commission.

China Rights Forum. (1995). *The property of men: The trafficking and domestic abuse of women.* New York: Human Rights in China.

Chiroro, P., G. Bohner, G. T. Viki, and C. Jarvis. (2004). Rape myth acceptance and rape proclivity: Expected dominance versus expected arousal as mediators in acquaintance rape situations. *Journal of Interpersonal Violence* 19(4): 427–42.

Cho, N. H. (1995). Consequences of a son preference in a low-fertility society: Imbalance of the sex ratio at birth in Korea. *Population and Development Review* 10(3): 17–42.

Choi, S. Y. (1998). Restoring virginity: Hymen repair surgery saves lives at the expense of deception. *Berkley Medical Journal.* Retrieved October 11, 2005 from http://www.ocf.berkeley.edu/~issues/fall98/hymenrep.html.

Chowdhry, D. P. (1991). Girl child: Victim of gender bias. *Girl Child in India.* New Delhi: Ashish Publishing House.

Chozik, A. (2005). U.S. women seek a second first time with hymen surgery. *Wall Street Journal.* December 15. www.post-gazette.com/pg/05349/622923.stm.

Chuan, K. E. (1995). Sex selection at birth. *Statistics Singapore Newsletter* 17 (3).

Cindoglu, D. (2000). Virginity tests and artificial virginity in modern Turkish medicine. In *Women and sexuality in Muslim societies,* ed. P. Ilkkaracan, 263–71. Istanbul, Turkey: Women for Women's Rights Publications.

Cleary, P. (2001). Honor killings happen here too. February 1. Retrieved from http://www.theage.com.au/news/2001/02/01/FFXALYSVLIC.html.

CNN. (1995). OJ Simpson main page. CNN.com. Retrieved December 28, 2004 from http://www.cnn.com/US/OJ/.

Coale, A. J. (1991). Excess female mortality and the balance of the sexes in the population. *Population Development Review* 17: 517–23.

Coale, A. J., and J. Banister. (1994). Five decades of missing females in China. *Demography* 31: 459–79.

Cohen, A. (2000). Excess female mortality in India: The case of Himachal Pradesh. *American Journal of Public Health,* 90 (9): 1369–71.

Commission on Human Rights. (2000). *Integration of the Human Rights of Women and the Gender Perspective.* United Nations, Economic and Social Council, February 29.

Commission on the Status of Women. (1993). Retrieved July 20, 2004 from http://www.earthsummit2002.org/toolkits/women/un-doku/un-comm/csw/csw199 3.htm.

Connors, J. (1994). Government measures to confront violence against women. In *Violence against women,* ed. M. Davis. London: Zed Books.

Cook, R. J., B. M. Dickens, and M. F. Fathalla. (2002). Female genital cutting (mutilation/circumcision): Ethical and legal dimensions. *International Journal of Obstetrics and Gynecology* 79: 281–87.

Cooke, M. (1996). *Women and the war story.* Berkeley: University of California Press.

Coomaraswamy, R. (1994). United Nations special rapporteur for the commission on human rights on violence against women, its causes and consequences. Retrieved from http://193.194.138.190/html/menu2/7/b/mwom.htm.

Council on Scientific Affairs, American Medical Association (1995). Council report: Female genital mutilation. *Journal of the American Medical Association,* 274: 1714–16.

Counts, D. C., J. K. Brown, and J. C. Campbell, eds. (1992). *Sanctions and sanctuary: Cultural perspectives on the beating of wives.* Boulder, CO: Westview.

Cousineau, M., and G. Rondeau. (2004). Toward a transnational and cross-cultural analysis of family violence. *Violence against women* 10 (8): 935–949. Thousand Oaks: Sage.

Criminal Code of the Kyrgyz Republic, Normative Acts. 1994. Bishkek, Kyrgyzstan.

Culchieworks. (2003). The Magdalene Story. http://www.netreach.net/~steed/magdalen.html.

Cummings, S. R., X. Ling, and K. Stone. (1997). Consequences of foot binding among older women in Beijing, China. *American Journal of Public Health,* 87(10): 1677–79.

Cunliffe-Jones, P. (2001). Islam in Nigeria: a child-mother caught in a storm. *Lagos.* http://www.mg.co.za/mg/za/archive/2001jan/features/12jan-sharia.html.

Das Gupta, M. (1987). Selective discrimination against female children in rural Punjab, India. *Population Development Review* 13: 77–100.

Davies, M. (1994). *Violence against women.* London: Zed Books.

Davis, G., J. Ellis, M. Hibbert, R. P. Perez, and E. Zimbelman. (1999). Female circumcision: The prevalence and nature of the ritual in Eritrea. *Military Medicine,* 64 (1): 11–16.

De Bruyn, M. (2003). Violence, pregnancy and abortion. *Issues of Women's Rights and Public Health,* 2nd ed. Chapel Hill, NC: Ipas.

Demleitner, N. (2001). The law at a crossroads: The construction of migrant women trafficked into prostitution. In *Global human smuggling: comparative perspectives,* ed. David Kyle and Rey Koslowski. Baltimore: Johns Hopkins University Press.

Diamantopoulou, A. (2001). Trafficking in women second conference on women in democracy. Retrieved August 2, 2001 from http://diamantopoulou.gr/corpus/europe/europe_en2/01/e2_en_27.htm.

Dierie, W. (1998). *Desert flower.* New York: William Morrow.

Dixon-Mueller, R. (1993). The sexuality connection in reproductive health. *Studies in Family Planning* 24 (5): 269–82.

Dobash, R. E., and R. P. Dobash. (1992). *Women, violence and social change.* London: Routledge.

———. (1998). *Rethinking violence against women.* Thousand Oaks, CA: Sage.

Dogar, Rana. (1999). After a life of slavery. *Newsweek,* April 5. Retrieved April 10, 2003 from http://www.freetheslaves.nt/after_life_of_slavery.htm.

Dongfang, M. (2002). Statement of Ma Dongfang: Victim of planned birth policy. Laogai Research Foundation. Retrieved December 16, 2004 from http://www.laogai.org/news/newsdetail.php?id = 1933.

Dorkenoo, E. (1994). *Cutting the rose: female genital mutilation.* London: Minority Rights.

Dottridge, M. (2002). Trafficking in children in West and Central Africa" *Gender and Development* 10, 1: 38–42.

Dovlo, E., and A. K. Adzoyi. (1995). *Report on Trokosi Institution.* Department for the Study of Religions, University of Ghana, Legon.

Doyal, L. (1995). *What makes women sick: Gender and the political economy of health.* New Brunswick, NJ: Rutgers University Press.

Drakulic, S. (1994). The rape of women in Bosnia. *Women and violence: Realities and responses worldwide,* ed. Miranda Davies, 181. London: Zed Books.

D'Souza, N., and R. Natarajan. (1986). Women in India, the reality. In *Women in the world, 1975–1985: The women's decade,* ed. L. B. Iglitzin and R. Ross. Santa Barbara, CA: ABC Clio Information Service.

Duzkan, A., and F. Kocali. (2000). An honor killing: She fled, her throat was cut. In *Women and sexuality in Muslim societies,* ed. P. Ilkkaracan. Istanbul, Turkey: Women for Women's Human Rights.

Edwards, C., and J. Harder. (2000). Sex slave trade enters the U.S. *Insight on the News,* as reported on NEXIS database. November 27.

Edwards, R. (2002). End of female circumcision? *New Scientist* 8.

Egyptian Fertility Care Society (EFCS). (1996). *Clinic based investigation of the typology and self-reporting of FGM in Egypt.* Cairo: EFCS.

El Mundo. (2004). Terrorismo domestico: Alerta. Retrieved October 17, 2004 from http://www.elmundo.es/documentos/2004/06/sociedad/malostratos/alerta.

Elchalal, U. (1997). Ritualistic female genital mutilation: Current status and future outlook. *Obstetrical and Gynecological Survey* 52: 643–51.

El-Zanaty, F., et al. (1996). *Egypt demographic and health survey.* Calverton, MD: Macro International.

Estrich, S. (1987). *Real rape.* Cambridge, MA: Harvard University Press.

European Commission. (2002). Trafficking in women. The misery behind the fantasy: from poverty to sex slavery. Retrieved from http://europa.eu.int/comm/justice_home/news/8mars_en.htm.

European Study Group on Heterosexual Transmission of HIV. (1992). Comparison of female to male and male to female transmission of HIV in 563 stable couples. *British Medical Journal* 304: 809–13.

Farah, J. (1997). Cover-up of China's gender-cide. Western Journalism Center. Retrieved September 29, 1997 from http://www.freerepublic.com/forum/a8896.html.

Farley, M., I. Baral, M. Kiremire, and U. Sezgin. (1998). Prostitution in five countries: Violence and post-traumatic stress disorder. *Feminism & Psychology* 8(4): 405–26.

Farley, M., and H. Barkan. (1998). Prostitution, violence, and posttraumatic stress disorder. *Women and Health* 27(3): 37–49.

Fattah, E. (1991). *Understanding criminal victimization.* Ontario, Canada: Prentice Hall Canada, Inc.

Federal Prohibition of Female Genital Mutilation Act of 1996. (1996). Public Law 104–140, 1, 10 STAT 1327.

Feehan, M., S. Nada-Raja, J. A. Martin, and J. D. Langley. (2001). The prevalence and correlates of psychological distress following physical and sexual assault in a young adult cohort. *Violence and Victims* 16(1): 49–62.

Feminist.com. (2002). Spotlight on: Honor killings. Retrieved February 7, 2005, from http://www.feminist.com/violence/spot/honor.html.

Fester, G. (1989). The United Women's Congress. In *Lives of courage: Women for a new South Africa,* ed. D. Russell. New York: Basic Books.

Fineman, M., and R. Mykitunk. (1994). *The Public Nature of Private Violence.* New York: Routledge.

Finnegan, F. (2001). *Do penance or perish.* Piltown, Co. Kilkenny, Ireland: Congrave Press.

FitzRoy, L. (1997). Mother/daughter rape. In *Women's encounters with violence: Australian experiences,* ed. S. Cook and J. Bessant. Thousand Oaks, CA: Sage.

Flake, D. (2005). Individual, family and community risk markers for domestic violence in Peru. *Violence against women* 11(3): 353–73.

Flattum, J. (1999). Honor killing demands global response. *Minnesota Daily.* January 29.

Fletcher, A. (1995). *Gender, sex, and subordination in England, 1500–1800.* New Haven: Yale University Press.

Fox, V. C. (2002). Historical perspectives on violence against women. *Journal of International Women's Studies* 4(1): 15–34.

Frank, M., H. M. Bauer, N. Arican, S. K. Fincanci, and V. Iacopino. (1999). Virginity examinations in Turkey. *JAMA,* 28: 485–90.

Frantz, D. (2000). Turkish women who see death as a way out. *New York Times.* November 3.

French, H. W. (1997). The ritual: Disfiguring, hurtful, wildly festive. *New York Times,* A4, January 31.

Frese, B., M. Moya, and J. L. Megius. (2004). Social perception of rape: How rape myth acceptance modulates the influence of situational factors. *Journal of Interpersonal Violence* 19(2): 143–61.

Freymond, Patrick. (2005). Research and environment news from China. *Science, Technology and Environment News,* The People's Republic of China, no. 9, March.

Gado, Marc. (1987). The killing of Lisa Steinberg. Retrieved November 18, 2002 from http://www.crimelibrary.com/notorious_murders/family/lisa_steinberg/3.htm.

Gangrade, K. D. and H. Chandler. (1991). The dowry system in India. In *Social Problems in the Asia Pacific Region,* ed. S. Sewell and A. Kelly, 260–83. Brisbane, Australia: Boolarong.

Gao, X. (2002). Statement of Gao Xiaoduan. Laogai Research Foundation. Retrieved January 5, 2005 from http://www.laogai.org/news/newsdetail.php?id=1932.

Garcia, A. M. (1985). *La operacion* [videotape]. L.A. Film Project.

Garel, M., S. Gosme–Seguret, M. Kaminski, and M. Cuttini. (2003). Ethical decision-making in prenatal diagnosis and termination of pregnancy: A qualitative survey among physicians and midwives. *Obstetrical and Gynecological Survey* 58(3): 168–70.

Garner, K. (2003). Where are the women in post-war Iraq? Women's Center at FIU. Retrieved July 23, 2004 from http://www.fiu.edu/~ippcs/karen_garner.html.

Gautam, D. N., and B. V. Trivedi. (1986). Unnatural deaths of married women with special reference to dowry deaths: A sample study of New Delhi. New Delhi: Bureau of Police Research and Development, Ministry of Home Affairs, Government of India.

George, S., A. Rajaratnam, and B. D. Miller. (1998). Female infanticide in rural South India. *Search Bulletin* 12(3), July-Sept, 18–26. Mumbai, India: SNDT Churchgate.

Ghana: United States condemns Trokosi. *Africa Online.* Retrieved August 23, 2001 http://www.africaonline.com/site/Articles/1,3,27442.jsp.

Gil, V., and A. Anderson. (1999). Case study of rape in contemporary China: A cultural-historical analysis of gender and power differentials. *Journal of Interpersonal Violence* 14 (11): 1151–71.

Gilmartin, C. (1990). Violence against women in contemporary China. In *Violence in China: Essays in culture and counterculture,* ed. J. Lipman and S. Harrell, 203–25. Albany: State University of New York Press.

Girshick, L. (2002). *Woman-to-woman sexual violence.* Boston, MA: Northeastern University Press.

Glenn, David. (2004). A dangerous surplus of sons? *Chronicle of Higher Education*, research publishing. http://chronicle.com/free/v50/i34/34a01401.htm.

Global Fund for Women. (1995). *Sisters and daughters betrayed*. Video.

Goltzman, J. C. (1998). Cultural relativism or cultural intrusion? Female ritual slavery in Western Africa and the international covenant on civil and political rights: Ghana as a case study. *New England International and Comparative Law Annual* 4: 53–72.

Gondolf, E., and D. Shestakov. (1997). Spousal homicide in Russia. In *Violence against women* 3 (5). Thousand Oaks, CA: Sage.

Goodenough, P. (1999). Middle East women campaign against family honor killings. Conservative News. Retrieved from http://www.conservativenews.net/InDepth/archive/199903/IND19990308e.html.

Goonesekere, R. K. W. (2001). Prevention of discrimination and protection of indigenous peoples and minorities. *Economic and Social Council*. http://www.unhchr.ch/Huridocda.PDF.

Green, D. (1999). *Gender violence in Africa: African women's responses*. New York: St. Martin's Press.

Griffin, S. (1975). Rape: The all American crime. In *Rape victimology*, ed. L. Schultz, 19–39. Springfield, IL: Charles Thomas.

Gruenbaum, E. (1982). The movement against clitoridectomy and infibulation in Sudan. *Medical Anthropology Newsletter* 13(2): 4–12.

———. (1988). Reproductive ritual and social reproduction: Female circumcision and the subordination of women in Sudan. In *Economy and class in Sudan*, ed. N. O'Neill and J. O'Brien. London: Avebury.

Gunning, I. R. (1992). Arrogant perception, world-travelling and multicultural feminism: the case of female genital surgeries. *Columbia Human Rights Review* 23: 189–248.

Haeri, S. (1995). The politics of dishonor: Rape and power in Pakistan. In *Faith and freedom: Women's human rights in the Muslim world*, ed. M. Afkhami, 161–74. Syracuse, NY: Syracuse University Press.

Haj-Yahia, M. M. (2000). Implications of wife abuse and battering for self-esteem, depression, and anxiety as revealed by the second Palestinian national survey on violence against women. *Journal of Family Issue*, 21(4): 435–463.

Halaby, J. (2000). Two women, one girl slain in honor crimes in Jordan. *Associated Press*. March 20.

Hales, A. (1981). Health care issues in Liberia. Lecture given at Cornell University.

Hautzinger, S. (2002). Criminalising male violence in Brazil's women's police stations: from flawed essentialism to imagined communities. *Journal of Gender Studies* 11(3): 243–51.

Hedge, R. S. (1999). Marking bodies: Reproductive violence: A feminist reading of infanticide in south India. *Violence against women* 5 (5): 506–24.

Hegland, M. E. (2000). Review of "Crimes of honor and our honor and his glory" in Middle East Women's study review, Spr./Sum. 15(1/2): 15–19.

Heise, L. (1993). Violence against women: The missing agenda. In *The health of women: A global perspective*, ed. M. Koblinsky, J. Timyan, and J. Gay, 171–95. Boulder: Westview Press.

———. (1994a). Gender-base abuse: A global epidemic. In *Reframing women's health: Multidisciplinary research and practice*, ed. A. Dan. Thousand Oaks, CA: Sage.

————. (1994b). Violence against women: The hidden health burden. Background paper for the World Bank, Washington, DC.

————. (1996). Health workers: Potential allies in the battle against woman abuse in developing countries. *JAMA*, 51: 120–22.

Heise, L., and J. R. Chapman. (1992). Reflections on a movement: The U.S. battle against women abuse. In *Freedom from violence: Women's strategies from around the world*, ed. M. Schuler. Washington, DC: OEF International.

Heise, L., M. Ellsberg, and M. Gottemoeller. (1999). Ending violence against women. *Population Reports*. Series L. no. 11. Baltimore, MD: Population Information Program, Johns Hopkins School of Public Health.

Heise, L., J. Pitanguy, and A. Germain. (1994). *Violence against women: The hidden health burden.* Washington DC: World Bank.

Heise, L., A. Raikes, C. H. Watts, and Zwi. (1994). Violence against women: A neglected public health issue in less developed countries. *Social Science Medicine* 39: 1165–79.

Hellsten, S. K. (2004). Rationalising circumcision: From tradition to fashion, from public health to individual freedom-critical notes on cultural persistence of the practice of genital mutilation. *Journal of Medical Ethics* 30: 248–53.

Herzfeld, B. (2002). Slavery and gender: Women's double exploitation. *Gender and Development* 10: 50–55.

Herzog, S. (2004). Differential perceptions of the seriousness of male violence against female intimate partners among Jews and Arabs in Israel. *Journal of Interpersonal Violence* 19 (8), August: 891–900.

Heyzer, N. (2004). *Women's equality, development and peace: Achievements and challenges for Beijing + 10.* UNIFEM. Presentation at the *59th session of the UN General Assembly Third Committee*, October 12, 2004. Retrieved May 2006 from http://www.unifem .org/news_events/story_detail.php?StoryID = 174.

Hicks, G. (1994). *The comfort women.* New York: W. W. Norton.

Hill, P. (1986). Kerala is different. *Modern Asian Studies* 20(4): 779–92. Retrieved March 30, 2003 from http://www.jstor.org.

Hindu. Men without women. Retrieved August 31, 2003 from http://www.thehindu .com/thehindu/mag/2003/08/31/stories/2003083100250400.htm.

Hitchcock, A. (2001). Rising number of dowry deaths in India. http://www.wsws.org/ articles/2001/jul2001/ind-j04.shtml.

Hom, S. (1992). Female infanticide in China: The human rights specter and thoughts toward (an)other vision. *Columbia Human Rights Law Review* 23: 249–314.

————. (2001). Female infanticide in China: The human rights specter and thoughts toward (an)other vision. In *Femicide in Global Perspectives,* ed. D. E. H. Russell and R. A. Harmes, 138–45. New York: Teacher's College.

Honig, E., and G. Hershatter. (1988). *Personal voices: Chinese women in the 1980s.* Stanford, CA: Stanford University Press.

Horne, S. (1999). Domestic violence in Russia. *American Psychologist* 54(1): 55–61.

Hosken, F. (1993). *The Hosken report: Genital and sexual mutilation of females.* 4th ed. Lexington, MA: Women's International Network News.

————. (1999). Female genital mutilation. Women's International Network News. November.

Hughes, D. (2000). The "Natasha" trade: The transnational shadow market of trafficking in women. *Journal of International Affairs* 53, no. 2: 625–51.

Human Rights Watch. (1993). A modern form of slavery: Trafficking of Burmese women and girls into brothels in Thailand. New York: Human Rights Watch.

———. (1995). Rape for profit. New York: Human Rights Watch.

———. (1996). Shattered lives: Sexual violence during the Rwandan genocide and its aftermath. New York: Human Rights Watch, Women's Rights Project.

———. (1999a). Broken people: Caste violence against India's "Untouchables." New York: Human Rights Watch. http://www.hrw.org/reports/1999/india/.

———. (1999b). Crime or custom? Violence against women in Pakistan. Retrieved January 1, 2003 from http://www.hrw.org/reports/1999/pakistan/Pakhtml-01.htm#P160_8127.

———. (1999c). Human rights abuses committed by RUF rebels. http://www.hrw.org/reports/1999/sierra/SIERLE99-03.htm.

———. (2000a). Owed justice: Thai women trafficked into debt bondage in Japan. New York: Human Rights Watch.

———. (2000b). Seeking protection: Addressing sexual and domestic violence in Tanzania's refugee camps. New York: Human Rights Watch.

———. (2001a). Afghanistan humanity denied: Systematic violations of women's rights in Afghanistan 13(5). http://www.hrw.org/reports/2001/afghan3/afgwrd1001-01.htm#P85_1542.

———. (2001b). Asia's hidden apartheid. Retrieved April 17, 2003 from http://www.hrw.org/campaigns/caste/presskit.htm.

———. (2001c). Greece: Urgent action required on trafficking. New York: Human Rights Watch.

———. (2001d). Memorandum of concern: Trafficking of migrant women for forced prostitution into Greece. New York: Human Rights Watch.

———. (2001e). Protectors of pretenders? Government human rights commissions in Africa. http:///www.hrw.org/reports/2001/africa/overview/contributions.html.

———. (2001f). Sacrificing women to save the family: Domestic violence in Uzbekistan. *Human Rights Watch* 13(4). Washington, DC: Human Rights Watch.

———. (2001g). Women's human rights: Violence against women. Retrieved January 1, 2003 from http://www.hrw.org/wr2k1/women/women2.html.

———. (2001h). Women's human rights: Violence against women. Retrieved January 1, 2003 from http://www.hrw.org/wr2k1/women/women2.html

———. (2004a). "If we return, we will be killed." Consolidation of ethnic cleansing in Darfur, Sudan. http://www.hrw.org/campaigns/darfur/.

———. (2004b). Honoring the killers: Justice denied for "honor" crimes in Jordan. Retrieved January 3, 2005 from http://www.hrw.org/reports/2004/jordan0404/index.htm.

HumanTrafficking.org. (2004). Thailand. December, http://www.humantrafficking.org/countries/eap/thailand/.

Hussain, A. (2001). Kashmir women face acid attacks. Retrieved August 10, 2001 from http://news.bbc.co.uk/hi/english/world/south_asia/newsid_1484000/1484145.stm.

Igwegbe, A. O., and I. Egbuonu. (2000). The prevalence and practice of female genital mutilation in Nnewi, Nigeria: The impact of female education. *Journal of Obstetrics and Gynecolog* 20 (5): 520–22.

Ilkkaracan, P., ed. (2000). *Muslim Societies*. Turkey: Women for Women's Human Rights.

International Lesbian and Gay Association. (1999). World Legal Survey. Retrieved on December 22, 2003 from http://www.ilga.org/Information/Legal_survey/ilga_world_legal_survey%20introduction.htm.

International Programme on the Elimination of Child Labour (IPEC). (2001). Nepal: action against trafficking. IPEC support yields results. August 13. Retrieved December 4, 2004 from http://www.ilo.org/public/english/standards/ipec/about/fact sheet/facts12.htms02.

Ismail, M. (2004). Evidence on honor killings: Unreported cases in District Swabi, North-West Frontier, province of Pakistan. Paper presented at the International Conference on Violence against Women, April 26, Wellesley, MA.

Itano, N. (2003). Sex assault now a political act in Zimbabwe. *Women's enews*. Retrieved September 5, 2005 from http://www.womensenews.org/article.cfm?aid=1513.

Izett, S., and N. Toubia. (1999). *Learning about social change: A research and evaluation guidebook using female circumcision as a case study*. New York: Rainbo.

Jackson, C. (1991). Should angels fear to tread? *Health Visitor* 64(8): 251–53.

Jain, R. S. (1992). *Family violence in India*. New Delhi, India: Radiant.

Javeria, A. (2002). Violence against women: The high price of honor and dignity in Pakistan. *Journal of the International Institute* 10 (1). Retrieved December 10, 2004 from http:www.umich.edu/~iinet/journal/vol10no1/ameera.htm.

Jeeva, M., Gandhimathi, and Phavalam. (1998). Female infanticide: Philosophy, perspective and concern of SIRD. *Search Bulletin* 13 (3): 9–17.

Jehl, D. (1999). Arab's honor price: A Woman's blood. *New York Times*. Retrieved December 10, 2004 from http://www.library.cornell.edu/colldev/mideast/chastity .htm.

Jener. (2005). Personal communication.

Jensen, K., and N. Otoo-Oyortey. (1999). *Gender-based violence: An impediment to sexual and reproductive health*. Report for the International Planned Parenthood Federation Members' Assembly. Retrieved February 17, 2004 from http://www.ippf.org/resource/gbv/ma98/index.htm.

Jewkes, R. (2004). *Child sexual abuse and HIV in South Africa: Beyond virgin cleansing*. Paper presented at the 2004 International Research & Action Conference: Innovations in Understanding Violence against Women, April 25–28, Wellesley Centers for Women.

Jewkes, R., J. Levin, N. Mbananga, and D. Bradshaw. (2002). Rape of girls in South Africa. *Lancet* 359: 319–20.

Johansson, S., and O. Nygren. (1991). The missing girls of China: A new demographic account. *Population and Development Review* 17(1): 40–46.

Johnson, D. (1999). Trafficking of women into the European Union. *New England International and Comparative Law Annual*. Retrieved June 3, 2002 from http://www .nesl.edu/annual/vol5/johnson.htm.

Johnson, P. S., and J. A. Johnson. (2001). The oppression of women in India. *Violence against women* 7 (9): 1051–68.

Jolly, R. (1997). *Human development report*. New York: United Nations Development Program.

Jones, A. (1999–2000). Case study: Female infanticide. *Gendercide Watch*. http://www.gendercide.org/case_infanticide.html.

Jordan, A. (2002). Human rights or wrongs? The struggle for a rights-based response to trafficking in human beings. *Gender and Development* 10(1): 28–37.

Kahn, T. (2004). Marriage-related violence against girls in rural Pakistan examining role of family and community. Paper presented at the International Conference on Violence against Women, Wellesley, MA.

Kanics, J. (1998). Trafficking in women. *Foreign Policy: In Focus* 3, 30.

Kapadia, K. (2002). *The violence of development: The political economy of gender*. London: Zed Books.

Kasdon, L. (2006). A little piglet makes a big difference. *Christian Science Monitor*. March 8. Retrieved March 10, 1006 from http://search.csmonitor.com/search_content/0308/p14s03-lifp.html.

Kassindja, F., and L. M. Bashir. (1998). *Do they hear you when you cry?* New York: Delacorte Press.

Katz, J., and S. Jhally. (2000). Put the blame where it belongs: On men. Retrieved May 10, 2006, from http://www.jacksonkatz.com/blame.html.

Keenan, C., A. el-Hadad, and S. Bailan. (1998). Factors associated with domestic violence in low-income Lebanese families. *Image: Journal of Nursing Scholarship* 30(4).

Kelkar, G. (1992). *Violence against women: Perspectives and strategies in India*. Bangkok, Thailand: Asian Institute of Technology.

Kelly, L., and J. Radford. (1998). Sexual violence against women and girls: An approach to an international overview. In *Rethinking violence against women*, ed. R. E. Dobash and R. P. Dobash. Thousand Oaks, CA: Sage.

Kerala (1993). The Facts. *New Internationalist* 241: 1–4. Retrieved April 6, 2003 from http://www.newint.org.

Kerala State Literacy Mission. (2003). Official website of the Kerala Government. Retrieved April 11, 2003 from http://keralagov.in.

Kerber, L. K., and S. DeHart. (1995). *Women's America*. 4th ed. New York: Basil Blackwell. [dup.]

Kersenboom-Story, S. C. (1987). *Nityasumangali: Devadasi tradition in South India*. Delhi, India: Motilal Banarsidass.

Kesselman, M., and J. William. (2000). *Introduction to comparative politics*. New York: Houghton Mifflin.

Khalid, R. (1997). Perceived threat of violence and coping strategies: A case of Pakistan women. *Journal of Behavioural Sciences* 8(1-2): 43–54.

Khan, T. S. (1999). Wedding hells. *Review* March, 4–10. Conference presentation, April 28, 2004.

Khodyreva, N. (1996). Sexism and sexual abuse in Russia. In *Women in a violent world*, ed. C. Corrin. Edinburgh, Scotland: Edinburgh University Press.

Kiiti, N. (2005). Personal communication, January 25.

Kim, E. (2000). *Ten thousand sorrows*. Canada: Doubleday.

Kirloskar, S. and S. Cameroon-Moore. (1997). Cult supplies child sex trade. *India Times* 27: 22–29.

Kishwar, M., and R. Vanita. (1984). In search of answers: Indian women's voices from Manushi. In *Family violence,* ed. M. Kishwar and R. Vita, 203–42. London: Zed Books.

Kleinbach, R., and S. Amsler. (1999). Kyrgyz bride kidnapping. *International Journal of*

Central Asian Studies, 4. Retrieved March 6, 2006 from http://faculty.philau.edu/kleinbachr/new_page_1.htm.

Kome, P. (2002). Montreal massacre remembered throughout Canada. Retrieved February 6, 2002 from http://64.81.195.15/article.cfm/dyn/aid/363/context/archive.

Kopelman, L. (2002). Female circumcision/genital mutilation and ethical relativism. Second opinion (October 1994). In *Taking sides: Clashing views on controversial issues in human sexuality,* ed. W. Taverner. Dushkin, CT: McGraw-Hill.

Koss M. P., T. E. Dinero, and C. A. Seibel. (1988). Stranger and acquaintance rape: Are there differences in the victim's experience? *Psychology of Women Quarterly* 12: 1–24.

Koss, M. P., and J. Woodruff. (1991). Deleterious effects of criminal victimization on women's health and medical utilization. *Archives of Internal Medicine* 151: 342–47.

Krane, J. E. (1996). Violence against women in intimate relations: Insights from cross-cultural analyses. *Transcultural Psychiatric Research Review* 33(4): 435–65.

Krasula, J. (2002). Four wives slain in 6 weeks at Fort Bragg. CBSNews.com. Retrieved January 28, 2004 from http://www.cbsnews.com/stories/2002/07/31/national/printable517033.shtml.

Krau, N. (1998). Honor killings threaten dozens. http://www.gsnonweb.com/gsnbase/98_08/980803/17359.html.

Krishna, S. (1999). Gender bias is the socialization process of girl child in Bihar. *IASSI Quarterly* 12 (2).

———. (2002). Death wish for daughters: Son preference and daughter aversion in Bihari folk songs. Manus, 131. Retrieved August 4, 2004 from http://free.freespeech.org/manushi/131/deathwish.html.

Krishnakumar, A. (2002). Life and death in Salem. Hindu 19 (04). Retrieved March 2, 2006 from http://www.hinduonnet.com/fline/fl1904/19041300.htm

Kristof, N. D. (1991). A mystery from China's census: Where have young girls gone? *New York Times*, A1, A8.

———. (2005a). Raped, kidnapped and silenced. *New York Times*. June 14.

———. (2005b) The Rosa Parks for the 21st century. *New York Times,* A1. p. 27, November 8.

Kulwicki, A. D. (2002). The practice of honor crimes: A glimpse of domestic violence in the Arab world. *Issues in Mental Health Nursing* 23(1): 77–87.

Kumar, R. (1993). *The history of doing: An illustrated account of movements for women's rights and feminism in India, 1800–1900.* London: Verso.

Kuo, M. (2002). Asia's dirty secret. *Harvard International Review* 22(2): 42–54.

Kwabena-Essem, A. (1995). African Traditional Religions. *Djembe Magazine* 13: 1–9.

Lacey, M. (2004). From broken lives, Kenyan women build place of unity. *New York Times*, December 7.

———. (2005). Sudan and southern rebels sign pact to end civil war. *New York Times*, International, January 1, p. 3.

Lang, J. (2003). Working with men to end gender-based violence: Lessons for the Asian context. UNECAP, United Nations paper. http://www.unescap.org/esid/GAD/publication/DiscussionPapers/15/series15-mai n-text.pdf.

La Strada. (2001). Trafficking in women. Retrieved August 2, 2001 from http://free.ngo.pl/lastrada/page2.html.

La Strada-Ukraine. (2004). About La Strada-Ukraine. Fact Sheet 2004. Retrieved December 6, 2004 from http://www.brama.com/lastrada/about.html.

Lawson, A. (2002). Bangladesh protest against acid attacks. BBC News, March 8. Retrieved January 25, 2005 from http://news.bbc.co.uk/1/hi/world/south_asia/1861157.stm

Lax, R. (2000). Socially sanctioned violence against women: Female genital mutilation is the most brutal form. *Clinical Social Work Journal* 28(4): 403–12.

Lazaridis, G. (2001). Trafficking and prostitution: The growing exploitation of migrant women in Greece. *European Journal of Women's Studies* 8 (1): 67–102.

Leclerc-Madlala, S. (2002). On the virgin cleansing myth: Gendered bodies, AIDS and ethnomedicine. *African Journal of AIDS Research* 1(2): 87–95.

Lederer, L. (1999a). Statement before the subcommittee on international operations and human rights, committee on international relations, United States House of Representatives. September 14. The Protection Project. Retrieved December 29, 2004 from http://209.190.246.239/testimonies/ljl/ljl.pdf.

———. (1999b). The Women's Freedom Network. Sept./Oct. and Nov./Dec. vol. 6, (5 and 6). National Conference on Sexual Trafficking. The Protection Project, Kennedy School of Government, Harvard University. Retrieved December 4, 2004 from http://www.womensfreedom.org/artic653.htm.

Lefkowitz, B. (1997). *Our guys.* New York: Vintage Books.

Lerner, G. (1986). *The creation of patriarchy.* Oxford: Oxford University Press.

———. (1990). Reconceptualizing differences among women. *Journal of Women's History* 1 (3).

Levinson, D. (1989). *Family violence in cross-cultural perspective.* Newbury Park, CA: Sage.

Liebling, H. (2002). Samanya Agnes—I did not know Agnes—Ugandan women's experiences of violence, rape and torture during war in Luwero district: Implications for health policy, welfare and human rights. Paper presented to the 8th International interdisciplinary Congress on women, women's world, July, Makere University, Kampala, Uganda.

Lightfoot-Klein, H. (1989). *Prisoners of ritual: An odyssey into female genital circumcision in Africa.* Binghamton, NY: Haworth Press.

Lobel, K., ed. (1986). *Naming the violence: Speaking out about lesbian battering.* Seattle, WA: Seal Press.

Lockhart, H. (2004). *Female genital mutilation: Treating the tears.* Middlesex, England: Middlesex University Press.

Logmans, A., A. Verhoeff, R. Bol Raap, F. Creighton, and M. van Lent. (1998). Ethical dilemma: Should doctors reconstruct the vaginal introitus of adolescent girls to mimic the virginal state? (Who wants the procedure and why). *British Medical Journal* 316: 459–60.

Lopez, I. (1997). Agency and constraint: Sterilization and reproductive freedom among Puerto Rican women in New York City. In *Situated Lives: Gender and culture in everyday lives,* ed. L. Lamphere, H. Ragone, and P. Zavella, 157–74. New York: Routledge.

Loue, S. (2001). *Intimate partner violence: Societal, medical, legal and individual responses.* New York: Kluwer Academic/Plenum Publishers.

Lukes, S. (1980). *Power: A radical view.* London: Macmillan Press.

Luo, T. (2000). Marrying my rapist? The cultural trauma among Chinese rape survivors. *Gender and Society* 14 (4): 581–97.

Lykes, M.B., M. Brabeck, T. Ferns, and A. Radan. (1993). Human rights and mental health among Latin American women in situations of state-sponsored violence. *Psychology of Women Quarterly* (17): 525–44.

Macharia, D. (2003). The film star with a difference. *Young Nation*, March 23.

Mackie, G. (1996). Ending footbinding and infibulation: A convention account. *American Sociological Review* 61(6): 999–1005.

———. (2000). Female genital cutting: The beginning of the end. In *Female "circumcision" in Africa: Culture, controversy and change*, ed. B. Shell-Duncan and Y. Hernlund. Boulder, CO: Lynne Rienner.

MADRE. (2003). Beyond collateral damage: Women's organization calls for humanitarian perspective on Iraq war. Retrieved January 24, 2005 from http://madre.org//press/pr/collateraldamage.html.

Magnier, M. (2002). Battery behind the shoji screen: After new legislation, Japan finally faces up to the prevalence and horror of domestic abuse. *Los Angeles Times*, p. 1C, June 17.

Maksymovych, L. (2004). Prevention trafficking in Ukraine. Paper presented at the Wellesley Centers for Women International Research and Action Conference: Innovations in Understanding Violence against Women, April 25–28, Wellesley, MA.

Malamuth, N. (1981). Rape proclivities among men. *Journal of Social Issues*, 37: 138–57.

Mandelbaum, G. D. (1998). *Women's seclusion and men's honor: Sex roles in North India, Bangladesh, and Pakistan.* Tucson: University of Arizona Press.

Mansoor, H. (2003). Infanticide the most ignored crime in Pakistan. *Daily Times.* Retrieved December 12, 2004 from http://www.dailytimes.com.pk/default.asp?page=story_5-4-2003_pg7_21.

Manthorpe, J. (1999). China battles slave trading in women: Female infanticide fuels a brisk trade in wives. *Vancouver Sun*, A1, January 11.

Mardorossian, C. M. (2002). Toward a new feminist theory of rape. *Signs* 3: 743–77. Retrieved December 23, 2004 from http://proquest.umi.com.

Mascarehnas, M. M. (1991). Feminism hijacked down the slippery slope: Feticide to infanticide. In *Violence against women*, ed. Sushma Sood, 93–104. Jaipur, India: Arihana Publishers.

Masciarelli, A., and I. Eveleens. (2004). Sudanese tell of mass rape. *BBC News,* June 10. http://news.bbc.co.uk/2/hi/africa/3791713.stm.

Mason, G. (1997). (Hetero)sexed hostility and violence toward lesbians. In *Women's encounters with violence: Australian experiences*, ed. S. Cook and J. Bessant. Thousand Oaks, CA: Sage.

Masood, S. (2003). Pakistan inquiry reveals details of a woman's honor killing. *New York Times International.* December 14.

Mattar, M. (2004).Global perspective. Dod Seminar on Globalization and Corruption. Johns Hopkins University, Paul H. Nitze School of Advanced International Studies, Sept. 14–15. Retrieved December 2, 2004 from http://www.protectionproject.org/main1.htm.

Mattar, Y. M. (2003). Comparative analysis of the anti-trafficking legislation in foreign countries: towards a comprehensive and effective legal response to combating trafficking in persons. Statement to the House Committee on International Relations Subcommittee on International Terrorism, Nonproliferation, and Human Rights,

June 25. Retrieved March 17, 2006 from http://www.protectionproject.org/vvv.html.

Mayell, H. (2002). Thousands of women killed for family "honor." *National Geographic News*. Retrieved December 16, 2004 from http://news.nationalgeographic.com/news/2002/02/0212_020212_honirkilling.html.

Maynard, M. (1994). Methods, practice and epistemology: The debate about feminism and research. In *Researching women's lives from a feminist perspective*, ed. M. Maynard, and J. Purvis, 10–26. London: Taylor and Francis.

Mbacke, C., P. Adongo, P. Aeongo, and F. Binka (1998). Prevalence and correlates of female genital mutilation in the Kassena-Nankana District of Northern Ghana. *African Journal of Reproductive Health* 2: 13–24.

Mbugua, I. (1997). Ending the mutilation. *People and the Planet* 6 (1).

McClelland, S. (2001). Inside the sex trade. *Maclean's* (Library of Congress InfoTrac OneFile). December 3.

McCurry, J., and R. Allison. (2004). One child policy leaves China with huge shortage of women. *Taipei Times*. July. Retrieved January 24, 2005 from http://www.taipeitimes.com/News/edit/archives/2004/03/23/2003107449.

McDonald, B. (1999). My nightmare life in an orphanage: Woman tells how nuns cruelly beat the children. *Irish Independent*, January 27. http://www.childlink.co.uk/website/welfare/news/my.htm.

McGirk, T., and S. Plain. (2002). Lifting the veil on Taliban sex slavery. *Time Magazine*, February 18.

McWilliams, M. (1998). Violence against women in societies under stress. In *Rethinking violence against women*, ed. R. M. Dobash and R. P. Dobash. Thousand Oaks, CA: Sage.

McWilliams, M., and J. McKiernan. (1993). *Bringing it out in the open: Domestic violence in Northern Ireland*. Belfast, Northern Ireland: HMSO Publications.

McWilliams, M., and L. Spence. (1996). *Taking domestic violence seriously: Issues for the civil and criminal justice system*. Centre for Research on Women, University of Ulster, Jordanstown.

Mehrotra, A. (2001a). Health: The risks of gender based violence. Retrieved May 27, 2002 from http://www.undp.org/rblac/gender/genderbased.htm.

———. (2001b). Gender violence. Retrieved December 21, 2004 from http://www.undp.org/rblac/gender/legislation/violence.htm.

Meng, L. (1999). Ending violence and staying in marriage: Stories of battered women in rural China. *Violence against Women* 5:1469–93.

Menon, P. (1999). Inside the burn wards. *Frontline* 16 (17). Retrieved January 15, 2002 from http://www.indianterrorism.mybravenet.com/burnsward.htm.

Metcalf, C. (1996). At the cutting edge of change, fighting female genital mutilation in Uganda. *Human Rights Tribune* 3 (4), August.

———. (1997). Changing ways in Uganda. *People and the Planet* 6(1). Retrieved January 30, 2005, from http://www.womenaid.org/press/info/fgm/fgm-uganda.htm.

———. (1999). Ethiopia: Revenge of the abducted bride. *BBC World*. Retrieved June 18, 2005 from http/www.bbc.co.uk.

Mezey, G., and E. Stanko. (1996). Women and violence. In *Planning community mental health services for women: A multiprofessional handbook*, ed. K. Abel, M. Buszewicz, S.

Davison, S. Johnson, and E. Staples, 160–75. Florence: Taylor and Francis/Routledge.

Mikhail, S. (2002). Child marriage and child prostitution: Two forms of sexual exploitation. *Gender and Development* 10,1: 43–49.

Miko, F. T., and G. Park. (2000). *Trafficking in women and children: The U.S. and international response.* Washington: Congressional Research Service Report (U.S. Department of State).

Miller, B. D. (1992). Wife beating in India: Variations on a theme. In *Sanctions and sanctuaries: Cultural perspectives on the beating of wives,* ed. D. Counts, J. K. Brown, and J. C. Campbell, 173–184. Boulder, CO: Westview.

Ministry of Health. (1999). National plan of action for the elimination of female genital cutting in Kenya, 1999–2019. Ministry of Health, Government of Kenya, Nairobi.

Mitra, A. (1993). Female foeticide: A primitive trend practiced the world over. *Down to Earth*, 31.

Mladjenovic, L., and D. Matijasevic. (1996). SOS Belgrade July 1993–1995: Dirty streets. In *Women in a violent world,* ed. C. Corrin. Edinburgh, Scotland: Edinburgh University Press.

Moghissi, H., and M. J. Goodman. (1999). Cultures of violence and diaspora: Dislocation and gendered conflict in Iranian-Canadian communities. *Journal of Humanity and Society* 23 (4): 297–398.

Mojab, S. (2002). Honor killing: Culture, politics and theory. Association for Middle East Women's Studies. http://www.amews.org/review/reviewarticles/mojabfinal.htm.

Mojab, S., and A. Hassanpour. (2002a). The politics and culture of "honor killing." The murder of Fadime Sahindal. *Pakistan Journal of Women's Studies* alam-e-Niswan, 9(1): 57–77.

———. (2002b). Thoughts on the struggle against "honour killing." *International Journal of Kurdish Studies* 16 (1 and 2): 83–97.

Moniaga, N. C. (2002). A woman's right to health. *Journal of the American Medical Association,* 288: 1134.

Moreau, R. (2002). Of tribes, trials, and tribulations. *Newsweek.* August 5.

Morris, B. (1996). The closing of girls' schools in Afghanistan. *Off Our Backs* 26(10): 7.

Morris, M. (2002). Violence against women and girls. Fact sheet for the Canadian Research Institute for the Advancement of Women. Retrieved January 30, 2003 from http://www.criaw-icref.ca/Violence_fact_sheet.

Moschovis, P. P. (2002). When cultures are wrong. *Journal of the American Medical Association* 288: 1131–32.

Mullally, S. (2005). Gendered citizenship: Debating reproductive rights in Ireland. *Human Rights Quarterly* 7(1): 78.

Murphy, E., and K. Ringheim, eds. (2001). Reproductive health, gender and human rights: A dialogue. *Women's Reproductive Health Initiative.* Washington, DC: PATH. Retrieved December 28, 2004 from http://www.path.org/files/RH-GHR-08.pdf.

Muslim Women's League position paper on honor killing. (1999). http://www.mwlusa.org/pub_hk.html.

Mydans, S. (2001). Vengeance destroys faces, and souls, in Cambodia. *New York Times* section 1, column 1, p. 3, July 22.

Narasimhan, S. (1994). India: From sati to sex determination tests. In *Women and violence,* ed. M. Davies, 43–52. London: Zed Books.

Natarajan, M. (1995). Victimization of women: A theoretical perspective on dowry deaths in India. *International Review of Victimology* 3: 297–308.

Nazar, M., and D. Lewis. (2003). *Slave.* New York: Perseus Books Group.

New Internationalist. (1993). Respect and respectability. *New Internationalist.* Retrieved April 6, 2003 from http://www.newint.org/issue241/respect.htm.

Northern Ireland Human Rights Commission. (2001). Making a bill of rights for Northern Ireland, A consultation by the Northern Ireland Human Rights Commission. Belfast, Northern Ireland.

Northern Ireland Women's Aid Federation. (2004). Retrieved February 20, 2004 from http://www.niwaf.org/Domesticviolence/factsfigures.htm.

Nowrojee, B. (1996). *Shattered lives: Sexual violence during the Rwanda genocide and its aftermath.* New York: Human Rights Watch. Retrieved March 6, 2006 from http://www.hrw.org/reports/1996/Rwanda.htm.

Nwajei, S. D., and A. I. Otiono. (2003) Female genital mutilation: Implications for female sexuality. *Women's Studies International Forum* 26 (6): 575–80.

Nyangweso, M. (2002). Christ's salvific message and the Nandi ritual of female circumcision. *Theological Studies* 63: 579–600.

O'Neill, R. A. (1999). International trafficking in women to the United States: A contemporary manifestation of slavery and organized crime. Washington, DC: U.S. Department of State, Bureau of Intelligence and Research.

Odoi A., S. P. Brody, and T. E. Elkins. (1997). Female genital mutilation in rural Ghana, West Africa. *International Journal of Obstetrics and Gynecology* 56: 179–180.

Odujinrin, O. M.T., C. O. Akitoye, and M. A. Oyediran. (1989). A study on female circumcision in Nigeria. *West African Journal of Medicine* 8: 183–92.

Office to Monitor and Combat Trafficking in Persons. (2004). *Trafficking in Persons Report.* U.S. State Department. June 14. Retrieved December 6, 2004 from http://www.state.gov/g/tip/rls/tiprpt/2004/33192.htm.

Ogiamien, T. (1988). A legal framework to eradicate female circumcision. *Medical Science and Law* 28(2): 115–19.

Ojiambo Ochieng, R. (2002). The scars on their minds . . . and their bodies. The battleground: Women's roles in post conflict reconstruction. Paper presented at the 19th international peace research conference, July 1-5, Kyung Hee University, South Korea.

Oldenburg, V. T. (2002). *Dowry murder: The imperial origins of a cultural crime.* Oxford, UK: Oxford University Press.

Olesen, V. (2000). Feminisms and qualitative research at and into the millennium. In *Handbook of qualitative research,* ed. N. Denzin and Y. Lincoln, 215–55. Thousand Oaks, CA: Sage.

Oprah: The Oprah Winfrey Show. (2003). *Women held captive in Africa.* March 12 Transcript. Chicago: Harpo Productions.

Ortner, S. B. (1978). The virgin and the state. *Feminist Studies* 4: 19–35.

Panchanadeswaran, S., and C. Koverola. (2005) The voices of battered women in India. *Violence against women,* 11(6): 736–58.

Pandey, R. (1969). Hindu samskaras: Socio-religious study of the Hindu sacraments. New Delhi, India: Motilal Banarsidass.

Parker, R. (1996). Bisexuality and HIV/AIDS in Brazil. In *Bisexualities and AIDS: International perspectives,* ed. P. Aggleton, 148–60. Bristol, PA: Taylor and Francis.

Patel, V. (1997). Technology in service of female infanticide. *Humanscape,* 19–20.

PATH. (1997). Alternative rituals raise hope for eradication of female genital mutilation. Retrieved March 11, 2003 from http://www.path.org/resources/press/19771020-fgm.htm.

PATH. (2003). Harmful Traditional Health Practices. In *Reproductive Health Outlook.*

Peacock, D. (2002). Men as partners: South African men respond to violence against women and HIV/AIDS. EngenderHealth. Retrieved December 21, 2004 from www.engenderhealth.org.ia.wwm/pdf/map-hiv-sa.pdf.

Physicians for Human Rights. (1998). The Taliban's war on women: Health and human rights crisis in Afghanistan. http://www.yorku.ca/iwrp/afghan/Behindtheveil.htm.

Piispa, M. (2004). Age and meaning of violence; Women's experiences of partner violence in Finland. *Journal of Interpersonal Violence* 19(1): 30–48.

Ping, W. (2002). *Aching for beauty: Footbinding in China.* Minneapolis: University of Minnesota Press.

Pitcher, G., and M. G. Bowley. (2002). Infant rape in South Africa. *Lancet* 359 (9303): 274–75.

Pleck, E. (1987). *Domestic tyranny: The making of social policy against family violence from colonial times to present.* New York: Oxford University Press.

Population Communications International (PCI). (2003). India. http://www.population.org/programs_india.shtml.

Population Council. (2002). FGC excisors persist despite entreaties: Mali female genital cutting, or summary 2. *Frontiers in Reproductive Health.*

Porras, M. (1996). *Female Infanticide and Foeticide.* Retrieved from http://web.archive.org/web/19990508183744/http://sorrel.humboldt.edu/~lfs1/e thnog/marina/re search.html.

Poudel, Meena. (1994). Trafficking in women in Nepal: An overview. WATCH (Women Acting Together for Change, Nepal). Paper prepared for the First Planning Meeting of Regional Project Against the Trafficking in Women in East, South East and South Asia, organized by International Movement Against All Forms of Discrimination and Racism (IMADR), March 15–16, 1994. Tokyo, Japan.

Poudel, M., and I. Smyth. (2002). Reducing poverty and upholding human rights: a pragmatic approach. *Gender and Development* 10(1): 80–85.

Powell, C. (2004). Letter from the Secretary of State. Trafficking in persons report. U.S. Department of State. Retrieved January 2, 2005 from http://www.state.gov/g/tip/rls/tiprpt/2004/33285.htm.

Power, C. (2000). Becoming a 'Servant of God'; Devadasis are Dalit women sold into sexual slavery. Is this the end of a cruel tradition? *Newsweek.* June 25.

Pratap, A. (1995). Killed by greed and oppression. *Time Magazine,* 146 (11), September 11.

Priyadarshini, A. (2005). Personal communication. Ithaca, NY.

Protection Project. (2002). Survivor Stories. Testimony provided by U.S. House of Representatives, committee on international relations hearing on the implementation of the trafficking victims protection act. November 28, 2001. Retrieved December 30, 2004 from http://www.protectionproject.org/main1.htm.

————. (2004). Country reports: Nepal. Retrieved December 6, 2004 from http://www.protectionproject.org/main1.htm.

Puhar, A. (1993). On childhood origins of violence in Yugoslavia: II. The Zadruga. *Journal of Psychohistory* 21: 171–97.

Puri, D. (1999). Gift of a daughter: Change and continuity in marriage patterns of two generations of North Indians in Toronto and Delhi. PhD dissertation, University of Toronto.

Pyong Gap, M. (2003). Korean comfort women: The intersection of colonial power, gender and class. *Gender and Society* 17 (6): 938–57.

Quashigah, E. K. (1999). Legislating religious liberty: The Ghanaian experience. *Brigham Young University Law Review* 2: 589–606.

Queen Noor, H. M. (1999). Crimes of honor attracting national and international attention. January 11. Retrieved December 10, 2004 from http://www.noor.gov.jo/main/honorcrm.htm.

Qur'an, translation. (1999). ed. Sayed A. Razwy, trans. Abdullah Yusufali. Tahrike Tarsile Qur'an, 14th ed.

Quy, L. T., ed. (2000). *Prevention of trafficking in women in Vietnam.* Hanoi: Labour and Social Affairs Publishing House.

Radford, J. (1992). Womanslaughter: A license to kill? The killing of Jan Asher. In *Femicide: The politics of woman killing,* ed. J. Radford and D. E. H. Russell, 139–56. New York: Twayne.

Radhakrishnan, J. (2002). A merely legal approach cannot root out female infanticide. *Frontline* 19, 4. Retrieved January 20, 2004 from http://www.frontlineonnet.com/fl1904/19041320.htm.

Raj, A., and J. Silverman. (2002). Violence against immigrant women: The roles of culture, context and legal immigrant status on intimate partner violence. *Violence against Women* 8(3): 367–98.

Ralph, R. E. (2000). Jordanian parliament supports impunity for honor killings. Human Rights Watch. Retrieved from http://www.hrw.org/press/2000/01/jord0127.htm.

Ramanamma, A. (1991). Female foeticide and infanticide—A silent violence. In *Violence against women.* ed. Sushma Sood, 71–92. Jaipur, India: Arihana Publishers.

Rao, V. (1997). Wife beating in rural south India: A qualitative and econometric analysis. *Social Science Medicine* 44(8): 1169–80.

Rapaport, K. R., and D. C. Posey. (1991). Sexually coercive college males. In *Acquaintance rape: The hidden crime,* ed. A. Parrot and L. Bechhofer. New York: John Wiley and Sons.

Raphael, J., and R. M. Tolman. (1997). Trapped by poverty and abuse: New evidence documenting the relationship between domestic violence and welfare. University of Michigan Research and Development Center on Poverty, Risk and Mental Health.

Ren, X. (1999). Prostitution and economic modernization in China. In *Violence against women.* Thousand Oaks, CA: Sage.

Resolution condemning honor killings rejected by Pakistani Parliament. (1991). *Sisterhood is Global Institute* (SIGI). Retrieved August 31, 1999 from http://www.sigi.org/Alert/pak0899.htm.

Respect and Respectability. (1993). *New Internationalist* 241. Retrieved April 6, 2003 from http://www.newint.org/issue241/respect.htm.

Retlaff, C. (1999). Female genital mutilation: Not just over there. *Journal of the International Association of Physicians in AIDS Care* 5(5).

Reynolds, B. (1994). The move to outlaw female genital mutilation. *Ms. Magazine* (5)1, 92.

Rhode, D. L. (1989). *Justice and gender: Sex discrimination and the law.* Cambridge, MA and London: Harvard University Press.

Rice-Oxley, M. (2004). Britain examines "honor killings." *Christian Science Monitor.* Retrieved July 7, 2004 from http://www.csmonitor.com/2004/0707/p06s02-woeu .htm.

Richters, A. (1994). Women, culture and violence: A developmental, health, and human rights issue. Linden, Netherlands: Women and Autonomy Centre (VENA).

Rinaudo, B. (2003). Trokosi slavery: Injustice in the name of religion. African Studies Association of Australasia and the Pacific. 2003 Conference Proceedings: African on a global stage. Retrieved January 7, 2005 from http://www.ssn.flinders.edu.au/global/ afsaap/conferences/2003proceedings/rinau do.pdf.

Ristock, J. (2002). *No more secrets: Violence in lesbian relationships.* New York: Routledge.

————. (2003). Exploring dynamics of abusive lesbian relationships: Preliminary analysis of a multisite, qualitative study 1. *American Journal of Community Psychology* 31, (3–4), 329. Retrieved December 23, 2003 from http://proquest.umi.com.

Romito, P. (2000). Private violence, public complicity: The response of health and social services to battered women. In *Women, health and the mind,* ed. L. Sherr and J. St. Lawrence. Chichester, England: John Wiley and Sons.

Rosenthal, E. (2001). Harsh Chinese realities feed market in women. *New York Times,* May 6.

Rohtak. (2003). Missing sisters. *Economist,* April 17. Retrieved March 2, 2006 from http://econ.la.psu.edu/~broberts/courses/Econ471/PopChinaIndia.pdf.

Rozee, P. (1993). Rape in cross-cultural perspective. *Psychology of Women Quarterly* 17(4): 499–514.

Ruggi, S. (1998). Honor killings in Palestine. *Middle East Report.* Retrieved December 10, 2004from http://www.merip.org/mer206/ruggi.htm.

Russell, D. (1989). *Lives of courage.* New York: Basic Books.

————. (1990). *Rape in marriage.* Bloomington, IN: Indiana University Press.

Sabu, G., A. Rajaratnam, and B. D. Miller. (1998). Female infanticide in rural south India. *Search Bulletin,* July–Sept. 12(3): 18–26.

Sahebjam, F. (1994). *The stoning of Soraya.* New York: Arcade Publishing.

Sahinoglu Pelin, S. (1999). The question of virginity testing in Turkey. *Bioethics* 13: 256–61.

Salange. (2001). Women's health issues in Brazil. Personal Interview, Salvadore, Brazil. SS Universe Explorer. November, 19, 2001.

Sanday, P. (1981). *Female Power and Male Dominance.* Cambridge: Cambridge University Press.

————. (1990). *Fraternity gang rape: Sex, brotherhood, and privilege on campus.* New York: New York University Press.

Sanger, A. C. (2003). Surplus males and U.S./China Relations. Retrieved January 3, 2005 from http://www.alexandersanger.com/articles/2003_03_21.html.

Santos, C. (2004). Engendering the police: Women police stations and feminism in Sao

Paolo. *Latin American Research Review* 39 (3): 29–56. Retrieved December 23, 2004 from http://proquest.umi.com.

Sarhaddi Nelson, S. (2003). Another "honor" victim: Daughter, raped by brothers, killed by mother. *Persian Journal*. Retrieved May 18, 2004 from http://www.azcen tral.com/news/articles/1117HonorKilling17-ON.html.

Sarvate, S. (2000). Infanticide, bride burnings, suicides: Dowries, the root cause of abuse of women in India. *Pacific News Service*. http://wwwindianterrorism.mybravenet .com/IndianWomen2.htm.

Sati, N. (1997). The dark side of honor: Arabia culture. Retrieved from http://arabia .com/>http://arabia.com/content/culture/11_97/honor11.16.97.shtmlr.

Scheneck, L. (1986). An investigation into the reasons for dowry murder in India. In *Women and domestic violence: An annotated bibliography*, ed. M. Borst. Linden, Nether-lands: Women and Autonomy Centre (VENA).

Schild, M. (1991). Islam. In *Sexuality and eroticism among males in Moslem societies*, ed. A. Schmitt and J. Sofer. Binghamton, NY: Harrington Park Press.

Schipper, M. (2003) *Never marry a woman with big feet: Women in proverbs from around the world*. New Haven, CT: Yale University Press.

Sciolino, E. (2003). A crime of the young stalks France's urban wastelands. *New York Times*, October 24. Retrieved October 27, 2003 from http://www.nytimes.com/ 2003/10/24/international/europe/24FRAN.html?ex=106 802 6899andei=1anden =abc9c369bb7cb560.

Scott-Gliba, E., C. Minne, and G. Mezey. (1995). The psychological, behavioural and emotional impact of surviving an abusive relationship. *Journal of Forensic Psychiatry* 6(2): 343–58.

Seabrook, J. (1996). *Travels in the skin trade tourism and sex industry*. Chicago: Pluto Press.

Seligman, M. E. P. (1991). *Helplessness: On depression, development, and death*. 2nd ed. New York: W. H. Freeman.

Sen, A. (1990). More than 100 million women are missing. *New York Review of Books*, 61–66.

———. (1992). Missing Women. *British Medical Journal* 304: 587–88.

Sen, M. (2001). *Death by fire: Sati, dowry, death and female infanticide in modern India*. Lon-don: Weidenfeld and Nicolson.

Sev'er, A. (1997). Introduction. In *A cross-cultural exploration of wife abuse: Problems and prospectus*, ed. A. Sev'er, 1–26. Queenstown, Ontario, Canada: Edwin Mellen.

———. (2005). Personal communication, February 24.

Sev'er, A., M. Dawson, and H. Johnson. (2004, June). Lethal and nonlethal violence against women by intimate partners: Trends and prospects in the United States, The United Kingdom, and Canada. *Violence against Women*, 10(6): 563–76. Thousand Oaks, CA: Sage.

Sev'er, A., and G. Yurdakul. (2001). Culture of honor, culture of change: A feminist analysis of honor killings in rural Turkey. *Violence against Women* 7 (9): 964–98.

Sewell, H. (2000). Plea to save girl babies. *BBC*. http://wwwindianterrorism.mybravenet .com/femaleinfanticide.htm.

Sex-selective abortion and infanticide. (2004). *Wikipedia*. Retrieved January 3, 2005 from http://en.wikipedia.org/wiki/Sex-selective_abortion_and_infanticide.

Shanahan, K. (1992) *Crimes worse than death: How violence is terrorising Irish women*. Dublin: Attic Press.

Shankar, J. (1990). *Devadasi cult: A sociological analysis.* New Delhi: Ashish Publishing House.

Sharma, D. C. (2003). Widespread concern over India's missing girls. *Lancet* 362: 1553.

Shell-Duncan, B., and Y. Hernlund. (2000). Female circumcision in Africa: Dimensions of the practice and debates. In *Female circumcision in Africa: Culture, controversy, change,* ed. B. Shell-Duncan and Y. Hernlund, 1–40. London and Boulder, CO: Lynne Rienner.

Sheridan, K. (2004). Child marriage leading health risk for women in developing World. *Health and Medicine.* Retrieved March 6, 2006 from Voice of America News at http://www.voanews.com/english/archive/2004-06/a-2004-06-05-8-1.cfm.

Sibley, S. (1997). Let them eat cake: Globalization, postmodernism, colonialism, and the possibilities of Justice. *Law and Society Review* 31: 201–35.

Simmons, A. M. (1999). Ghana fights to end child slavery practice: A girl is given to a priest as 'wife of the gods.' *Los Angeles Times,* July 10. Retrieved March 10, 2006 from http://www.ghanaforum.com/news/simmons071099.htm.

Singh, K. (1994). Obstacles to women's rights in India. In *Human rights of women: National and international perspectives,* ed. R. J. Cook, 375–96. Philadelphia: University of Pennsylvania Press.

Sirohi, S. (2003). *Sita's Curse.* New Delhi, India: HarperCollins.

Sisterhood is Global Institute (SIGI). (1999). Resolution condemning honor killings rejected by Pakistani Parliament. Sisterhood is Global Institute (SIGI), August 31. http://www.sigi.org/Alert/pak0899.htm.

Skinner, B. F. (1953). *Science and Human Behavior.* New York: Macmillan Free Press.

Slavic Center for Law and Justice. (2002). Chinese province criticized for forced abortions, sterilizations. Slavic Center for Law and Justice. Retrieved January 27, 2005 from http://www.sclj.org/news/nr_010823_chinese.asp.

Smalley, S., and S. Mnookin. (2003). A house of horrors: In New York, runaways tell story of nightmarish abuse. May 5, www.msnbc.com/news/90832.asp.

Smith, H. (2004). Play shakes audience where women fall victim to gruesome honor killing. *Guardian,* January 28. www.quardean.co.uk/turkey/story/0,12700,1132772, 00.html.

Smith, J., and K. Kimsong. (2000). Acid laced vengeance. *Cambodia Daily Weekend,* February 5–6. Retrieved January 23, 2005 from http://www.camnet.com.kh/cambodia.daily/selected_features/acid_laced_vengeance.htm.

Snow, R. C., T. E. Slanger, F. E. Okonofua, F. Oronsaye, and J. Wacker. (2002). Female genital cutting in southern urban a peri-urban Nigeria: Self-reported validity, social determinants and secular decline. *Tropical Medicine and International Health* 7(1): 91–100.

Soh, C. S. (1997). The comfort women project. Retrieved February 6, 2003 from http://online.sfsu.edu/~soh/comfortwomen.html.

———. (2000). Human dignity and sexual culture: A reflection on the 'comfort women' issues. *ICAS.* Spring Symposium.

Solomon, A. (1991). Unreasonable doubt: Speaking out is the contested ground of credibility. *Village Voice,* August 6.

Song, Y. I. (1996). *Battered women in Korean immigrant families: The silent scream.* New York: Garland.

Sood, A. (2002). Audience involvement and entertainment-education. *Communication Theory* 12(2): 153–72.

SoonDock, K. (1995). *A lifetime of hatred.* http://www.hk.co.kr/event/jeonshin/w2/e_jsd_1.htm.

Spatz, M. (1991). A lesser crime: A comparative study of legal defenses for men who kill their wives. *Columbia Journal of Law and Social Problems, 24.*

Speth, J. G. (2000). The secret key: Poor women tend to those who tend to the future. WomenAid International. http://www.womenaid.org/fgmmain.html.

Spotlight on honor killing. (2002). http://www.feminist.com/violence/spot/honor.html.

Sridhar, L. (2004). Treating infanticide as homicide is inhuman. *InfoChange News.* Retrieved January 10, 2005 from http://www.infochangeindia.org/features211.jsp.

Statement of Gao Xiaoduan. (2002). Laogai Research Foundation. Retrieved January 5, 2005 from http://www.laogai.org/news/newsdetail.php?id = 1932.

Stein, B. (1996). Life in prison: Sexual abuse. *Progressive*, July 1. Available at: http://www.highbeam.com/library/docfree.asp?DOCID = 1G1:18410227&ctrlInfo = Round 19%3AMode19b%3ADocG%3AResult&ao.

Stein, D. (1988). Burning widows, burning brides: The perils of daughterhood in India. *Pacific Affairs* 61: 465–85.

Sterilization Safeguards. (1975). *Off Our Backs* 5(9): 3.

Stewart, D. E., and G. E. Robinson. (1996).Violence and women's mental health. *Harvard Review of Psychiatry* 4: 54–57.

Straus, M. A., and R. J. Gelles, eds. (1990). How violent are American families? Estimates from the national family violence resurvey and other studies. *Physical violence in American families: Risk factors and adaptations to violence in 8,145 families*, 95–112. New Brunswick, NJ: Transaction Publishers.

Sudha, S., and S. I. Raja. (1998). Intensifying masculinity of sex ratios in India: New evidence 1981–1991. *Forums Centre for Developement Studies.* Retrieved January 20, 2005 from http://www.hsph.harvard.edu/Organizations/healthnet/SAsia/forums/foeticide/articles/sexratio.html.

Swiss, S., P. Jennings, G. V. Aryee, G. H. Brown, R. M. Jappah-Samukai, M. S. Kamara, R. D. H. Schaack, and R. S. Turay-Kanneh. (1998). Violence against women during the Liberian civil conflict. *Journal of the American Medical Association* 279: 8625–29.

Tang, C. S. (1997). Psychological impact of wife abuse: Experiences of Chinese women and their children. *Journal of Interpersonal Violence* 12(3): 466–478.

Tang, C. S., F. M. Chueng, R. Chen, and X. Sun, (2002). Definition of violence against women: A comparative study in Chinese societies of Hong Kong, Taiwan, and the People's Republic of China. *Journal of Interpersonal Violence* 17(6): 671–88.

Tang, C. S., D. Wong, and F. M. Cheung. (2002). Social construction of women as legitimate victims of violence in Chinese societies. *Violence against Women*, 8(8): 968–96.

Tanveer, A. (2002). Death sentences for gang rape. *Independent* (London, England). Retrieved October 11, 2005 from http://www.highbeam.com/library/doc0.asp?docid = 1G1:90959982&dtype = 0~0&dinst = &author = Tanveer%2C%20Asim&title = Death%20sentences%20for%20gang%20rape.%28Foreign%20News%29&date = 09/02/2002&refid = ency_botnm.

Tanveer, K. (2005). Pakastani killed his 4 daughters for family 'Honor.' *Ithaca Journal*, p. 2, December 28.

Tanzeem, A. (2005). Rape victim wins respect and award. *BBC News,* November 3. Retrieved March 15, 2006 from http://news.bbc.co.uk/2/hi/south_asia/4404022 .stm.

Thomas, S. L. (1998). Race, gender, and welfare reform: The antinatalist response. *Journal of Black Studies*, 28(4): 419–46.

Tierney, W. (2000). Undaunted courage: Life history and the postmodern challenge. In *Handbook of qualitative research,* ed. N. Denzin and Y. Lincoln, 537–53. Thousand Oaks, CA: Sage.

Times of India. (2000). Female infanticide continues unchecked, unheard. http:// wwwindianterrorism.mybravenet.com/IndianWomen3.htm.

———. (2002). Housewife set ablaze by in-laws. Retrieved June 6, 2002, from http:// timesofindia.indiatimes.com/articleshow.asp?art_id = 12199524&sType q1.

Toubia, N. (1995). *Female genital mutilation: A call for global action.* 2nd ed. New York: Rainbo.

Turgut, P. (1998). Loss of honor means death in Turkish region. http://metimes.com/ issues98-17/reg/honor.htm.

UN Campaign on Women's Human Rights. (2002). Health: The risks of gender-based violence. Retrieved June 28, 2002 from http://www.undp.org/rblac/gender/gender based.htm.

UN Draft Declaration on the Elimination of Violence Against Women. (1993). UN Resolution 1993/10, Economic and Social Council, 43rd plenary meeting.

United Nations. (1994). Convention on the elimination of all forms of discrimination against women [CEDAW].

———. (1998). Report of the Special Rapporteur. http://www.unhchr.ch/huridocda/ hur . . . CN.4.1998.54.

———. (2003). Kenya: Increased public awareness of FGM. Office for the Coordination of Humanitarian Affairs. IRIN News Organization. Retrieved March 2, 2006 from http://www.irinnews.org/report.asp?ReportID = 32235.

United Nations Economic and Social Commission for Asia and the Pacific: Laws, Policies, and Regulations. (1994). http://www.unescap.org/pop/database/law_china/ ch_record021.htm.

United Nations Office for Drug Control and Crime Prevention (UNODCCP). (2002). The protocol to prevent, suppress and punish trafficking in persons. Retrieved July 30, 2002 from http://odccp.org//trafficking_protocol.html.

United Nations Population Fund. (2000a). Ending violence against women and girls. Retrieved June 4, 2002 from http://www.unfpa.org/swp/2000/english/ch03.html.

———. (2000b). The state of world population 2000 report, lives together, worlds apart: Men and women in a time of change. Retrieved from http://www.unfpa.org/ swp/2002/english/ch1/index.htm.

———. (2004). Working from Within: Uganda—Winning support from custodians of culture. Available at: http://www.un-ngls.org/UNFPA_Culture_2004.pdf.

United Press International. (2005). Women, children, sexually abused after tsunami. Retrieved January 24, 2005 from http://www.washtimes.com/upi-breaking/ 20050104-034636-5421r.htm.

USA Today. (1996). The Simpson trial timeline. October 18. Retrieved December 28, 2004 from http://www.usatoday.com/news/index/nns053.htm.

U.S. Department of State. (2004). Senegal, country reports on human rights practices—2003. Released by the Bureau of Democracy, Human Rights, and Labor. Retrieved October 11, 2005 from http://www.state.gov/g/drl/rls/hrrpt/2003/27748.htm.

Valerie, M., V. Hudson, and A. M. den Boer. (2003). *Bare branches: The security implications of Asia's surplus male population.* Cambridge, MA: MIT Press.

Van Willigen, J., and V. C. Channa. (1991). Law, custom, and crimes against women: The problem of dowry death in India. *Human Organization.* 50: 369–77.

Venkatesh, A. (2001). Tamil Nadu. *Frontline,* 18(9).

Vento, J. M. (1999). *Violence against women: A problem for theological anthropology.* PhD dissertation, Fordham University.

Vess, D. (1998). Women hold up half the sky. Retrieved December 4, 2004 from http://www.faculty.de.gcsu.edu/~dvess/gissues/wacch.htm.

Vetten, L. (2004). Mbeki and Smith both got it wrong. The Centre for the Study of Violence and Reconciliation. Retrieved December 21, 2004 from http://cavr.org.za/article/artvet15.htm.

Vickers, J. (1993). *Women and war.* London: Zed Books.

Vindhya, U. (2000). "Dowry Deaths" in Andhra Pradesh, India: Response of the criminal justice system. *Violence against women.* Thousands Oaks, CA: Sage.

Visaria, P. M. (1963). *The sex ratio of the population of India.* Thesis. Princeton, NJ: Princeton University.

Wadhwa, Soma (1995). Lambs to slaughter. *Outlook.* October 18. http://www.outlookindia.com/

Wallace, H. (1999). *Family violence: Legal, medical, and social perspectives.* Boston: Allyn and Bacon.

Wang, X. (1999). Why are Beijing women beaten by their husbands? A case analysis of family violence in Beijing. *Violence against women* 5: 1493–1501.

Watts, C. and C. Zimmerman,. (2002). Violence against women: Global scope and magnitude. *Lancet* 359 (9313): April 6: 1232–1237. April 6, 2002.

Weisskopf, M. (1985). China's birth control policy drives some to kill baby girls. *Washington Post,* A1, January 8.

Welch, L. (1999). Uppity women. *Ms. Magazine.* http://www.msmagazine.com/jun99/uppitywomen-jun.html.

Wennerholm, C. J. (2002). Crossing borders and building bridges: The Baltic region networking project. *Gender and Development* 10(1): 10–19.

Werner, C. (1997). Marriage, markets, and merchants: Changes in wedding feasts and household consumption in patterns in rural Kazakhstan. *Culture & Agriculture,* 19 (1-2): 6–13.

Wiafe, S. (2000). Slaves of tradition: Fetish priests are targets of campaign in Ghana. *New Internationalist,* Oxford, October 8.

Wiesner-Hanks, M. (2001). *Gender in history.* Oxford, UK: Blackwell Publishing.

Wijers, M., and L. Lap-Chew. (1997). *Trafficking in women forced labour and slavery-like practices in marriage, domestic labour and prostitution.* Netherlands: Foundation against Trafficking in Women.

Wikipedia. (2004). Sex-selective abortion and infanticide. Retrieved January 3, 2005, from http://en.wikipedia.org/wiki/Sex-selective_abortion_and_infanticide.

Williamson, L. (1978). An anthropological analysis. In *Infanticide and the value of life,* ed. Marvin Kohl, 61–75. Buffalo, NY: Prometheus Books.

WIN News. (2000). Reports from around the world: Asia and Pacific women's health, politics, poverty, education and danger. Women in Asia: Underpaid, undervalued and underemployed, Autumn. Retrieved September 27, 2005 from http:http://www .findarticles.com/p/articles/mi_m2872/is_4_26/ai_67380617.

Winkel, E. (1995). A Muslim perspective on female circumcision. *Women and Health,* 23 (1): 1–7.

Winrock International. (2004). Trafficking prevention project in Ukraine. Retrieved December 6, 2004 from http://www.winrock.org/fact/facts.cfm?CC=5162.

WomenAid International. (2000). Women and violence. http://www.womenaid.org/ press/info/violence/womenviolence.html.

———. (2003). Changing ways in Uganda. Retrieved January 30, 2005 from http:// www.womenaid.org/press/info/fgm/fgm-uganda.htm.

Women's International Network. (2000). Country reports on human rights practices for 1999: Paraguay. *WIN News* 26(2): 24.

Women's Rights International. (1999). Violence against women in times of war: A research study in Liberia. International Center for Research on Women and the Center for Development and Population Activities.

World Bank. (1998). IK notes: Senegalese women remake their culture. World Bank. December. Retrieved April 8, 2003 from http://www.worldbank.org/afk/ik/iknt3.pdf.

World Health Organization (WHO). (1996). Female genital mutilation: Information kit. Geneva: World Health Organization.

———. (1997). Female genital mutilation fact sheet N 153 http://www.who.org/in f-fs/en/fact153.htm.

———. (1999). Classification and definition for female genital mutilation. http://www .who.org/frh-whd/FGM/f-defini.htm.

———. (2001). Estimated prevalence rates for FGM. Geneva: World Health Organization.

Worth, D. (1989). Sexual decision-making and AIDS: Why condom promotion among vulnerable women is likely to fail. *Studies in Family Planning* 20 (6): 297–307.

Xu, X., F. Zhu, P. O'Campo, M. Koenig, V. Mock, and J. Campbell. (2005). Prevalence of and risk factors for intimate partner violence in China. *American Journal of Public Health* 95(1).

Yang, Y. Q. (2004). *Footbinding: Search for the Three-Inch Golden Lotus* [documentary]. Vancouver, BC: Moving Images.

Yirmibesoglu, V. (2000). Sevda Gok: Killed for honor in women and sexuality in *Muslim societies,* ed. P. Ilkkaracan. Istanbul, Turkey: Women for Women's Human Rights.

Yodanis, C. (2004). Gender inequality, violence against women, and fear: A cross-national test of the feminist theory of violence against women. *Journal of Interpersonal Violence* 19(6), June: 655–75.

Yoshihama, M. and S. Sorenson. (1994). Physical, sexual and emotional abuse by male intimates: Experiences of women in Japan. *Violence and Victims* 9(1). Springer.

Yoshimi, Y. (2000). *Comfort women: Sexual slavery in the Japanese military during World War II.* New York: Columbia University Press.

Youssef, N. (1973). Cultural ideals, feminine behavior and family control. *Comparative Studies in Society and History* 13: 326–47.

INDEX

Note: *Italic* page numbers indicate figures.

ABOUT THE AUTHORS

Andrea Parrot, Ph.D. is a professor in the Department of Policy Analysis and Management at Cornell University, where she has been on the faculty since 1981. She is also a clinical professor of Psychiatry at Upstate Medical University. Her work focuses on human sexuality and women's issues, specifically women's health and violence against women globally. She is the author of numerous books, monographs, training manuals, and articles. She has appeared on many television and radio programs, including *Face the Nation*, *Larry King Live*, *The Oprah Winfrey Show*, and *CBS This Morning*. Parrot has presented her work internationally and has been an invited lecturer to more than one hundred colleges and universities around the world. She has also been a faculty member for the Semester at Sea program through the Institute for Shipboard Education, affiliated with the Universities of Pittsburgh and Virginia.

Nina Cummings, MS, CHES is a health educator at Cornell University. With a specialty in women's health, she also serves as the university victim advocate. She is currently an adjunct faculty member at Ithaca College where she teaches a course on women's health each spring. For thirty years, her work has had a particular focus on violence against women—most notably intimate partner violence and sexual violence prevention and education—and she has presented at national and regional conferences on these topics. Cummings has collaborated on several publications with coauthor Andrea Parrot, including the training manual *Rape 101: Sexual Assault Prevention for College Athletes*.